Shirley Jackson's

"THE LOTTERY"

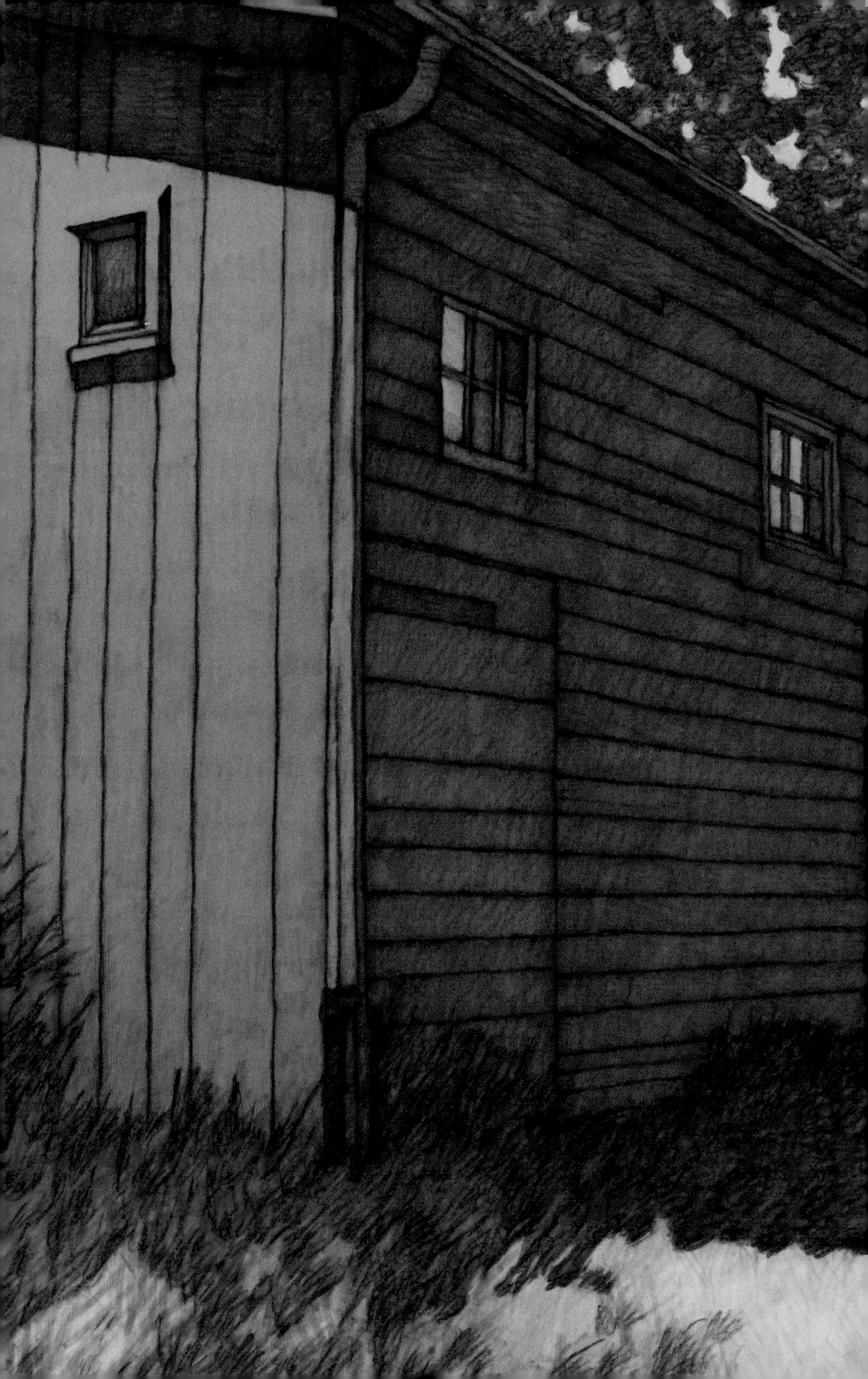

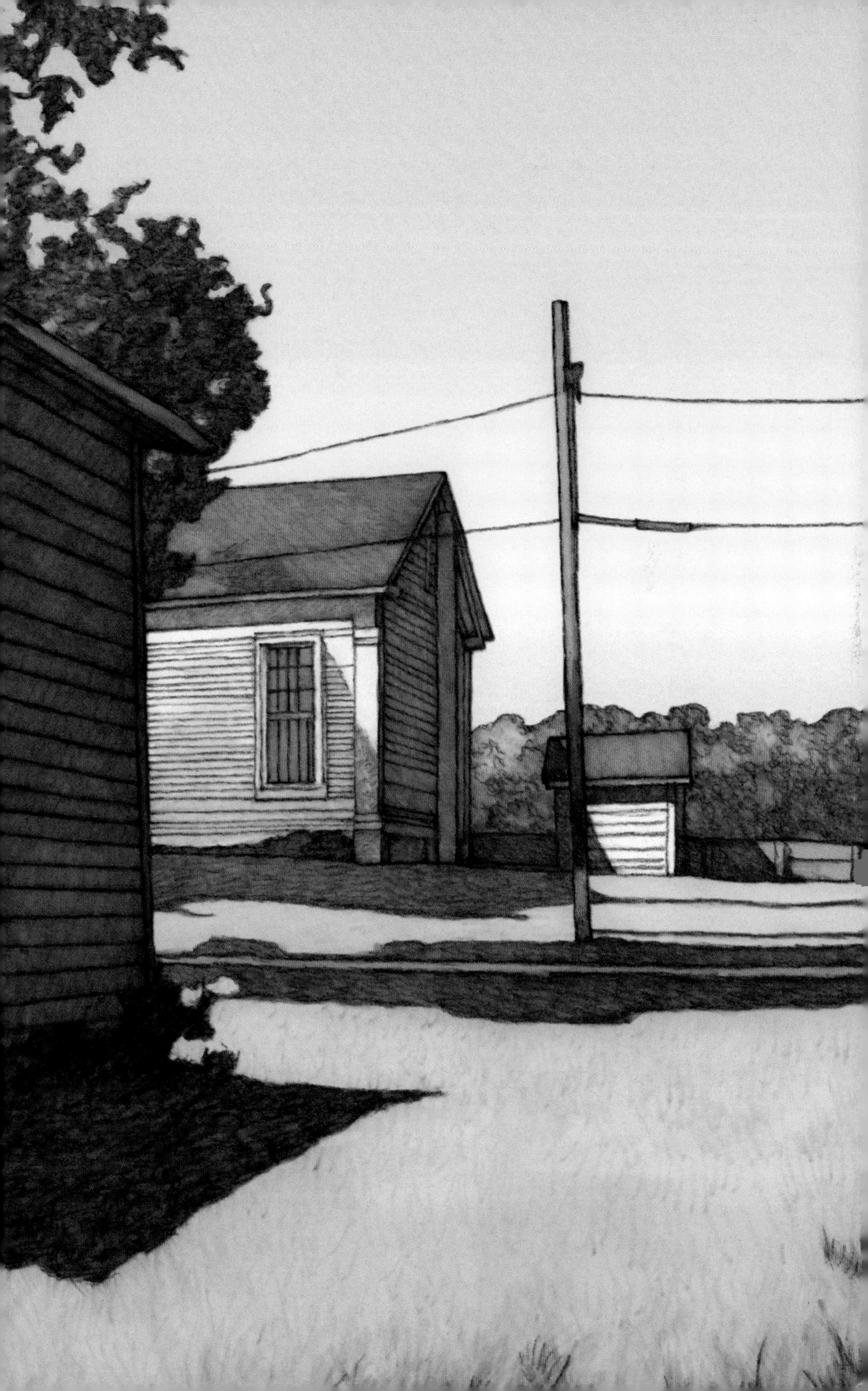

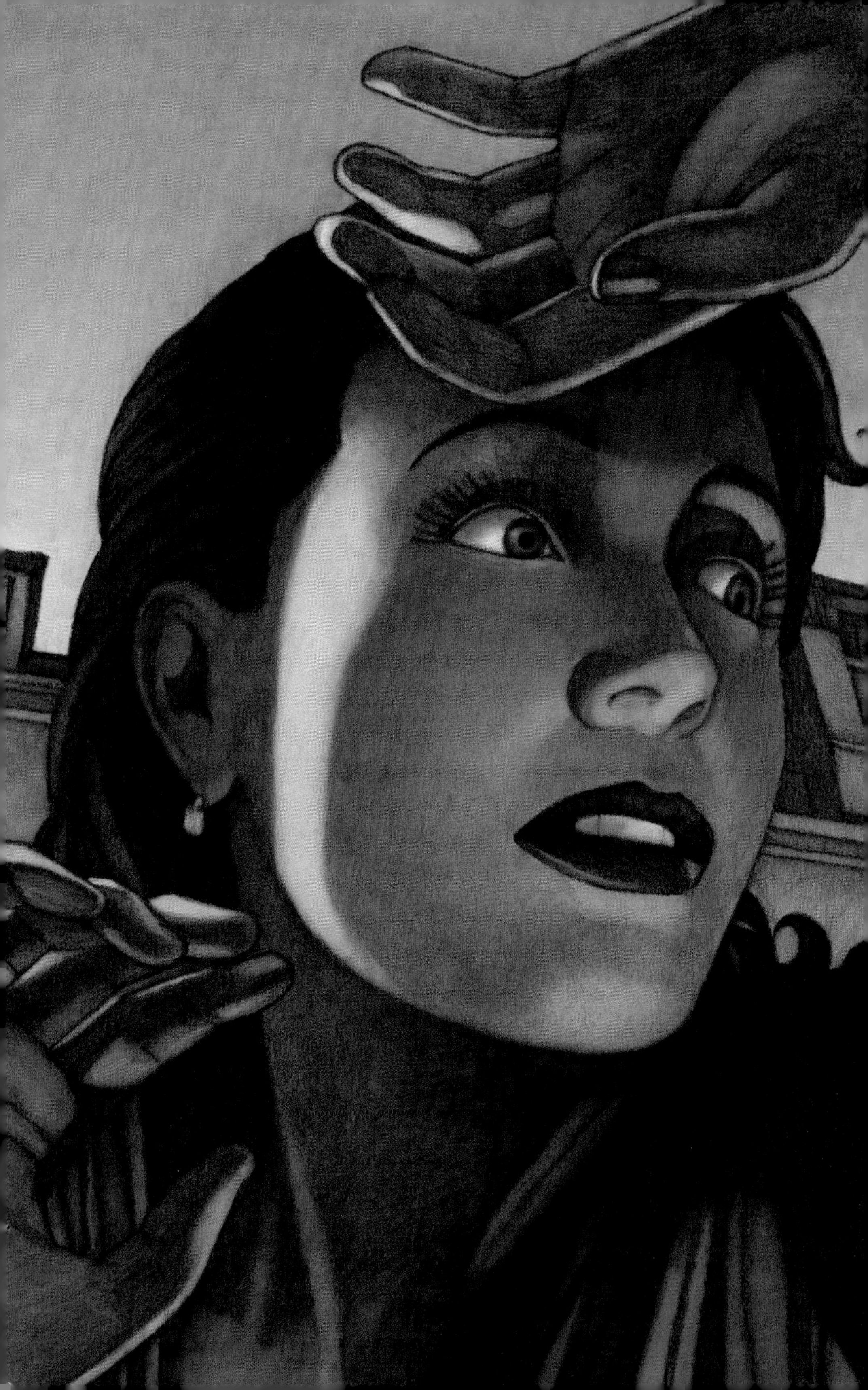

Also by Shirley Jackson

The Road Through the Wall

The Lottery and Other Stories

Hangsaman

Life Among the Savages

The Bird's Nest

Raising Demons

The Sundial

The Haunting of Hill House

We Have Always Lived in the Castle

The Magic of Shirley Jackson

Come Along with Me

Just an Ordinary Day

Let Me Tell You

The Witchcraft of Salem Village

The Bad Children

Nine Magic Wishes

Famous Sally

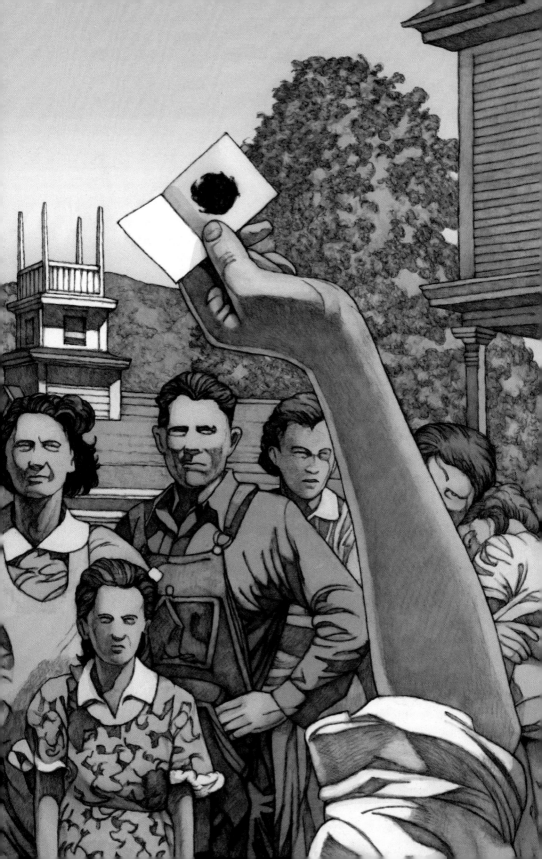

Shirley Jackson's

"THE LOTTERY"

THE AUTHORIZED GRAPHIC ADAPTATION
MILES HYMAN

A NOVEL GRAPHIC
FROM HILL AND WANG

A DIVISION OF FARRAR, STRAUS AND GIROUX
NEW YORK

Hill and Wang
A division of Farrar, Straus and Giroux
18 West 18th Street, New York 10011

Printed in the United States of America
Published simultaneously in hardcover and paperback
First edition, 2016

Library of Congress Cataloging-in-Publication Data
Names: Hyman, Miles, illustrator. | Jackson, Shirley, 1916–1965. Lottery.
Title: Shirley Jackson's "The Lottery" : the authorized graphic adaptation / Miles Hyman.
Other titles: Lottery
Description: First edition. | New York: Hill and Wang, 2016.
Identifiers: LCCN 2016007147 | ISBN 9780809066490 (hardback)
    ISBN 9780809066506 (paperback)
Subjects: LCSH: Graphic novels. | Comic books, strips, etc. |
    BISAC: COMICS & GRAPHIC NOVELS / Literary. | FICTION / Literary.
Classification: LCC PN6727.H96 S55 2016 | DDC 741.5/973—dc23
LC record available at http://lccn.loc.gov/2016007147

Contributing designer: Carole Schilling

Our books may be purchased in bulk for promotional, educational,
or business use. Please contact your local bookseller or
the Macmillan Corporate and Premium Sales Department
at 1-800-221-7945, extension 5442, or by e-mail at
MacmillanSpecialMarkets@macmillan.com.

www.fsgbooks.com
www.twitter.com/fsgbooks • www.facebook.com/fsgbooks

10 9 8 7 6 5 4 3 2 1

For my sister, Gretchen

I would like to thank my wife, Carole;
my parents, Corinne and Laurence;
and my children, Juliette, Charlotte, and Eliot.

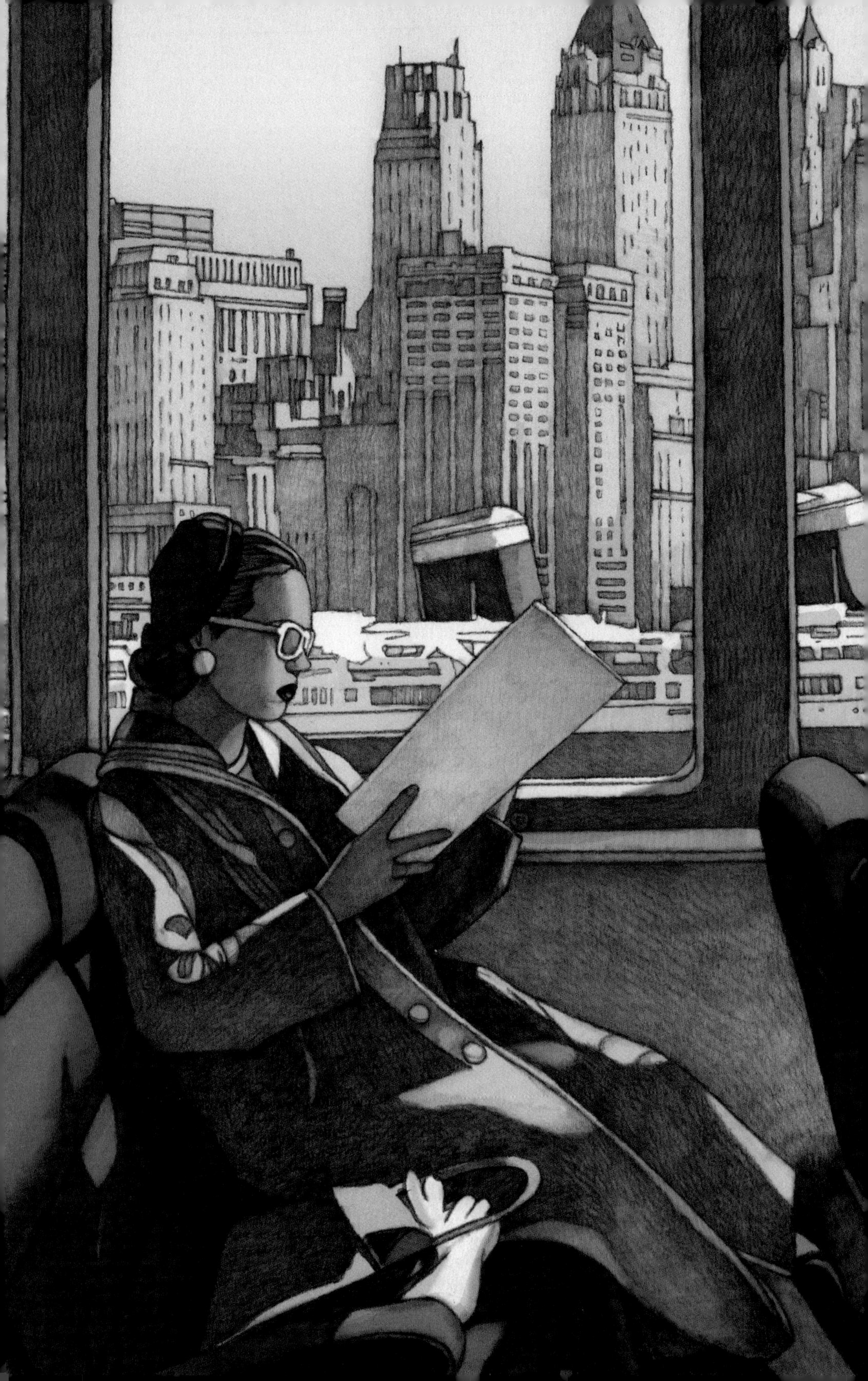

PREFACE

Visits with my father often include a ceremony, a unique sort of family séance. The tradition goes something like this: An ornate Victorian box is carefully carried from its corner resting place into the center of the living room. The box is placed on a table as my father and the rest of us—his children and grandchildren—gather around it.

By now even the youngest members of the family know what is afoot: we are about to listen to Grandma Shirley's music box. Etched with lace bunting and trim, roughly the size and shape of an old-fashioned gramophone that has lost its bell horn, the object we see resembles a relic from Hill House itself. Fashioned from dark exotic wood, the box has antique charm counterbalanced by a vaguely menacing quality that glows through years of dusting and varnish, making it inexplicably ageless—inanimate yet strangely alive.

After a careful winding up (which only my father is allowed to do), a metallic disk begins to rotate inside the box, a disk that is wider and thinner than a vinyl LP and riddled with an almost impercep-tible stubble, the surface illustrated to the edge with the frolic of some long-lost Italian *festeggiamento*.

At that point, something magical happens: the room fills with music, surging from the wooden box into the space around us. The vast flow of sound is incommensurate with the modest object we're standing around. The music itself—a highly ornamental arrangement of the once-popular tune "The Carnival of Venice"—is hard to describe, as if someone had condensed the ephemeral charm of a thousand ancient carousels into one acoustic rush. The original melody is all but lost under layers of labyrinthine harmony and counterpoint—an auditory experience so rich as to create what I can only describe as a visual effect on the senses that is as arresting as the box itself.

The music box was probably already an antique during my grandmother Shirley's lifetime and may indeed have been handed down by her mother, Geraldine—we grandchildren knew her as Grandmom—or from someone even higher up the Bugbee family tree. Whatever the facts of this obscure transmission, the music box must have seemed a relic even to Grandma Shirley—an heirloom, both elegant and sinister.

Beyond the haunting nature of the music itself, playing the music box is moving for other reasons. It represents a curious bond to the person who is *not* there with us, the most notable absence in the room: Grandma Shirley. It is perhaps the music box's dual capacity to attract and to repel, to enchant and to terrify, that makes it so fascinating—such a fitting representation for an artist whose own work so deftly treads the line between light and darkness, between humor and horror! That paradox—the dual creative vision that allows contrasting qualities to coexist so comfortably, almost festively, mutually enhancing each other's potent charm—permeates so much of what both Shirley and her husband, the literary critic Stanley Edgar Hyman, left behind them. As Shirley herself put it in an unpublished document: "I delight in what I fear." With time the mystery of her dual literary personae grew to be terribly vivid for me. How intriguing that the writer of "The Lottery" and

"Charles" was one and the same! How could the lighthearted *Raising Demons* and the dark *We Have Always Lived in the Castle* have sprung from the same creative mind?

My grandmother passed away unexpectedly during a nap on an August day in 1965. I was just shy of my third birthday. We really never got the chance to know each other and, to tell the truth, I have only one clear memory of her: I see her sitting on a chair or stool in her kitchen in what seemed to me like a palatial Victorian house on upper Main Street in North Bennington, Vermont. She seems to be onstage, framed by a doorway in the dim light as she talks to someone I can't see. Whenever I mention this image to my father or one of his siblings, they smile and nod in recognition. I've been told that, typically, after a day spent writing, doing housework, and parenting, Shirley would repair to the kitchen to begin preparing the family dinner, always sitting on the same stool, relaxing with a cigarette and a glass of J. W. Dant bourbon. It's not much, but it's one of my earliest, most clearest memories—of her or of anyone, I might add.

As a child, I lived surrounded by the physical resonance of my grandparents' lives: stacks and stacks of books, mountains of mystery stories with harrowing covers, books on the occult, erudite studies on ancient civilizations and obscure scholars. There was a formidable collection of blues and jazz records that filled an entire wall of the house I grew up in and which my grandparents and father had put together with the help of their dear friend Ralph Ellison—a collection that included Child Ballads and old English folk songs that would have played a fitting role in Shirley's work.

Then there are those impalpable things they left behind, including a ferocious love of Christmas, cats, cutthroat poker games, and spirited and intellectually rigorous (and sometimes stormy) dinner-table conversation. Most of the anecdotes are unverifiable—tainted evidence in the eyes of any seasoned researcher. But the truth is there somewhere, barely audible in the echoes of songs and dinner-party laughter, those late-night conversations about literature, myth, and ritual, ragtime and bedtime stories, pressed between the pages of a coffee-stained literary review or swept under the rug of the bar at the Algonquin Hotel.

There were always so many wonderful stories that included so many intriguing people: games of catch in the backyard with my father and J. D. Salinger, all-night poker games with celebrated painters and sculptors (debts were settled up with works of art at a time when Bennington College was the haunt of many an auspicious contemporary artist). There were countless dinners and parties with close friends—writers such as Ellison, Nemerov, and Bernard Malamud, to name a few. Brendan Gill, in his 1975 memoir, *Here at the New Yorker*, describes an inebriated Dylan Thomas pursuing my grandmother through the house until Stanley, who had been trying to watch a baseball game on television, grew irritated by the spectacle and subdued the rowdy Welsh bard by grabbing hold of his suspenders.

No one knew it then, but these were members of a disappearing tribe, an endangered species in the American cultural ecosphere: smoking, drinking, hard-partying midcentury intellectuals who were passionate about politics and ideas, art and literature, sports and good food. Between trips to New York City, where Shirley met with her agent while Stanley, a staff writer for *The New Yorker*, turned in copy, their North Bennington home was filled with literary figures, artists, critics, musicians. Their dinners became legendary: arguments broke out about jazz, baseball, and books, and were settled over dubious wagers. They threw outrageous, imaginative cocktail parties and generally lived large lives at a time when lives seemed larger across the board.

Of all the things left behind by my grandparents, Shirley's writing is particularly vivid. Her iconic masterpiece "The Lottery" naturally stands out, one of the most enduring works in American literature. For me, as an artist who has spent much of his professional life adapting novels and stories into graphic form, it would stand to reason that my grandmother's harrowing tale should entice over the years—not only because, like the music box, it had become a sort of family heirloom but because of how precise and nuanced the adaptation of this powerful piece of fiction would have to be to succeed. The story is such a perfect apparatus that it leaves little room for meddling. Some books sprawl and dream and carry on in ways that seem to invite imagery in spades. "The Lottery" does none of that—it is a no-nonsense, largely hermetic structure, words joined with a jeweler's precision.

So for nearly three decades, I passed.

Then a few years ago, while working on a graphic novel adaptation of James Ellroy's *The Black Dahlia,* based on a masterful script by the French comics writer Matz and the filmmaker David Fincher, I had a key insight into how I might adapt "The Lottery." The book you are about to read represents both a faithful rendering of the story and a complete visual restructuring of its delicate architecture, a meticulous visual retelling of the story in what is ultimately an entirely new language.

The experience has been daunting and immensely rewarding for me, both as a professional artist and as a grandson who has long grappled with this enigmatic, intangible inheritance. I waited thirty years to draw my grandmother's "The Lottery," but it was well worth the wait.

—Miles Hyman, Paris, June 2016

CHARA

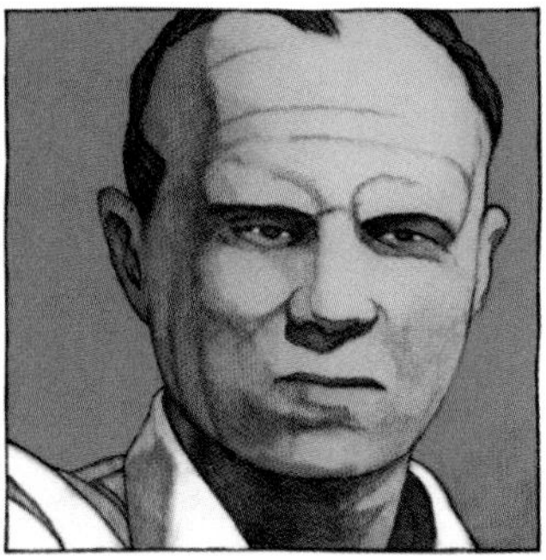

Mr. Joe Summers
Owner of the village coal business.
He runs the lottery.

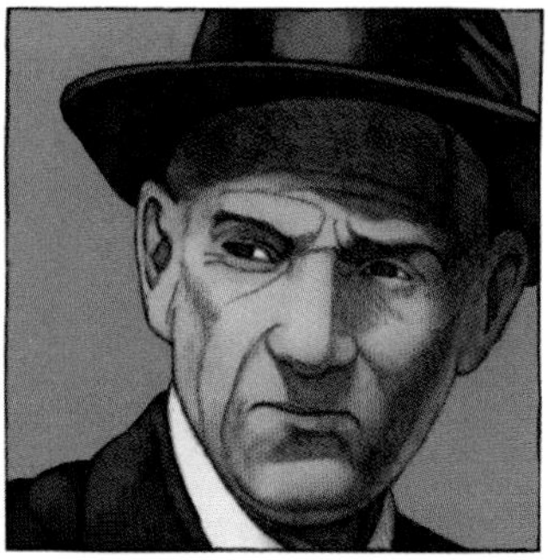

Mr. Harry Graves
The postmaster. He helps organize
and run the lottery.

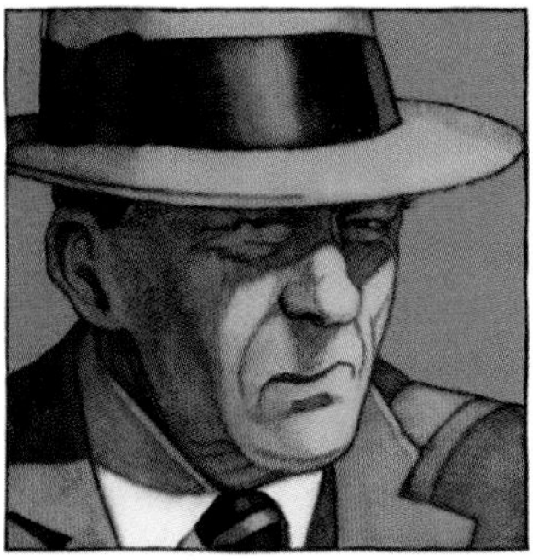

Old Man Warner
The village elder.
This is his seventy-seventh lottery.

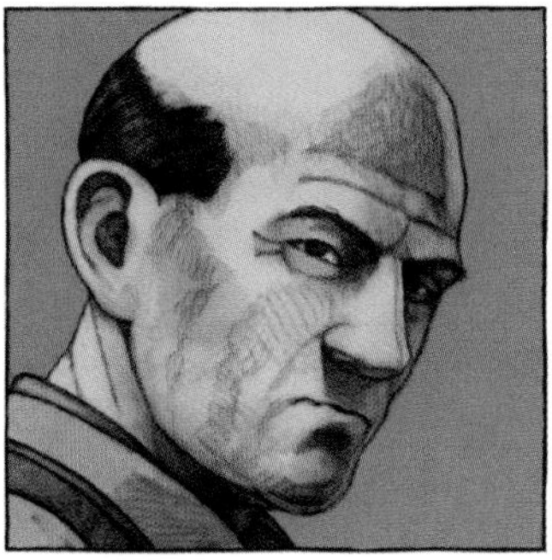

Steve Adams
First villager to be called
in the lottery.

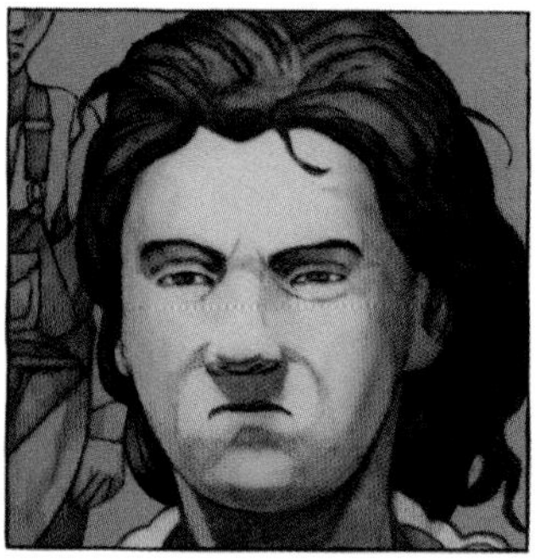

Jane Dunbar
Wife of Clyde,
mother of Horace.

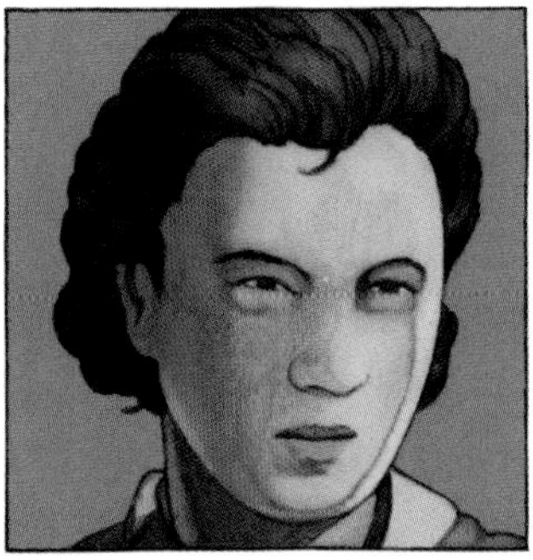

Mrs. Delacroix
Villager,
mother of Dickie.

CTERS

Tessie Hutchinson
Wife of Bill, mother of the three
Hutchinson children.

Bill Hutchinson
Head of the Hutchinson
household, Tessie's husband.

Bill Hutchinson, Jr.
Eldest son of Bill and
Tessie Hutchinson.

Nancy Hutchinson
Youngest daughter of Bill and
Tessie Hutchinson.

Dave Hutchinson
Youngest son
of Bill and Tessie Hutchinson.

Jack Watson
Eldest Watson son, drawing
this year as head of household.

Shirley Jackson's

"THE LOTTERY"

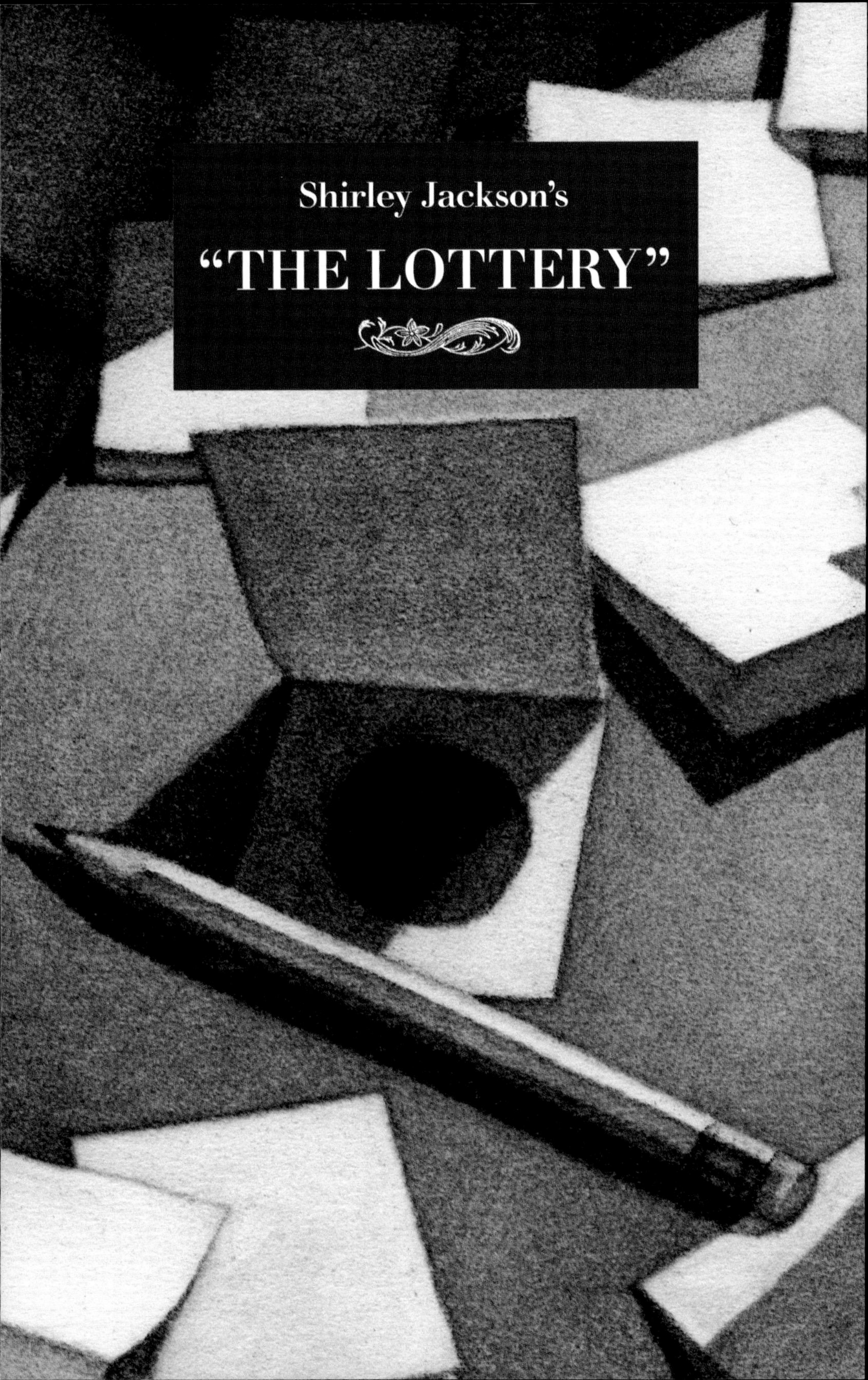

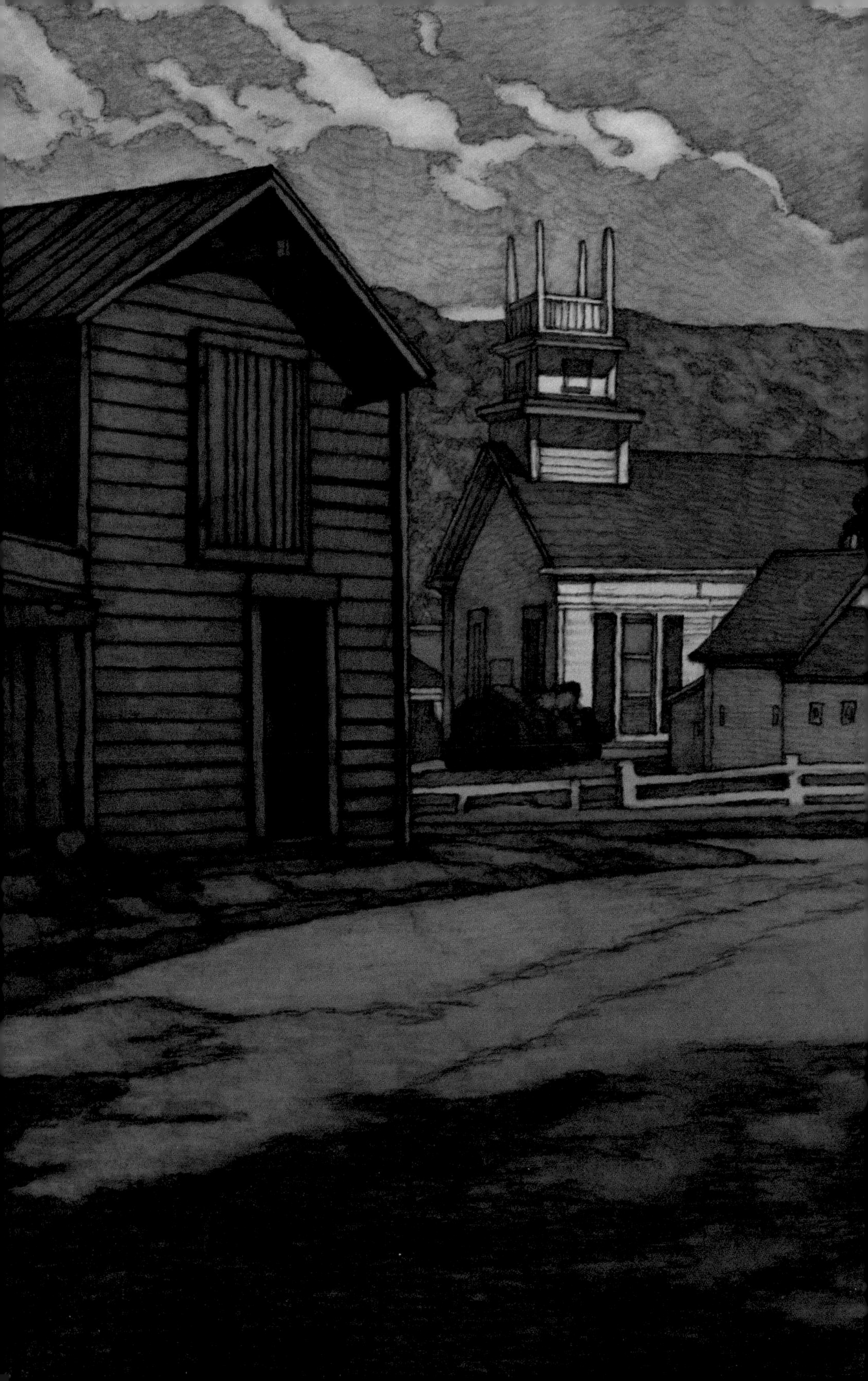

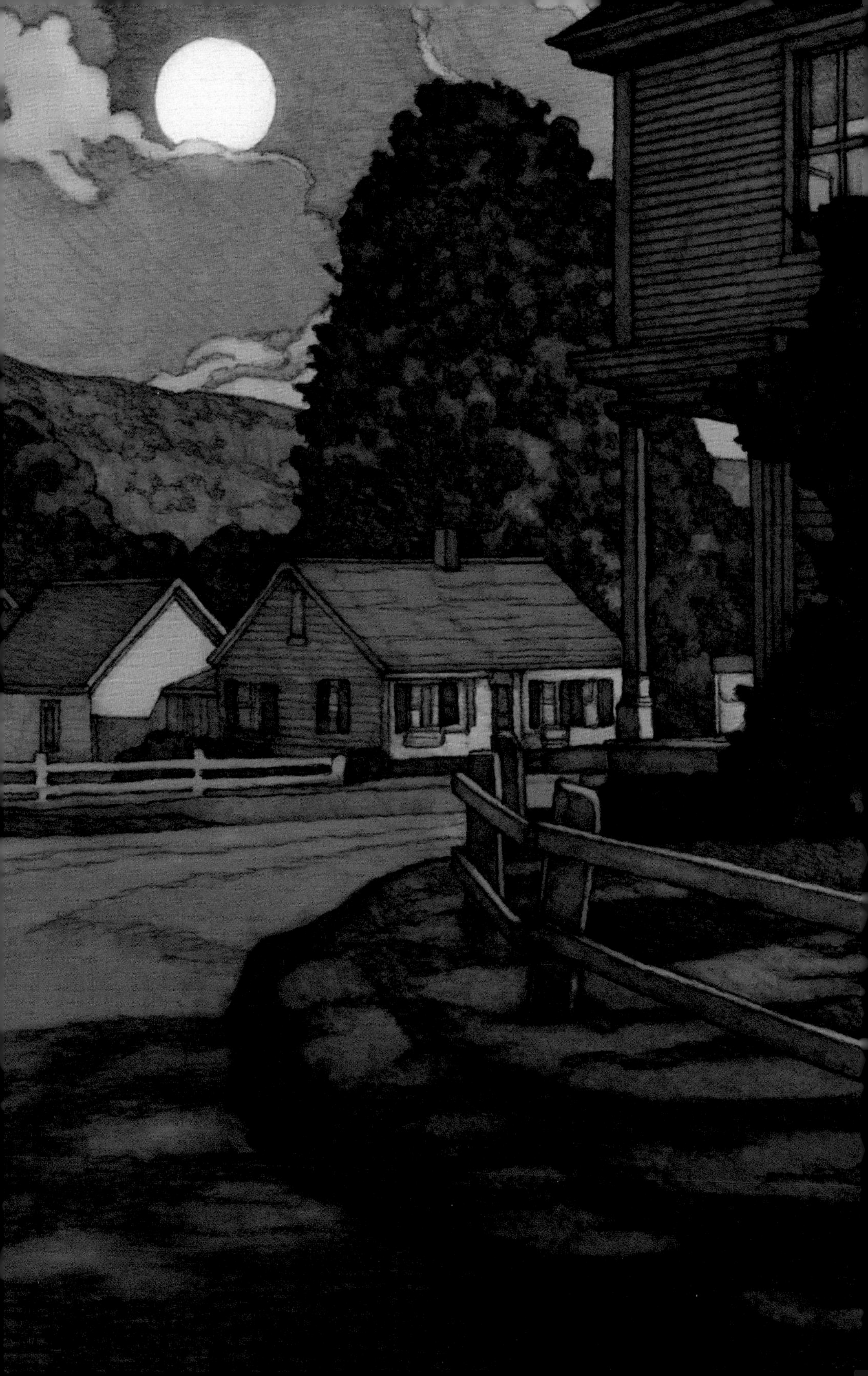

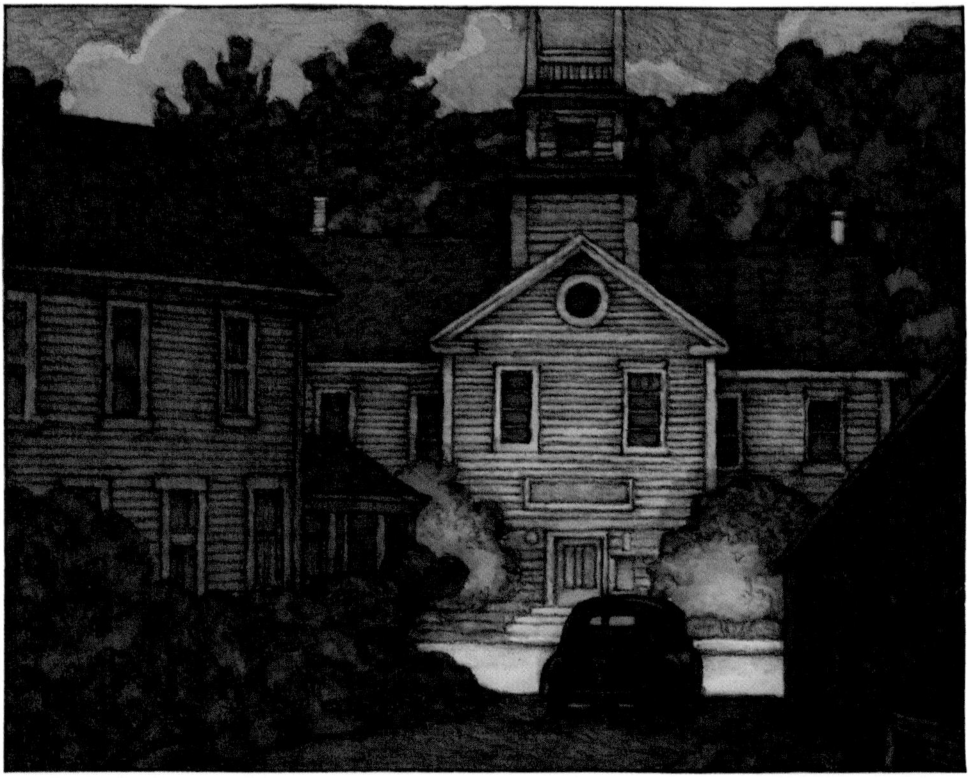

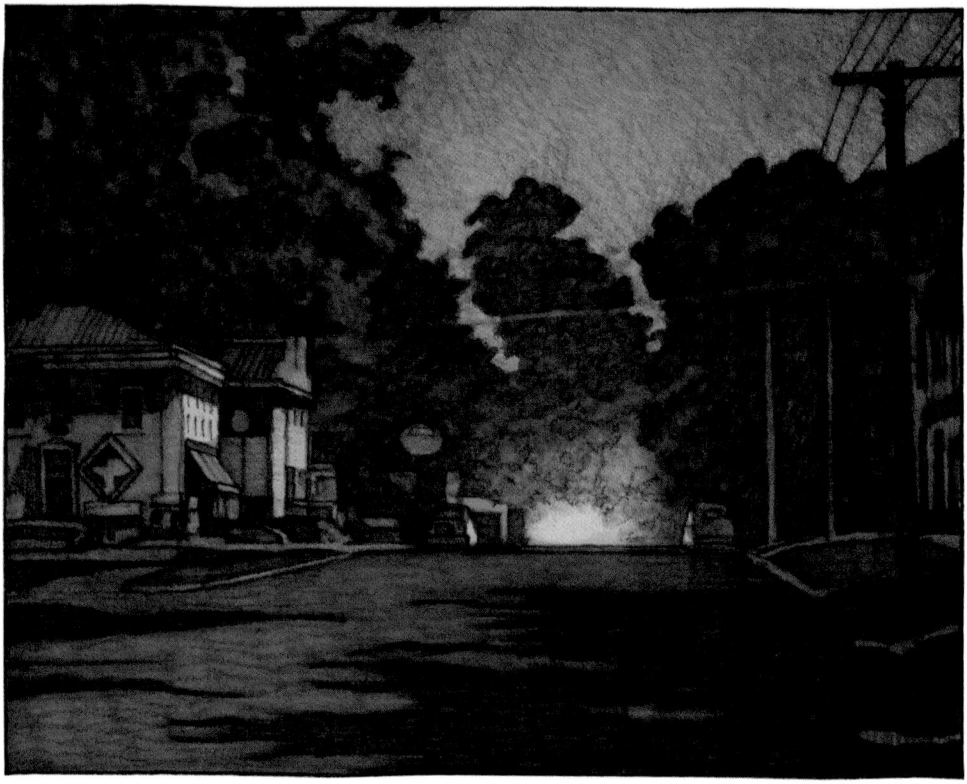

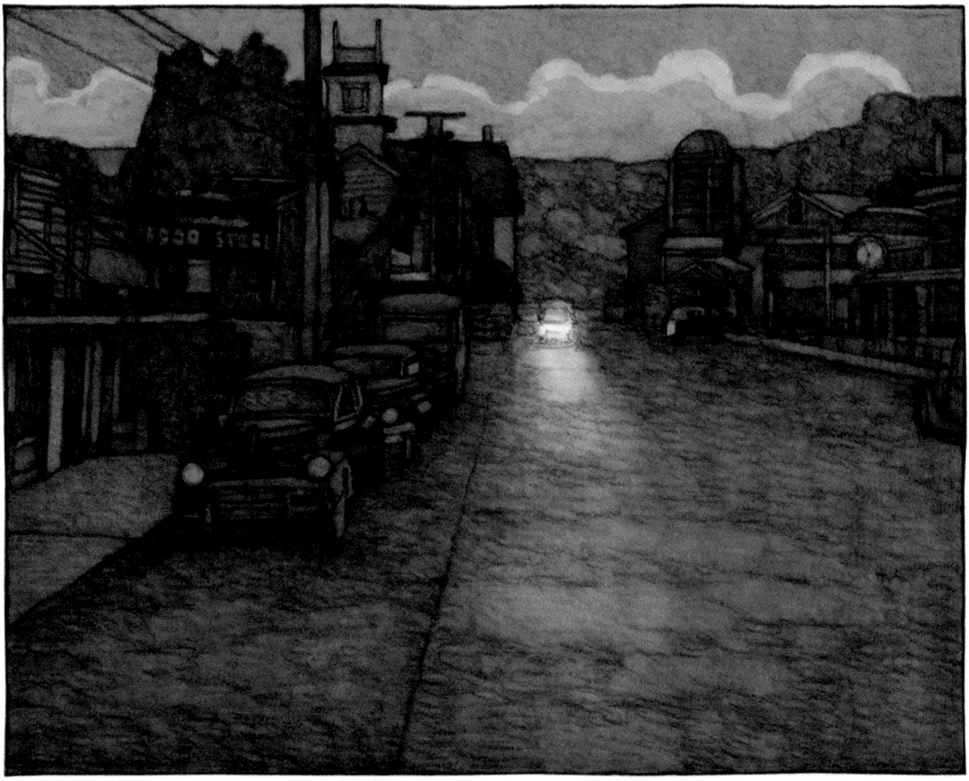

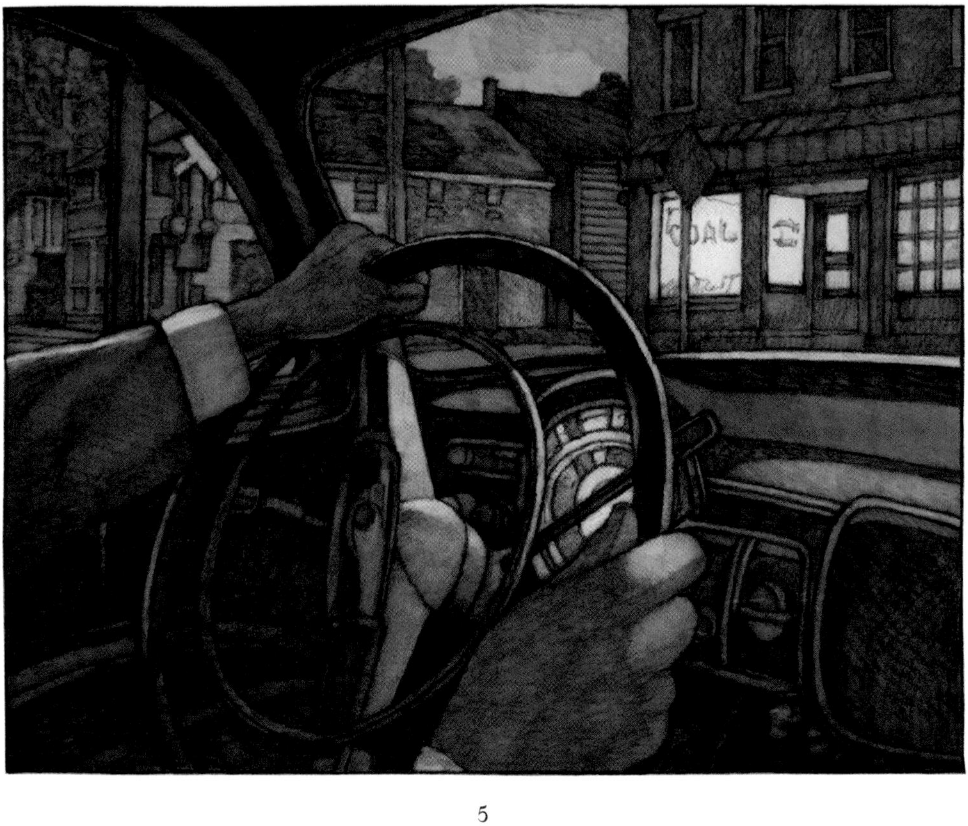

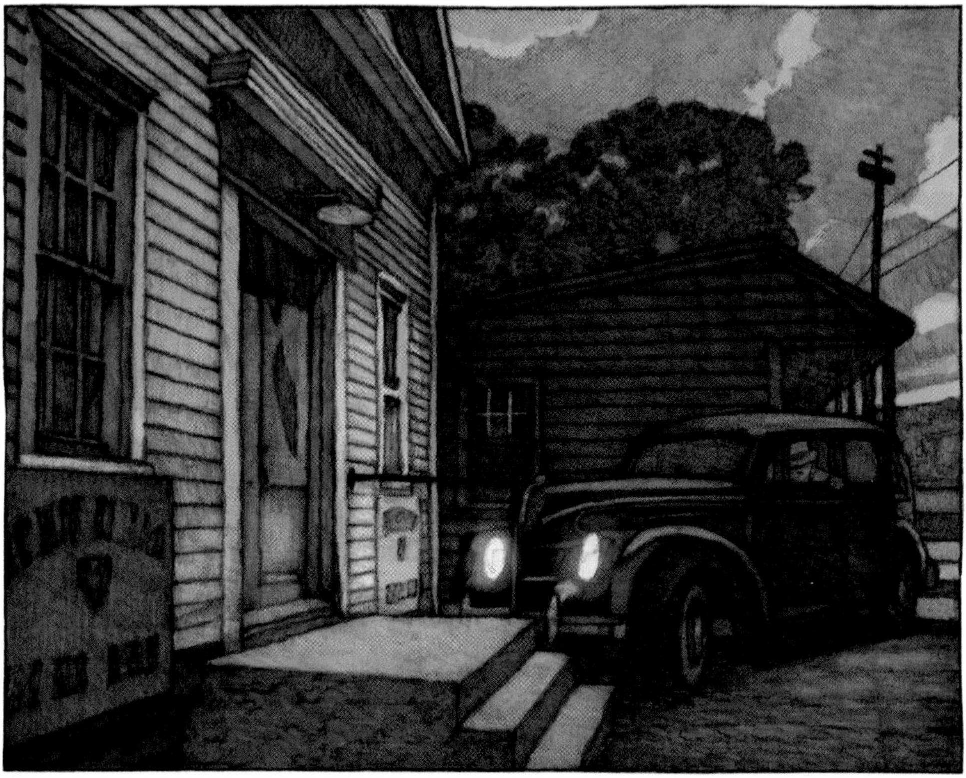

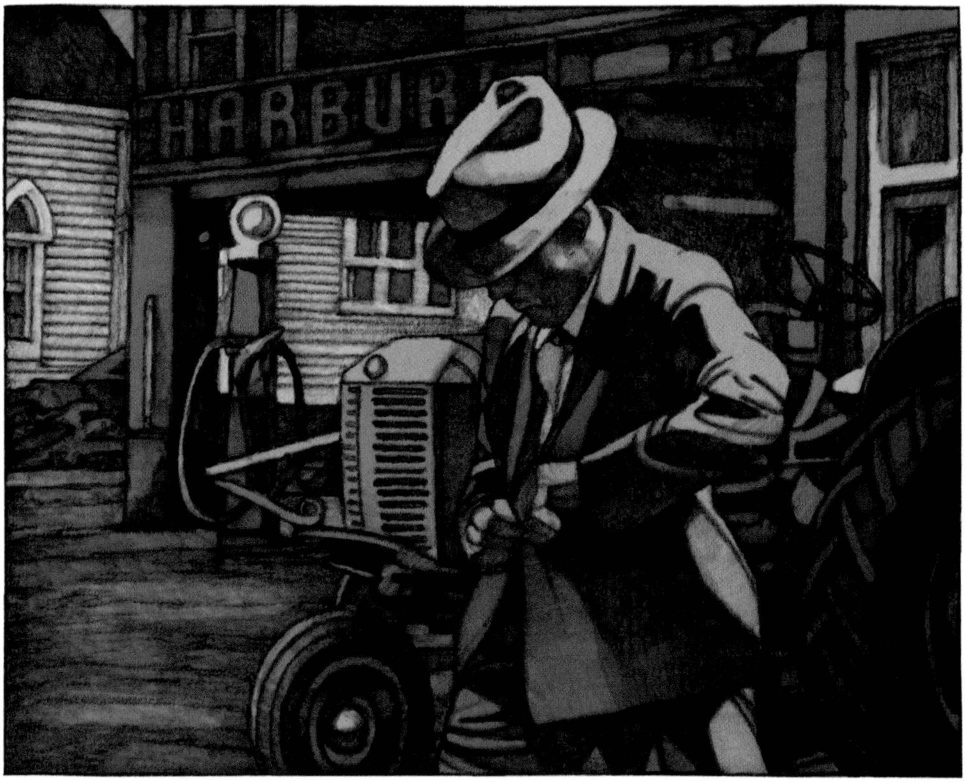
HARBUR

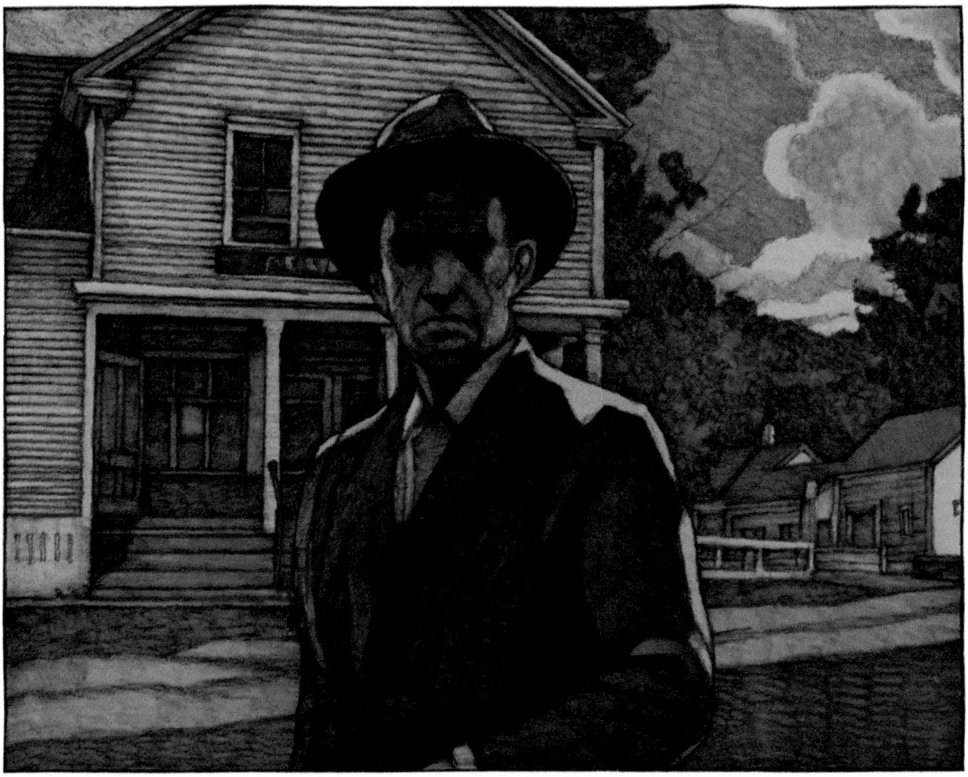

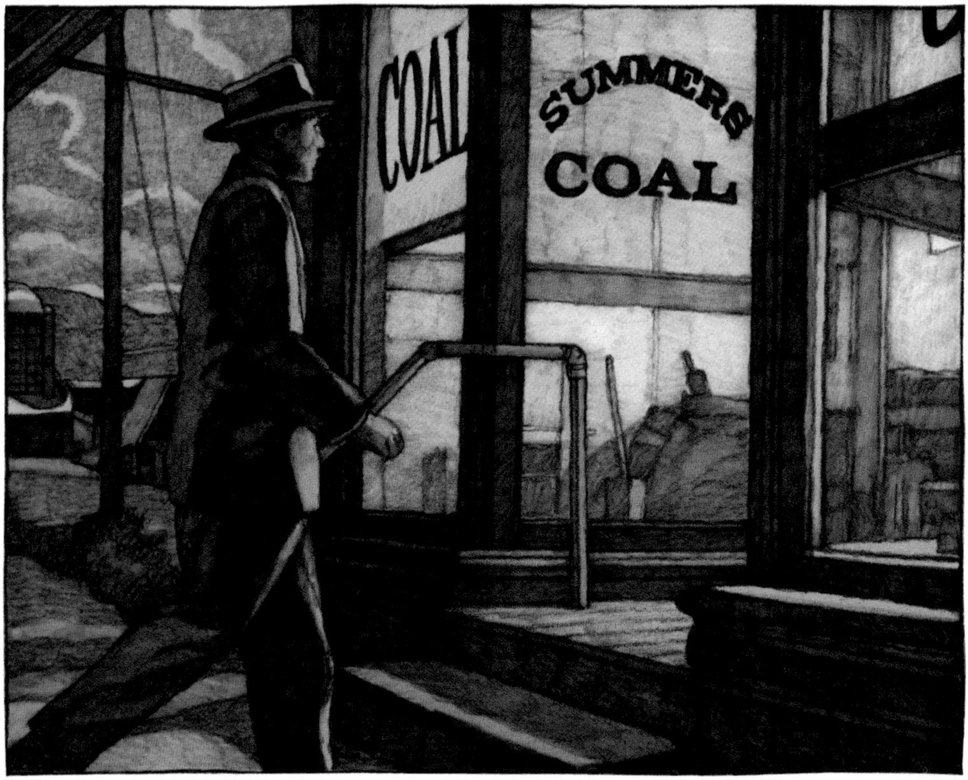
COAL
SUMMERS
COAL

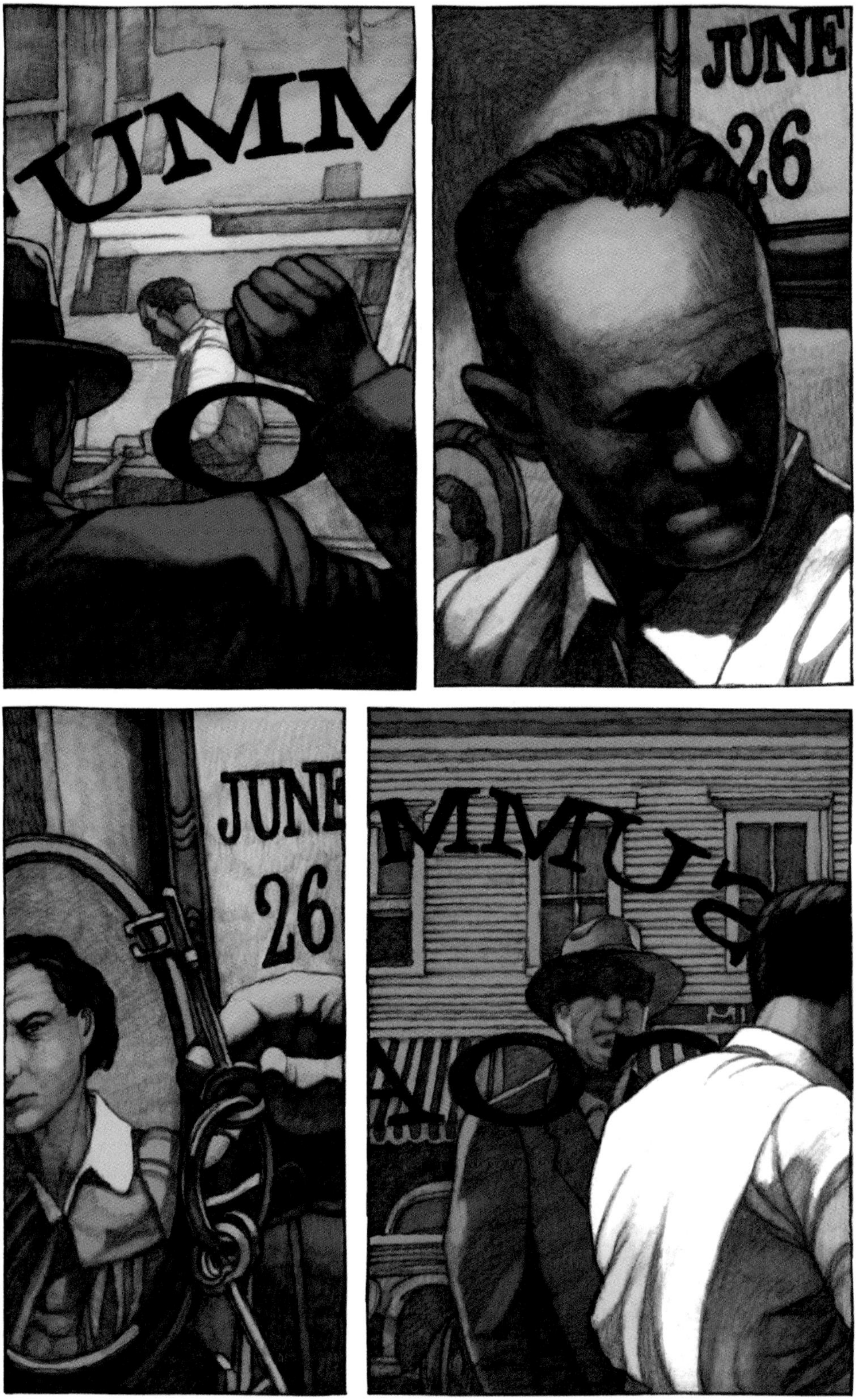
UMM
O
JUNE
26
JUNE
26
MMU
O

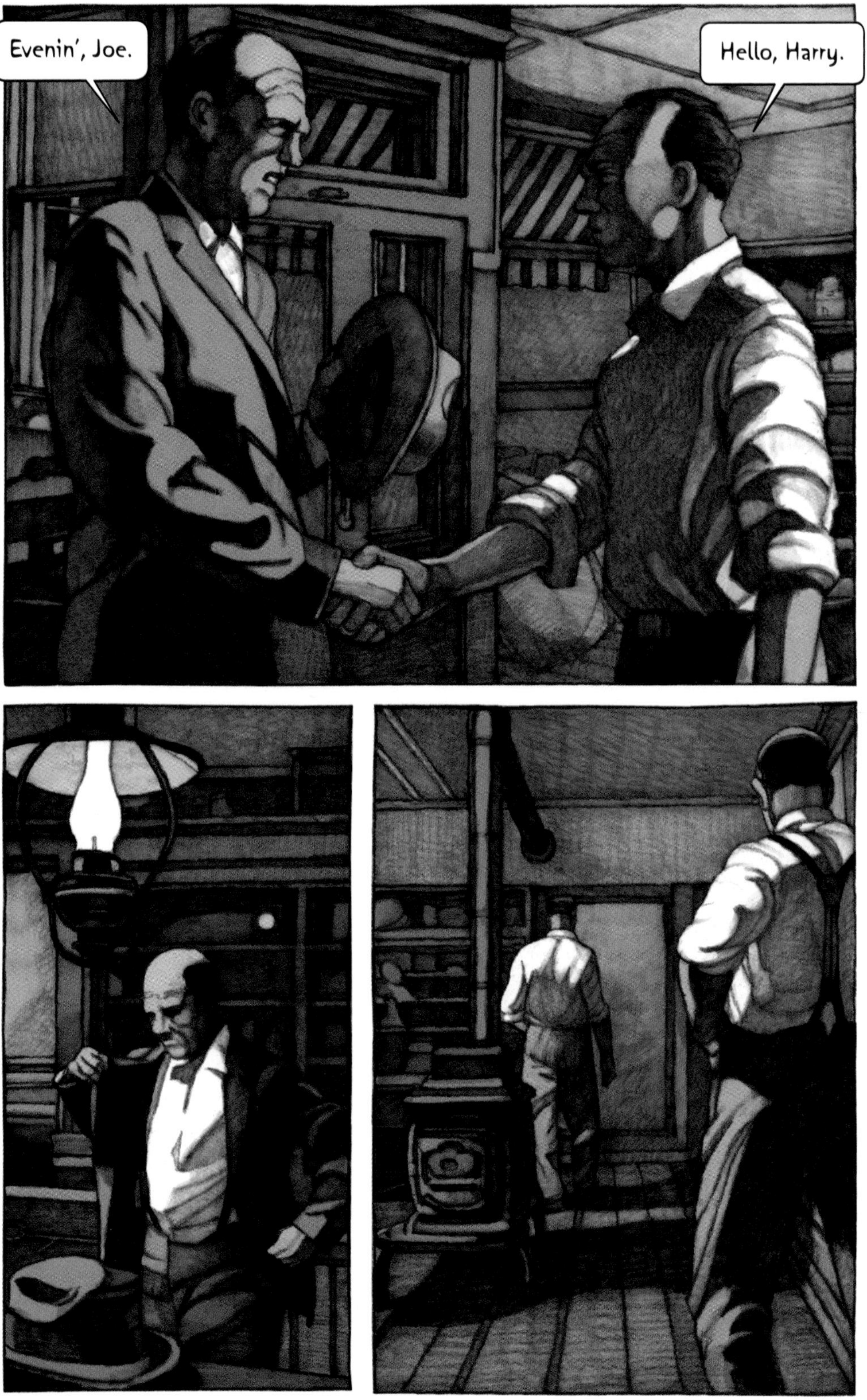
Evenin', Joe.
Hello, Harry.

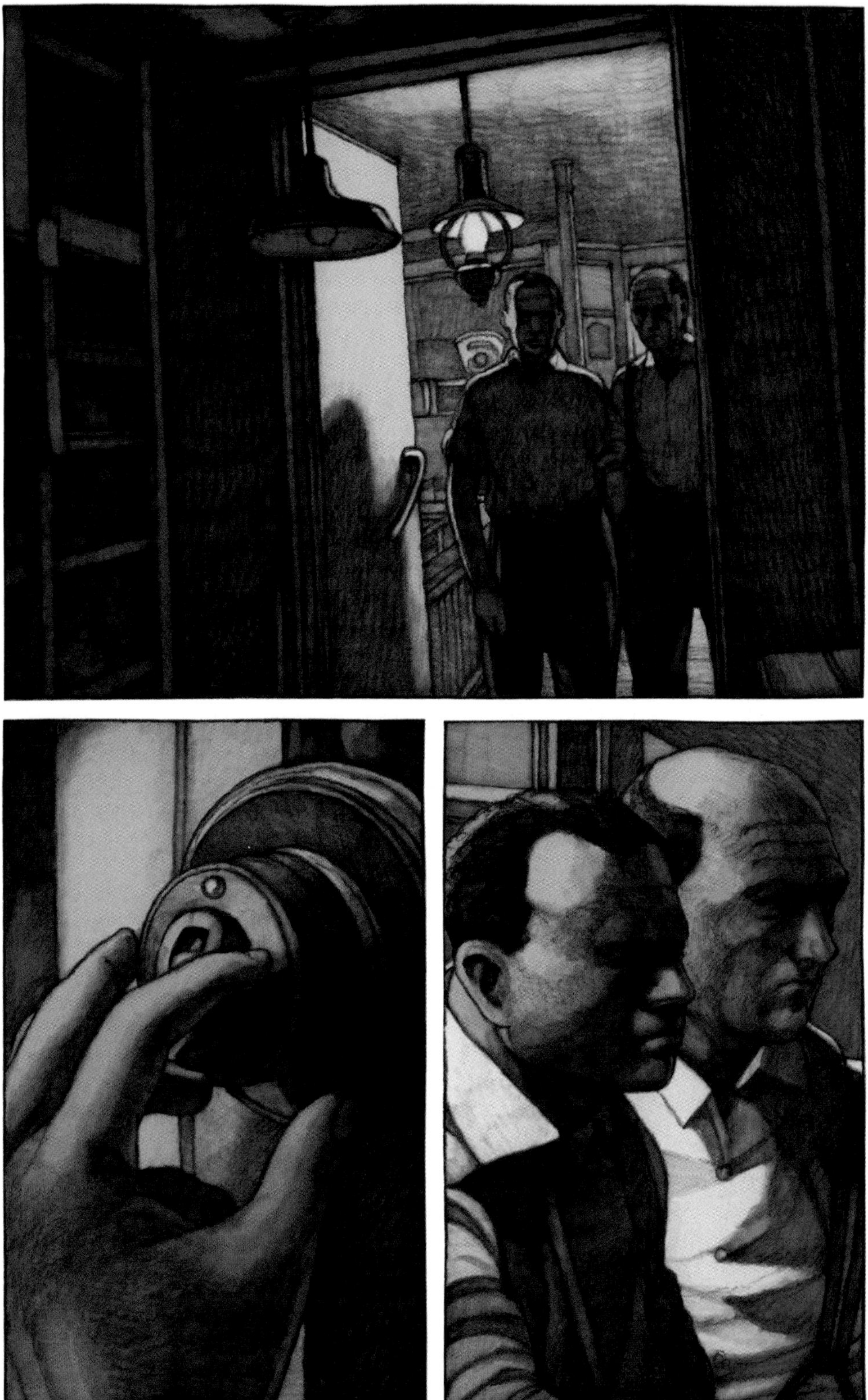

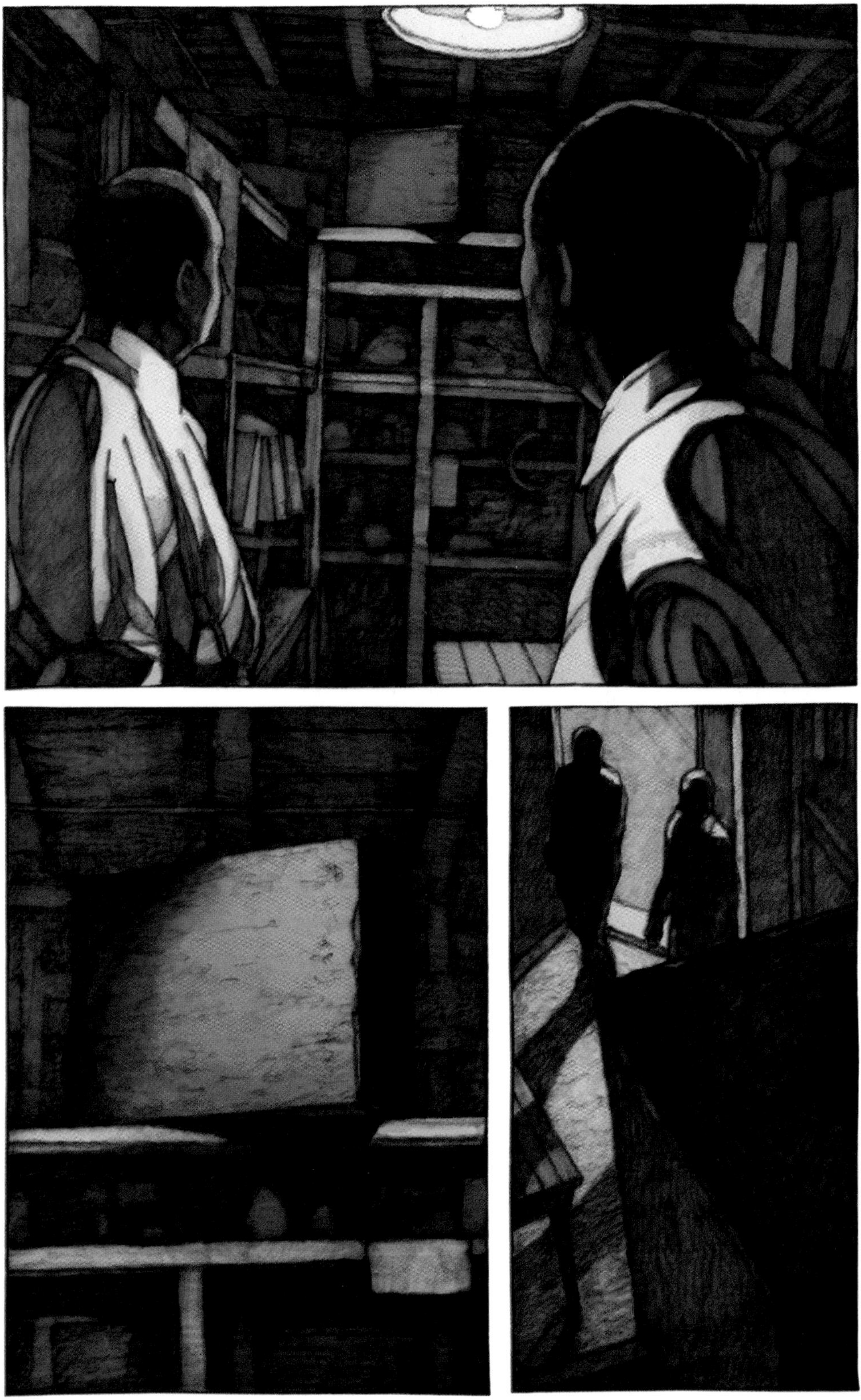

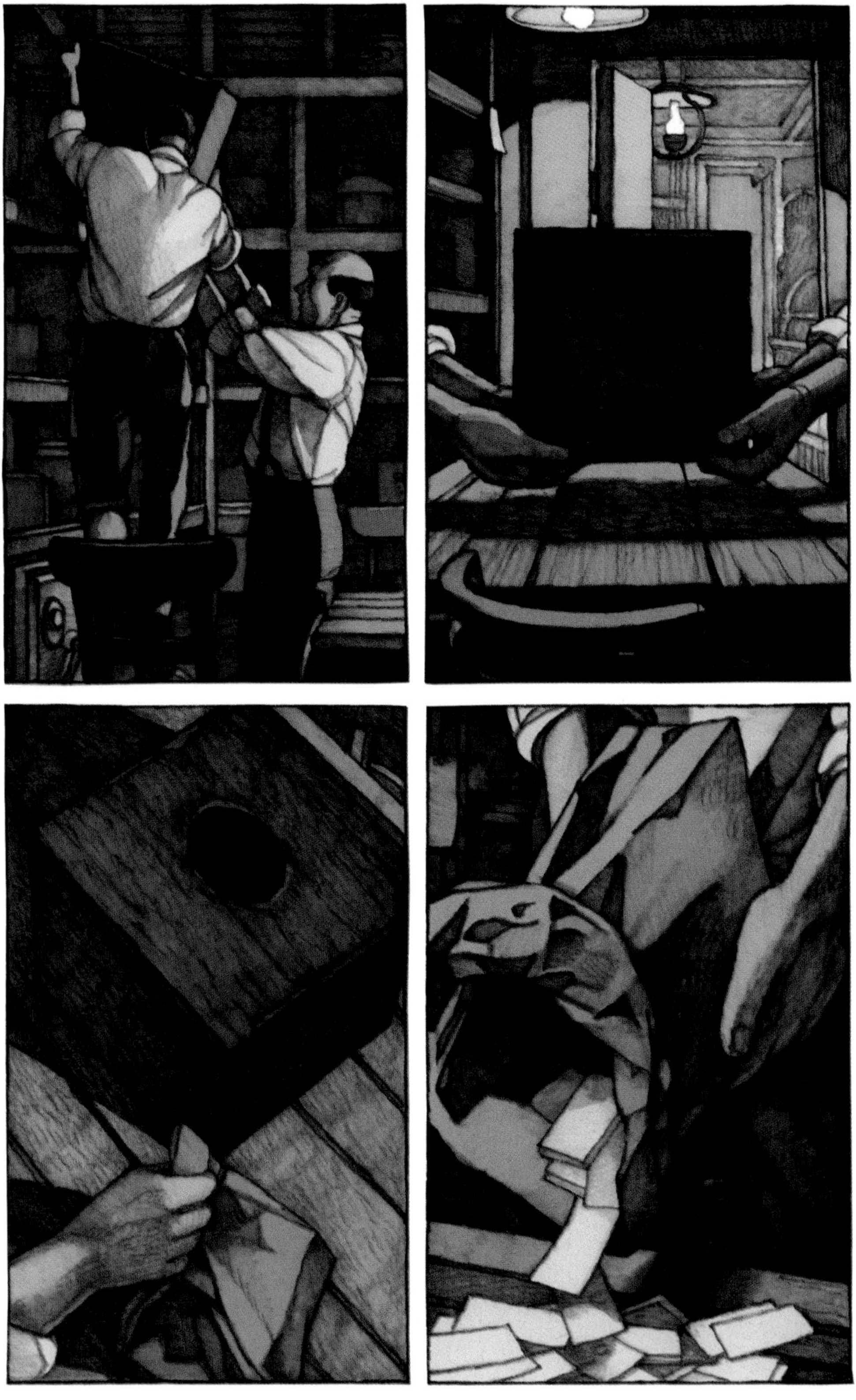

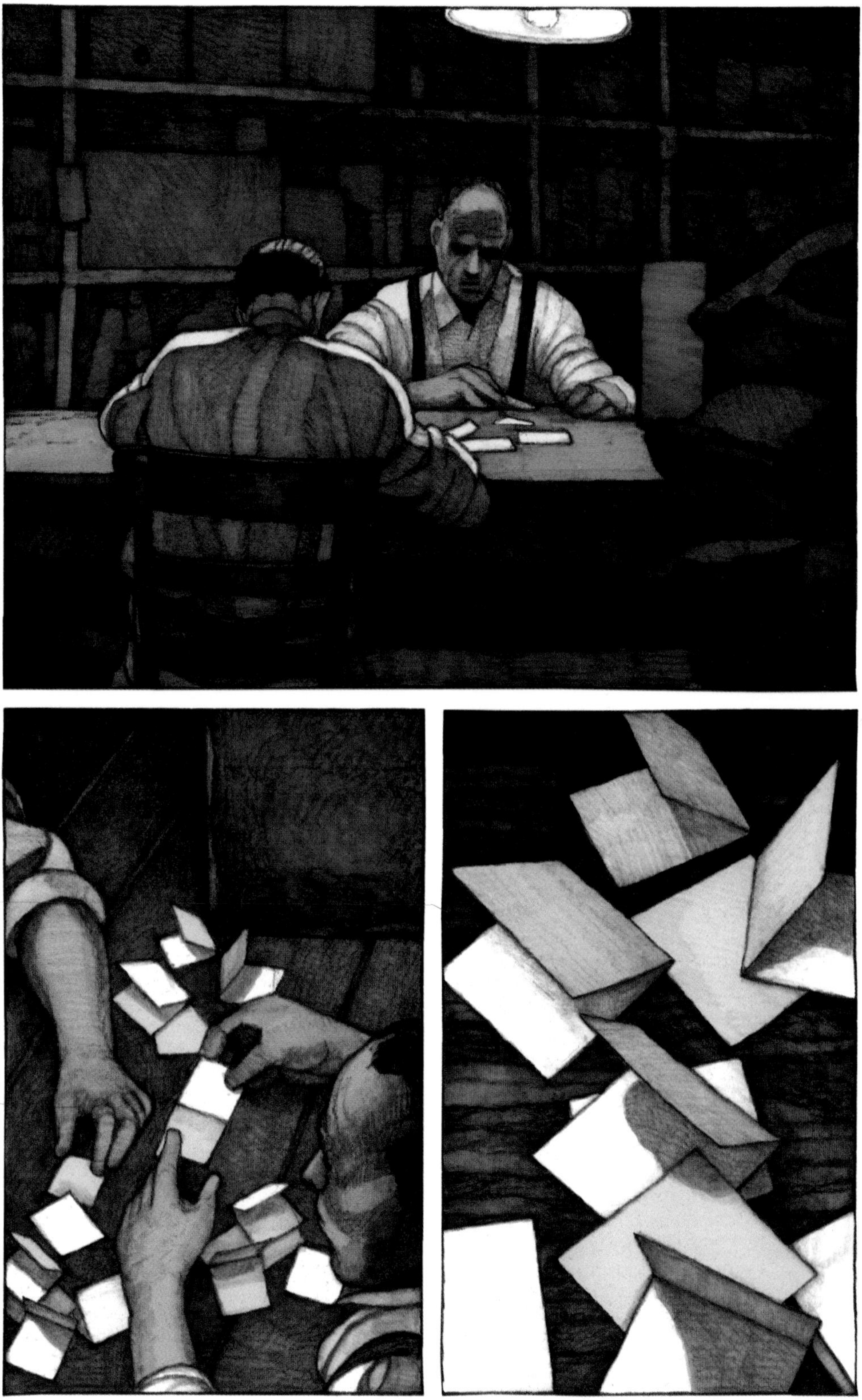

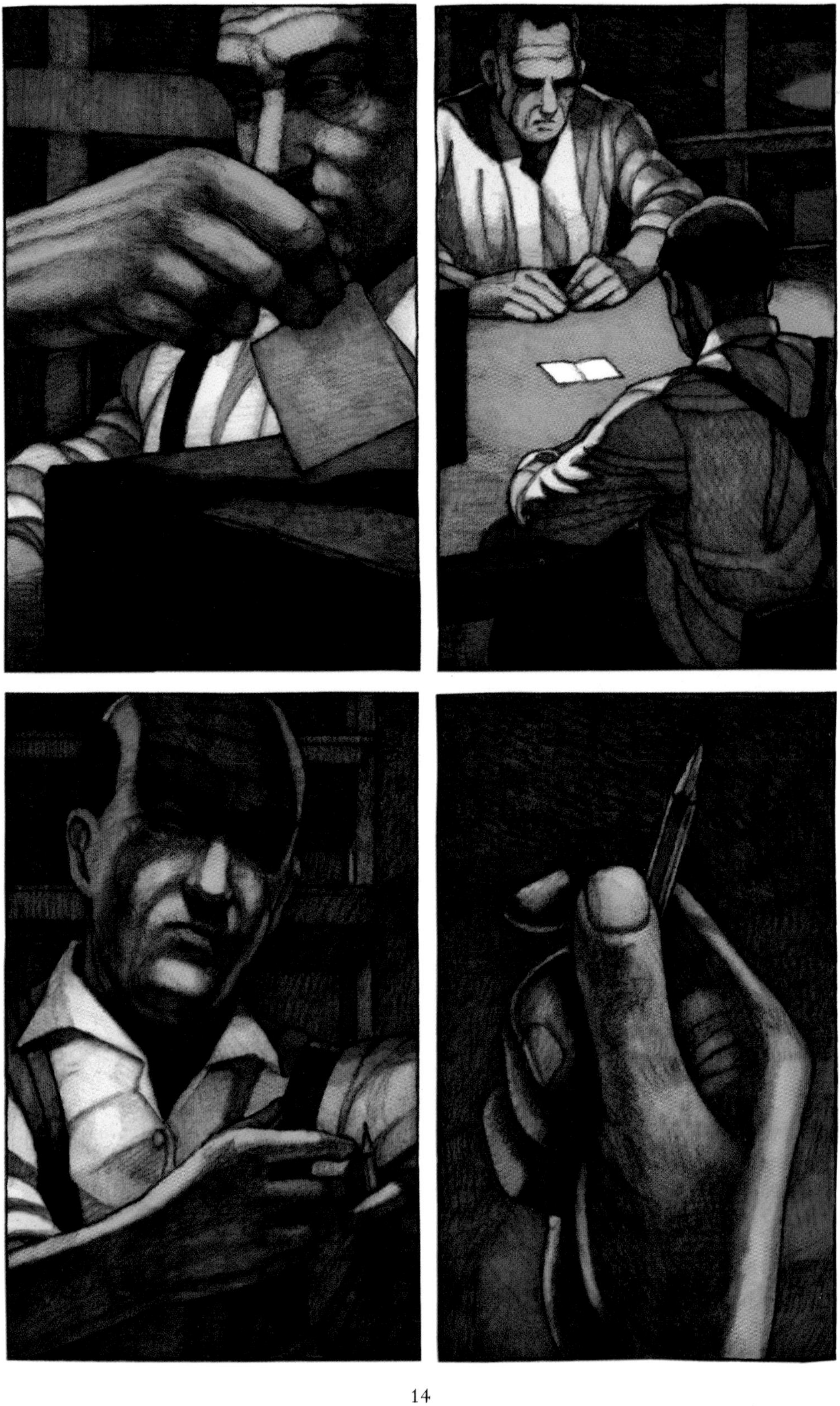

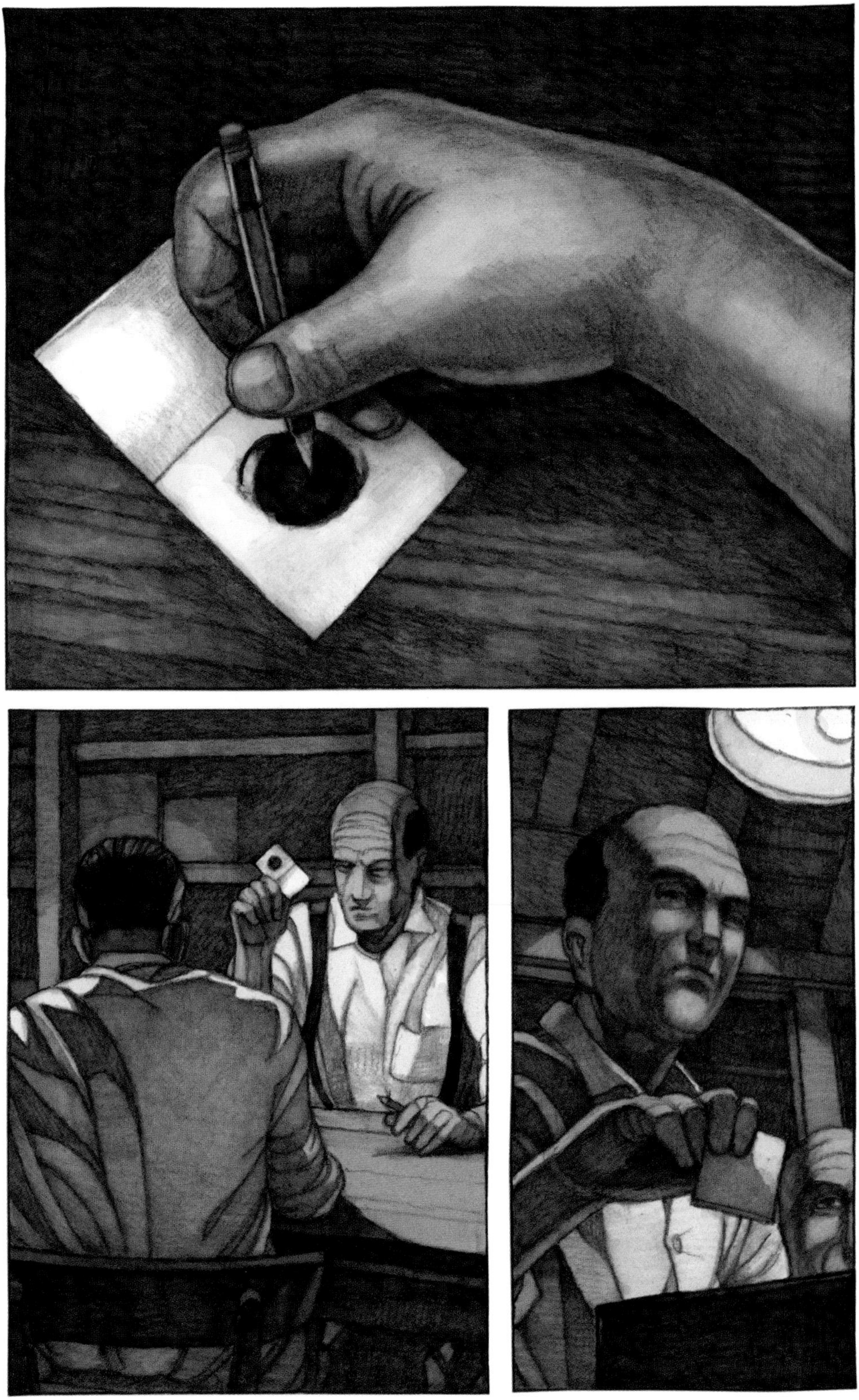

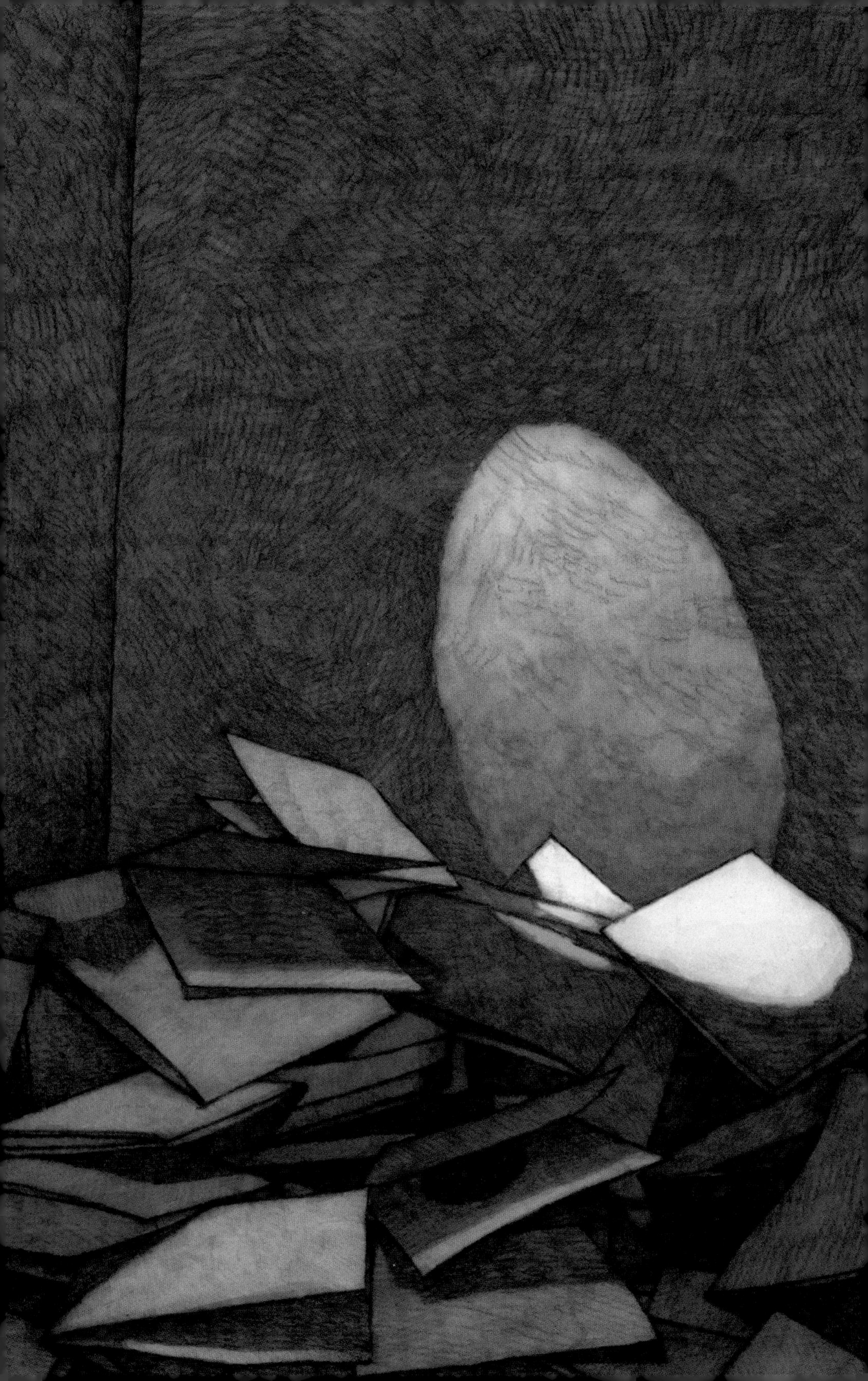

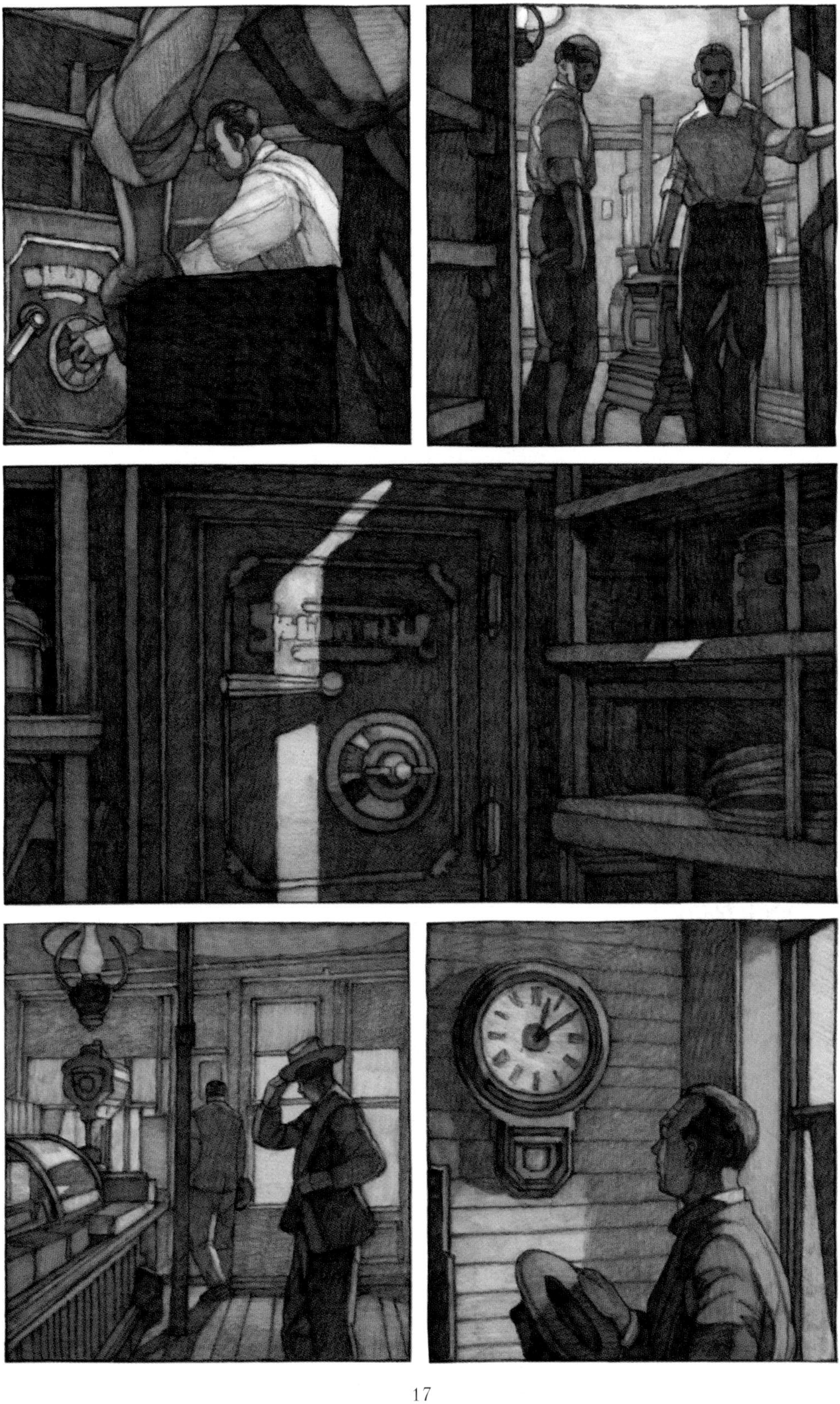

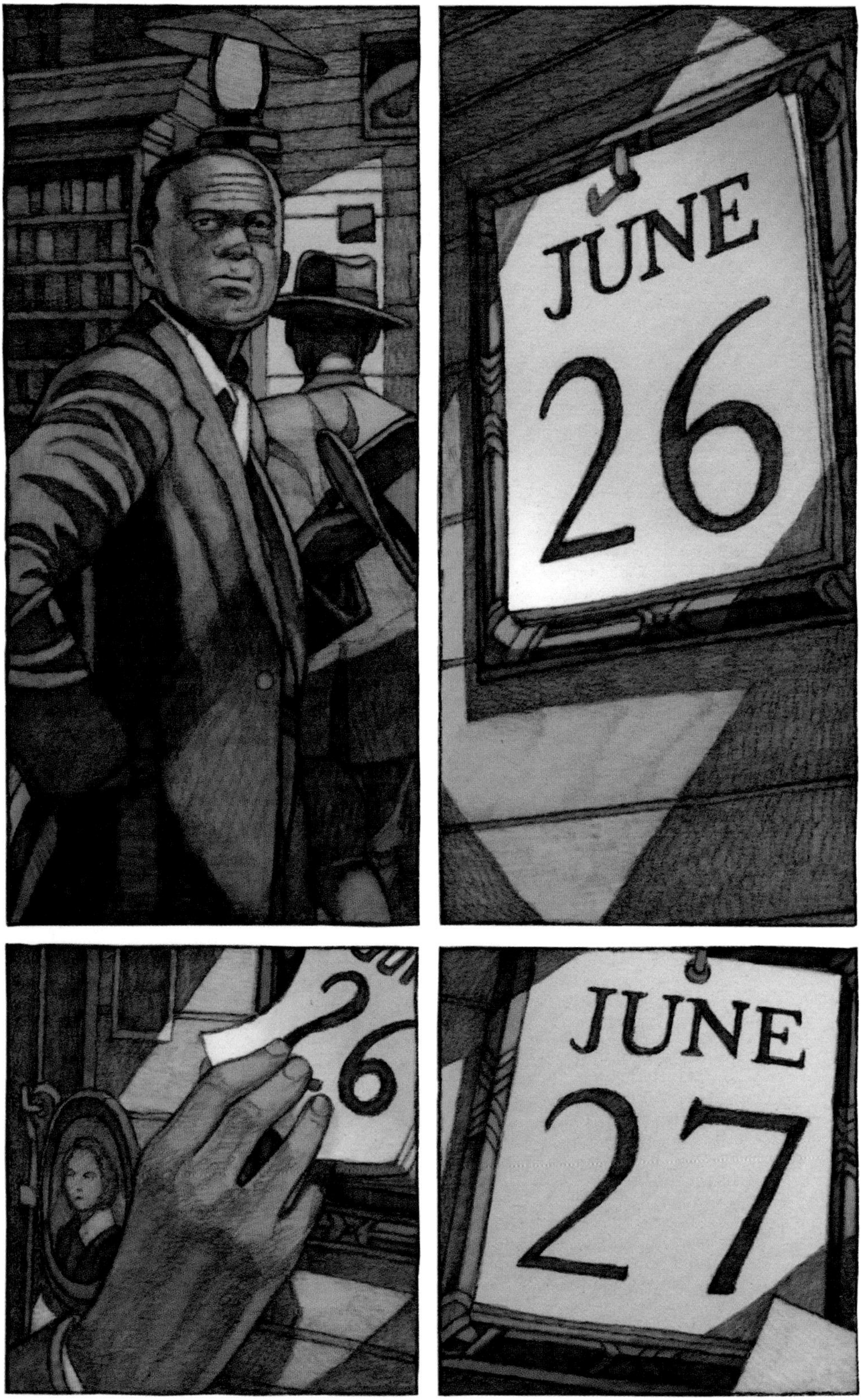
JUNE
26
JUNE
27

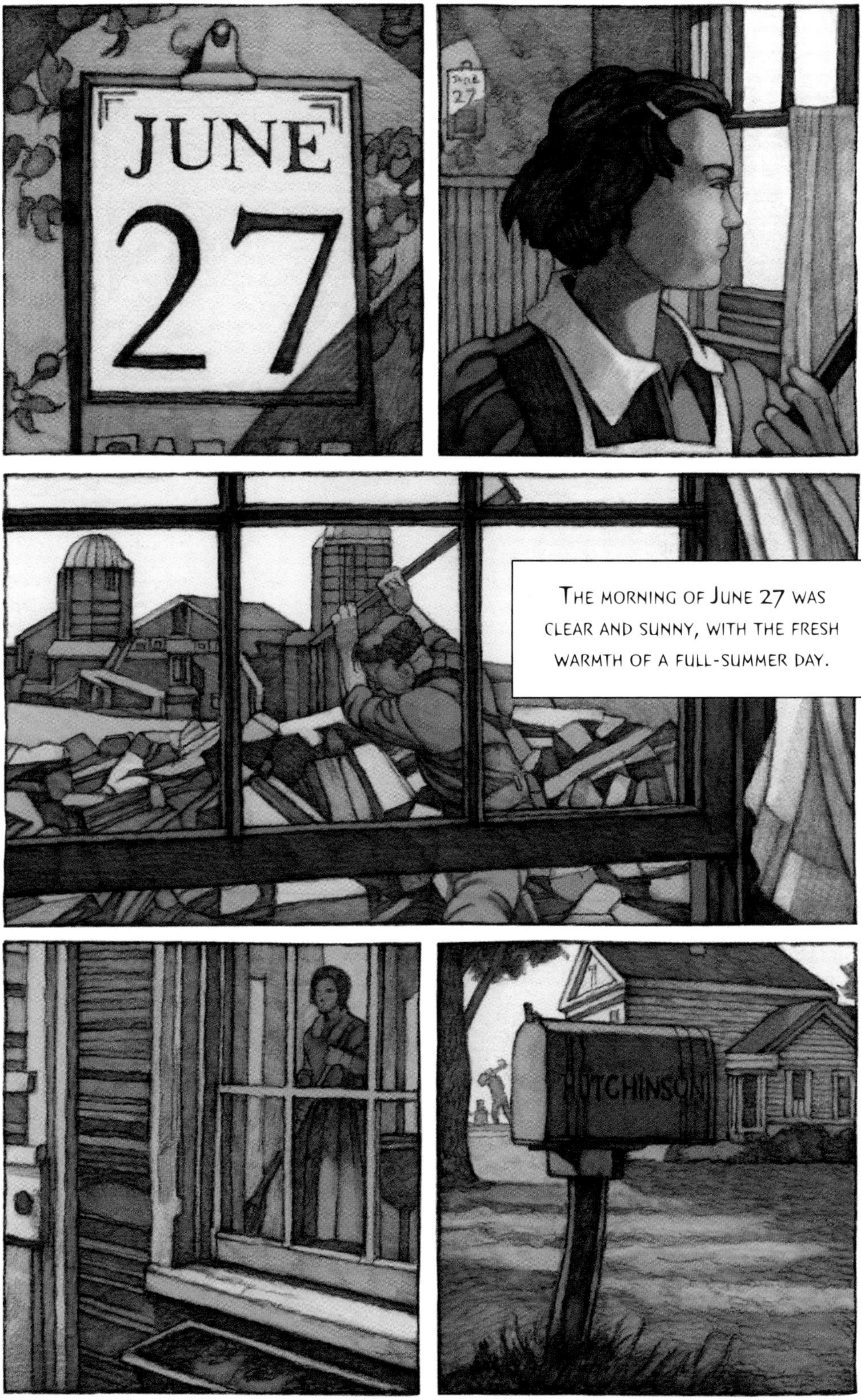
JUNE
27
THE MORNING OF JUNE 27 WAS CLEAR AND SUNNY, WITH THE FRESH WARMTH OF A FULL-SUMMER DAY.
HUTCHINSON

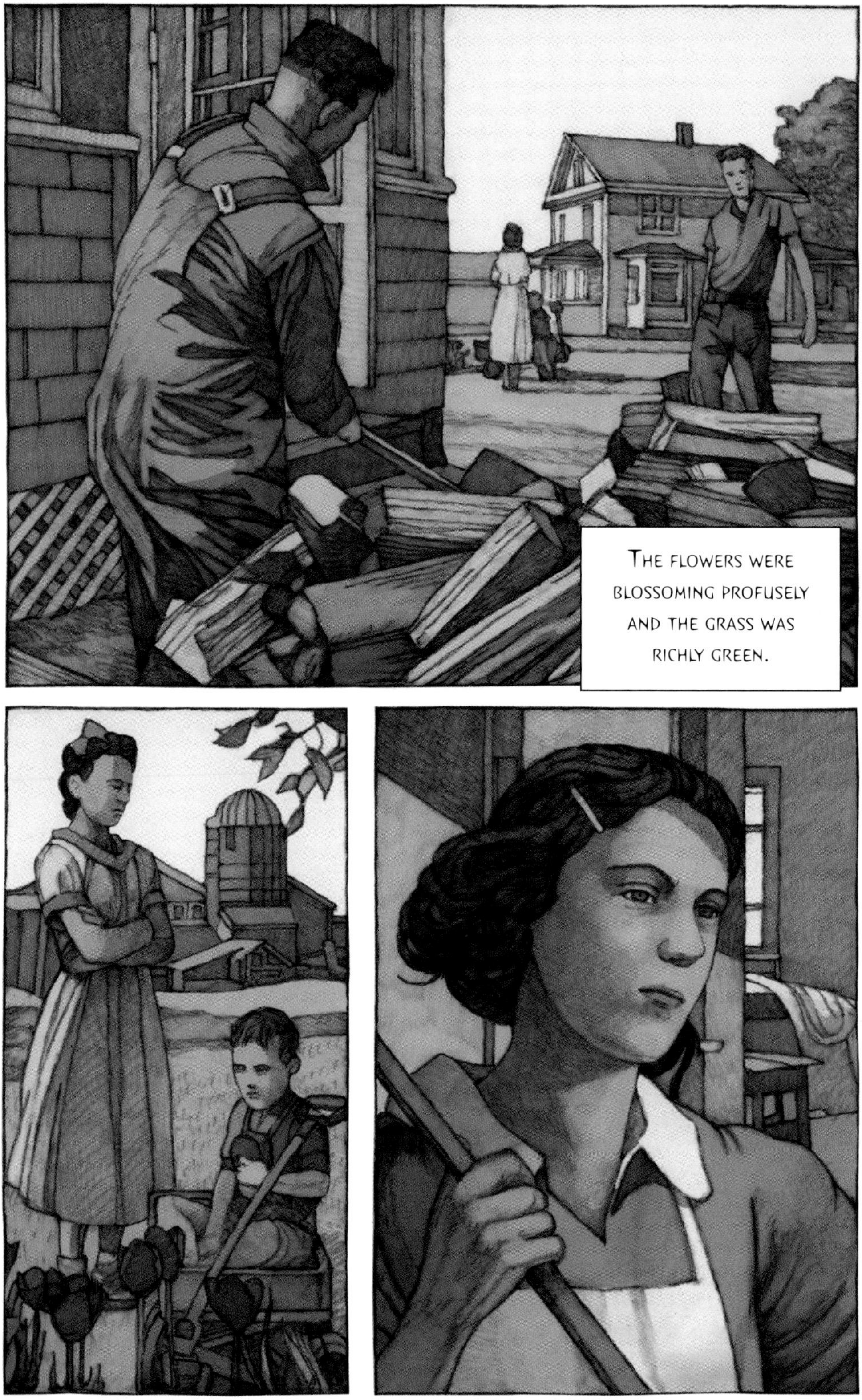
THE FLOWERS WERE BLOSSOMING PROFUSELY AND THE GRASS WAS RICHLY GREEN.

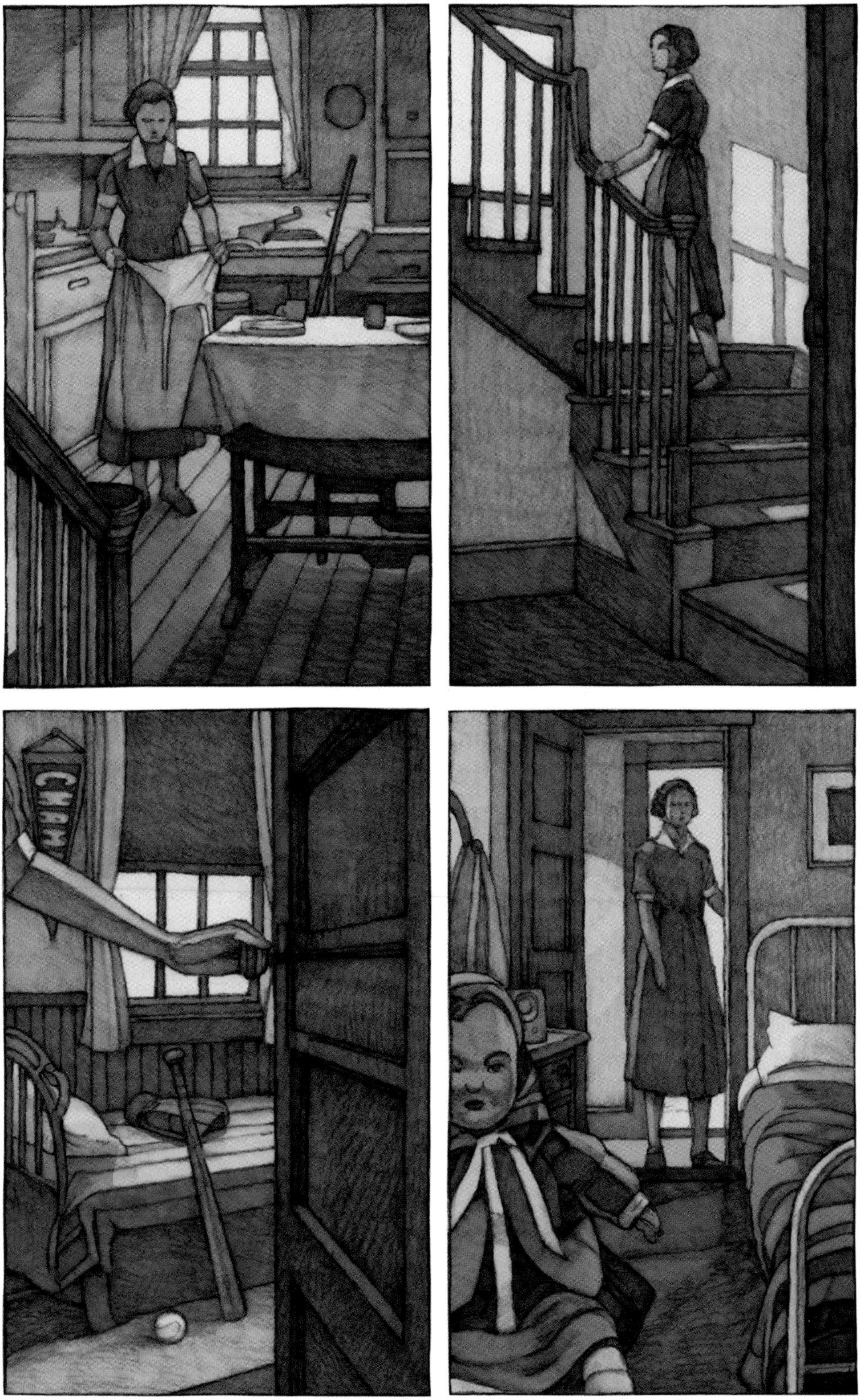

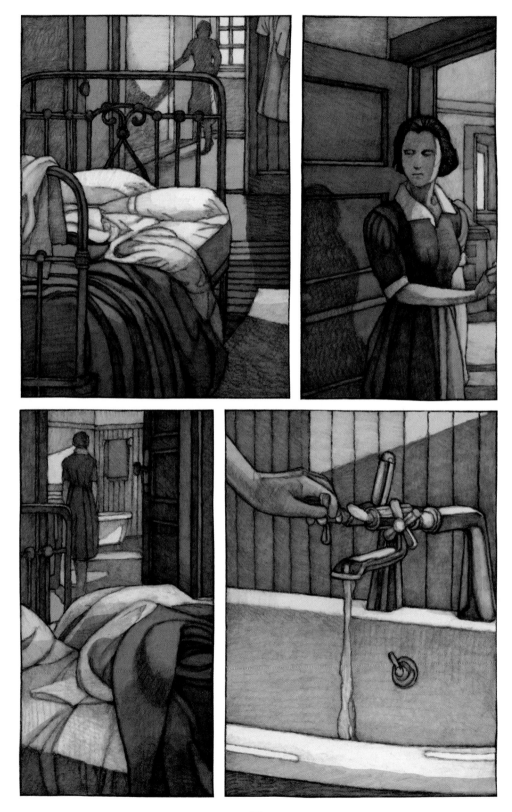

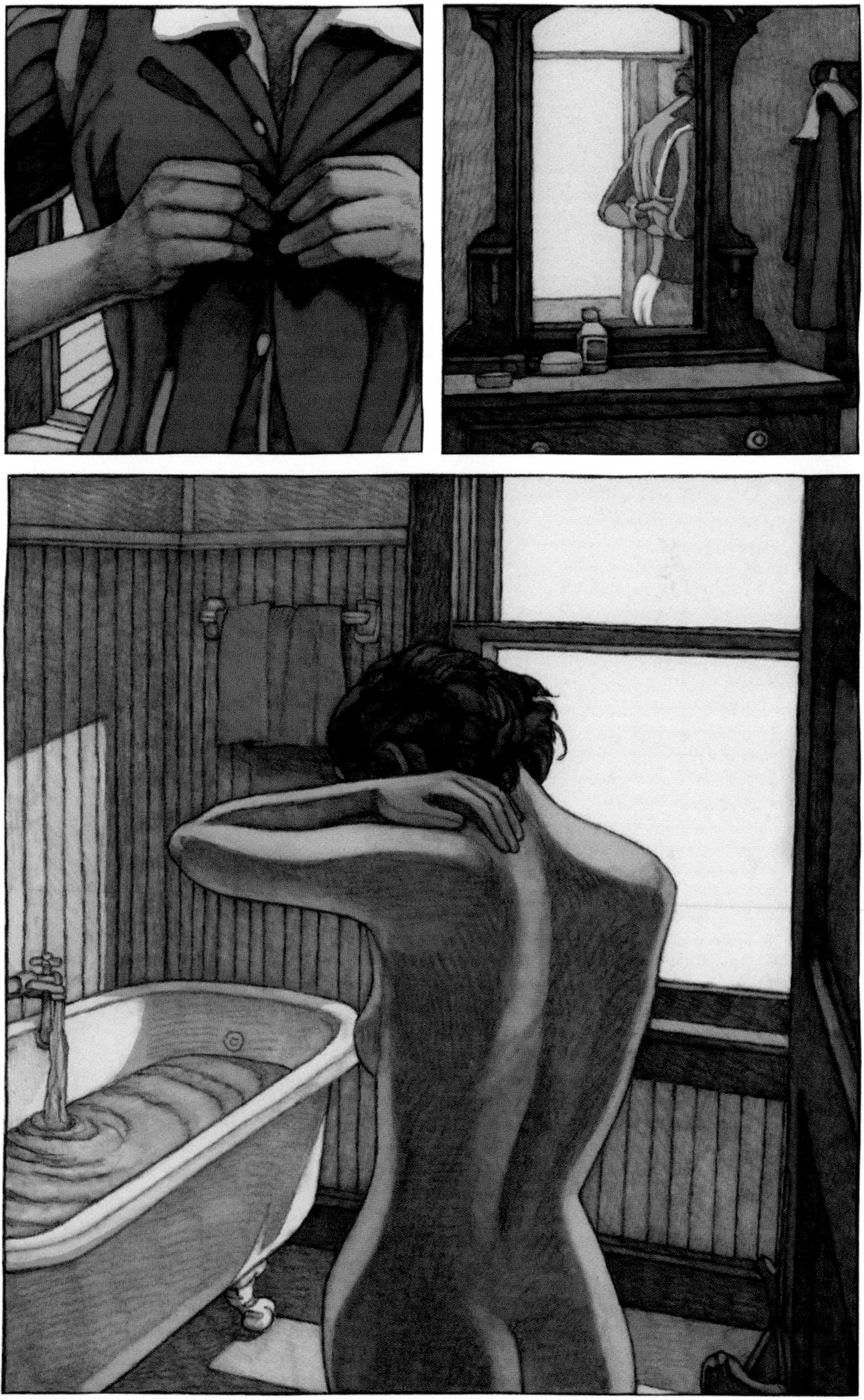

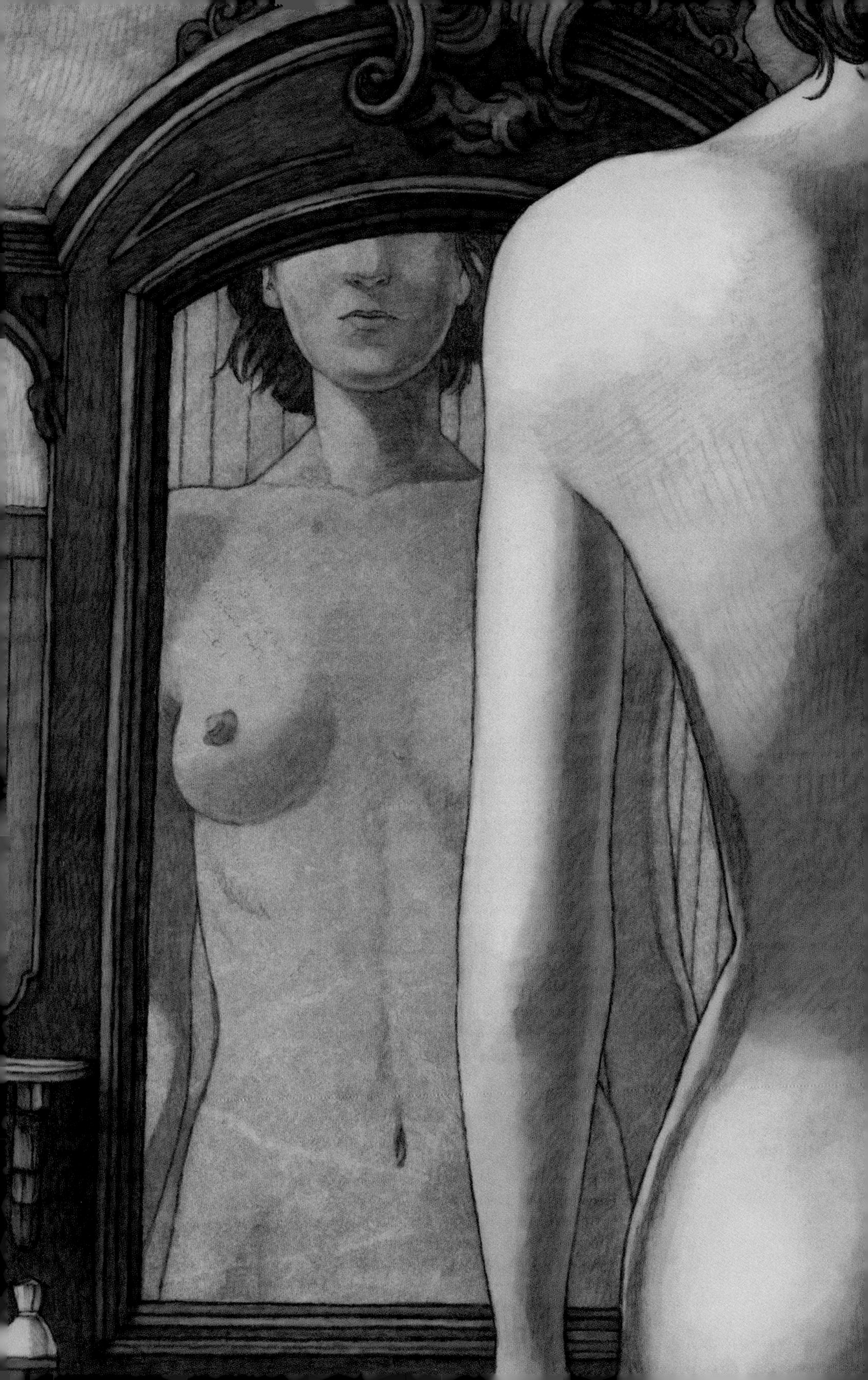

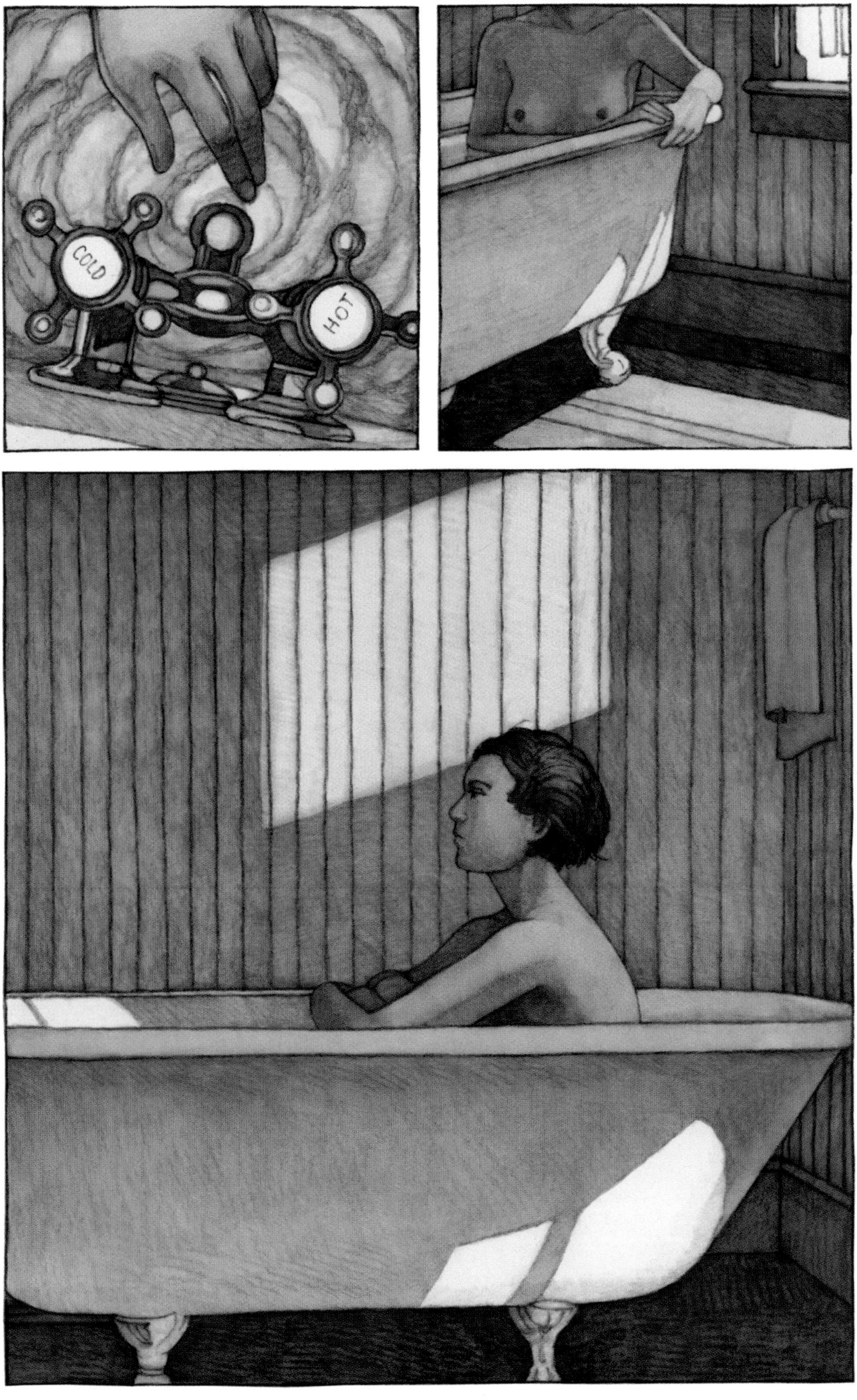
COLD
HOT

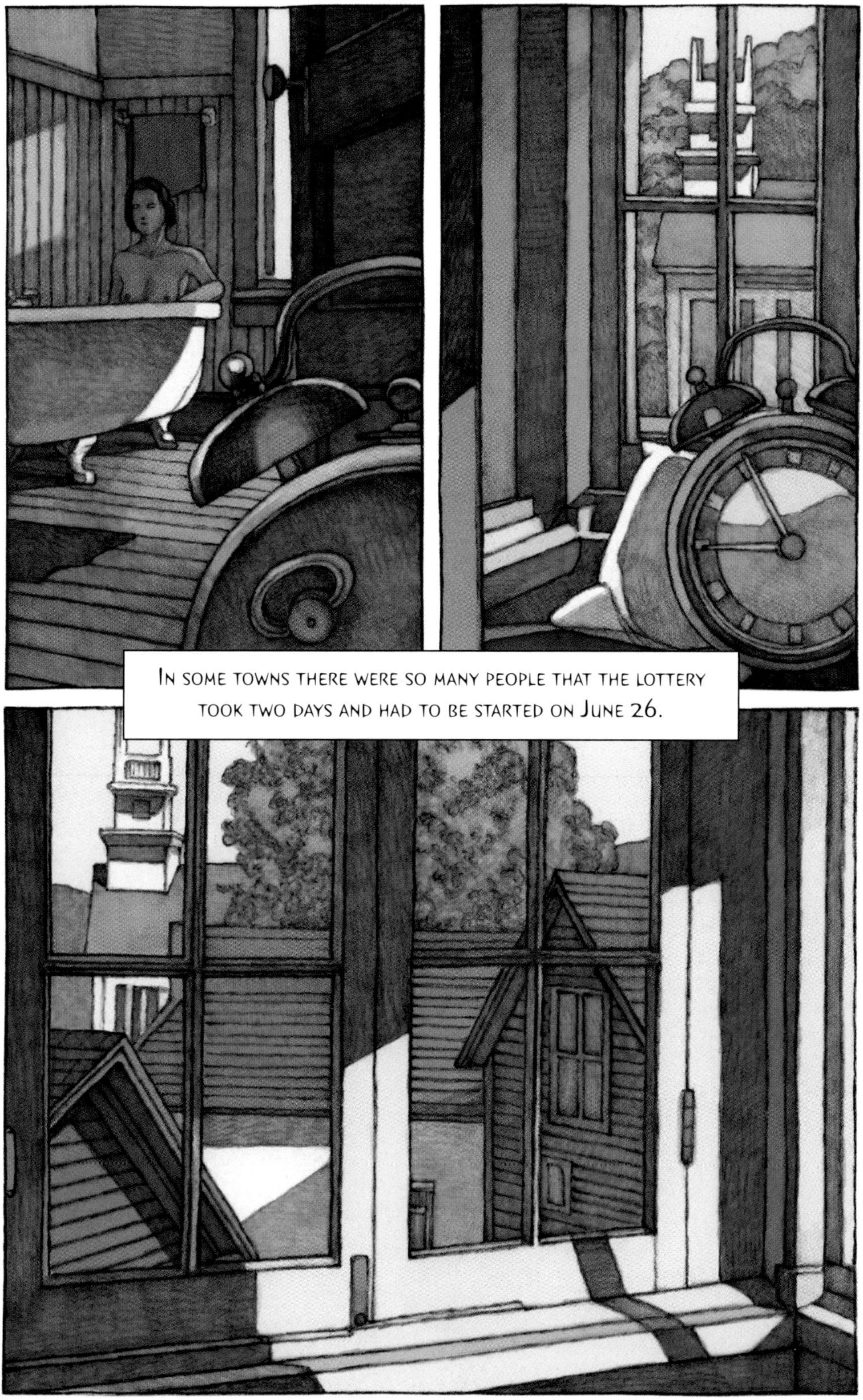
In some towns there were so many people that the lottery took two days and had to be started on June 26.

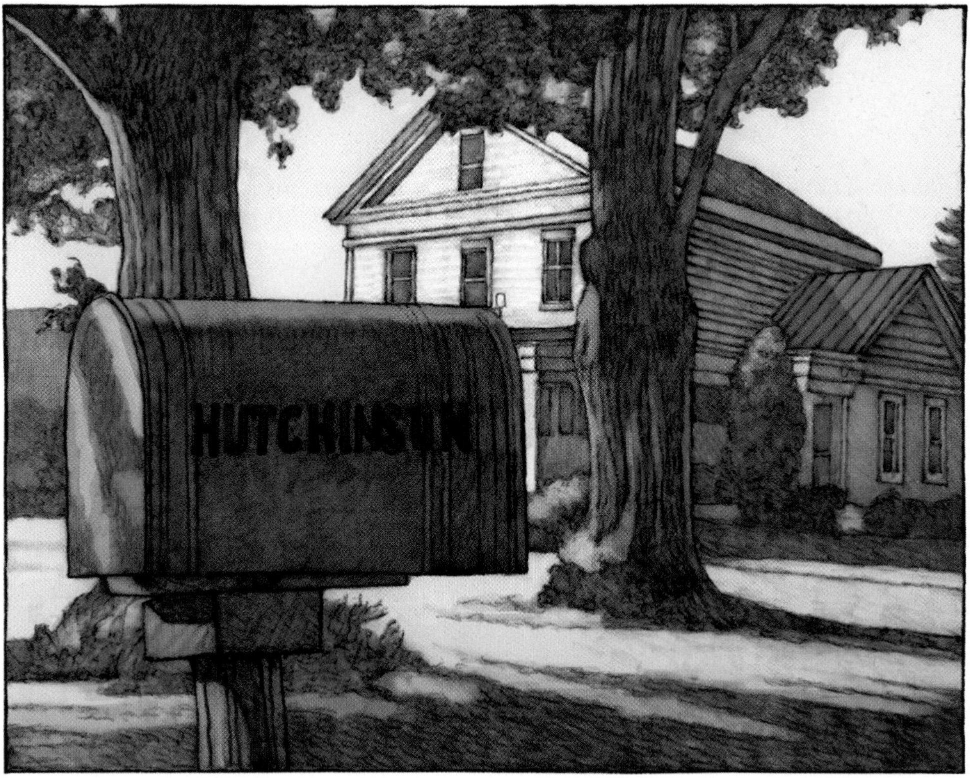
HUTCHINSON

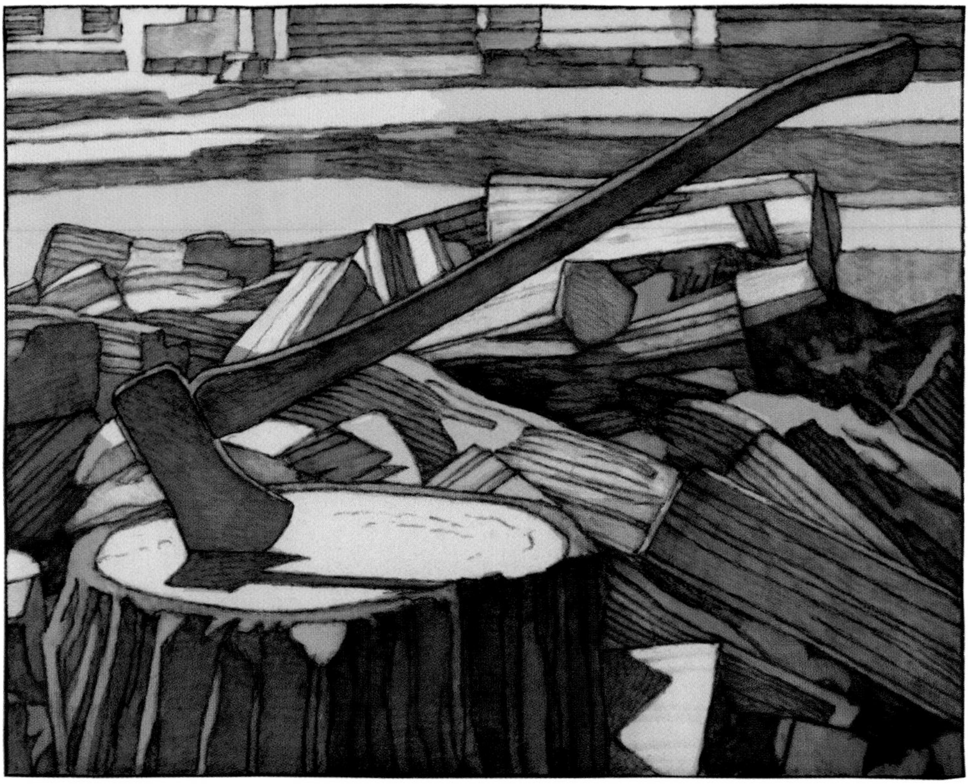

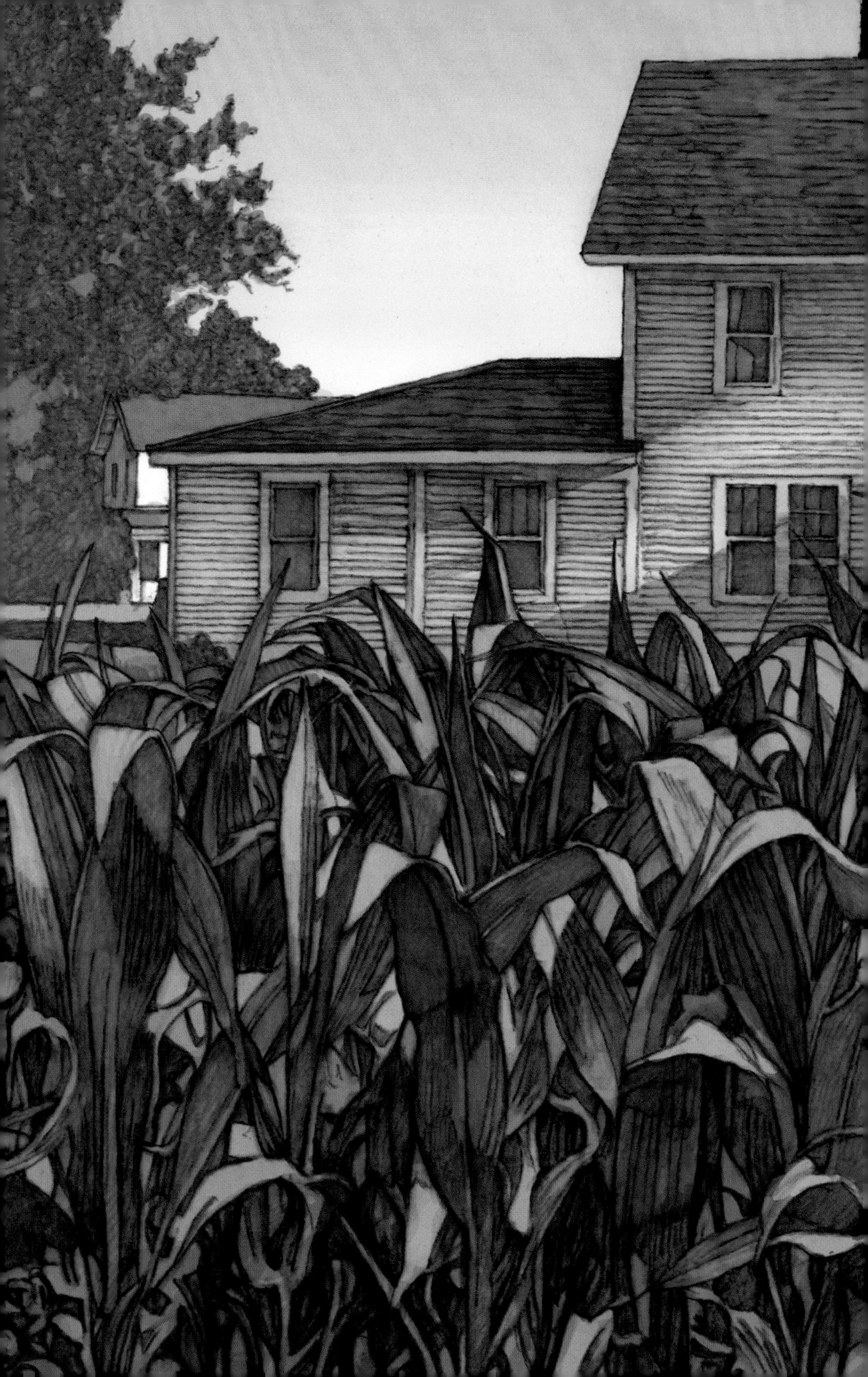

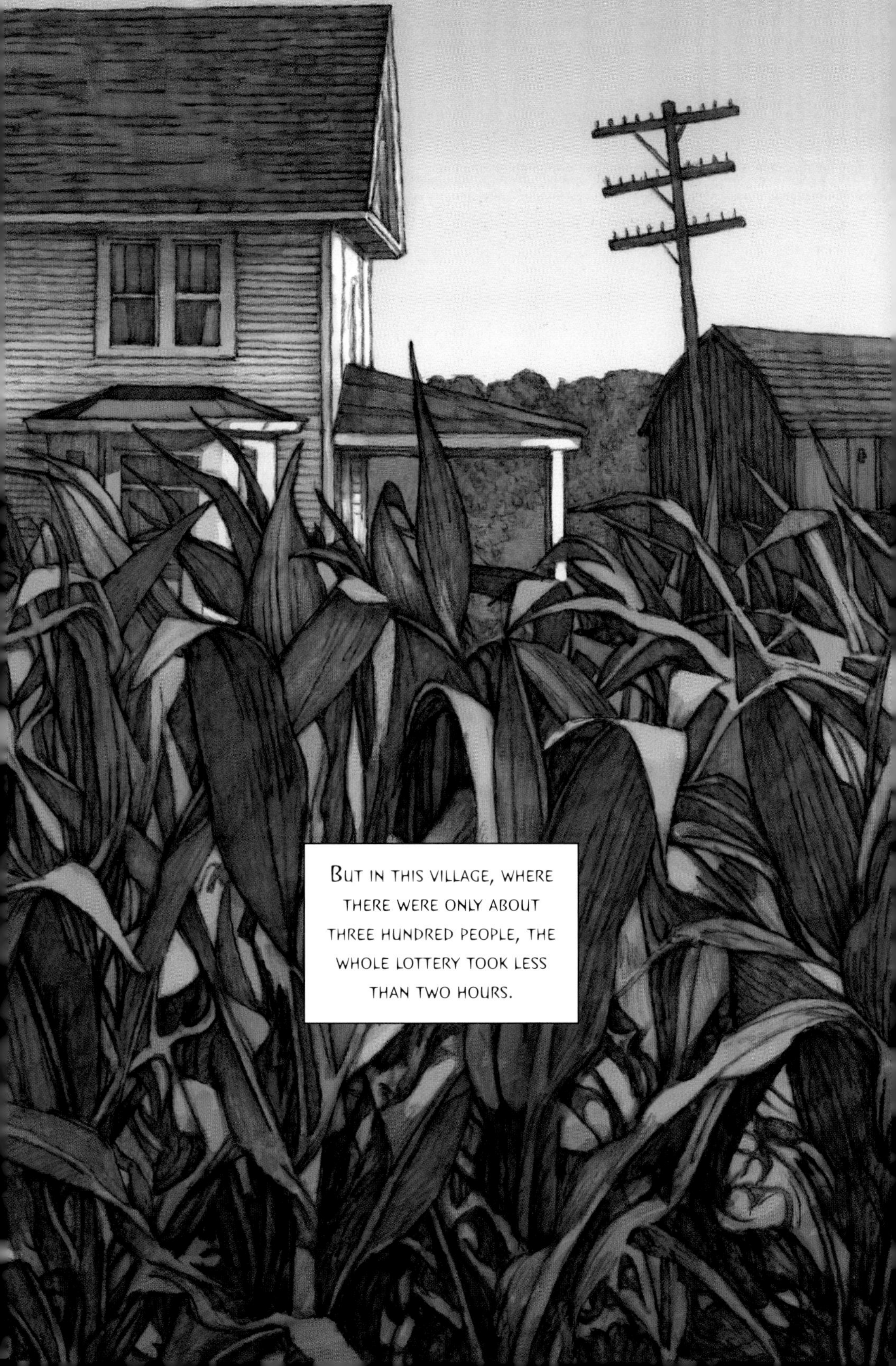
But in this village, where there were only about three hundred people, the whole lottery took less than two hours.

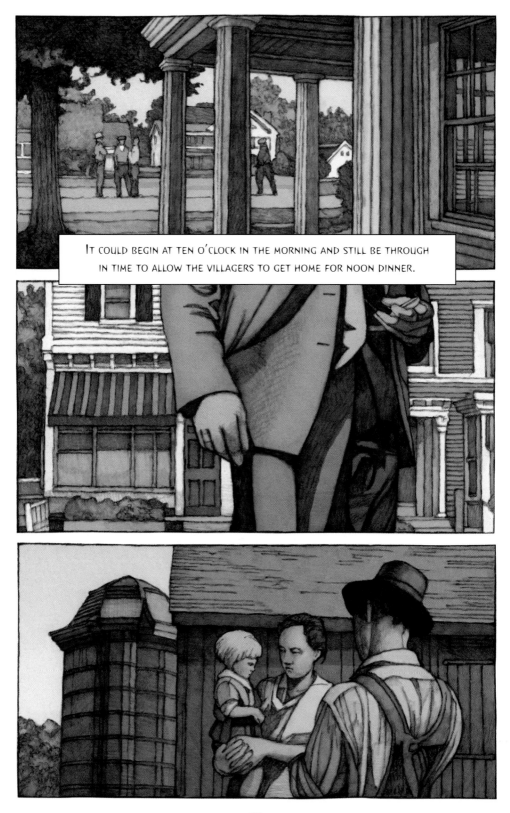

It could begin at ten o'clock in the morning and still be through in time to allow the villagers to get home for noon dinner.

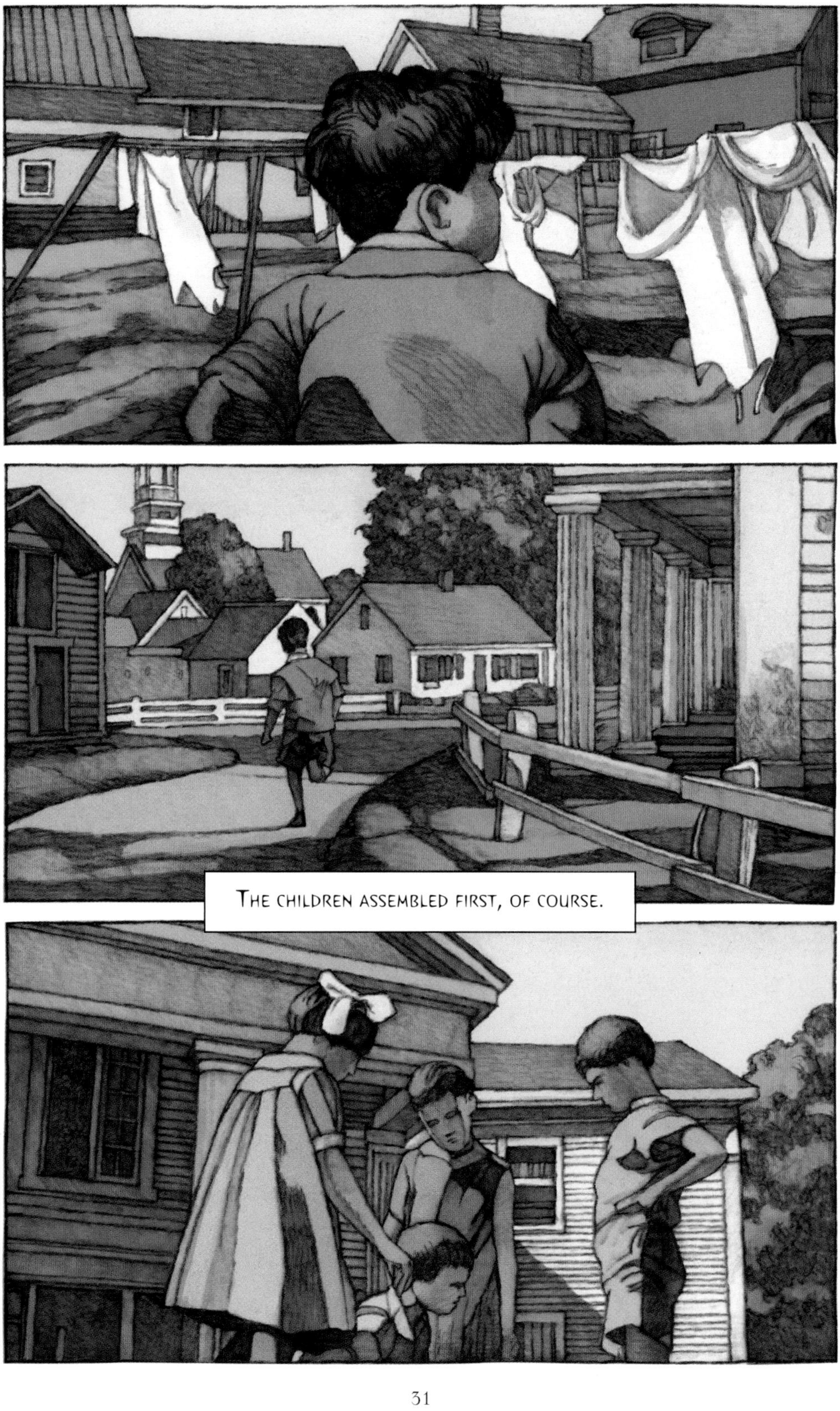
THE CHILDREN ASSEMBLED FIRST, OF COURSE.

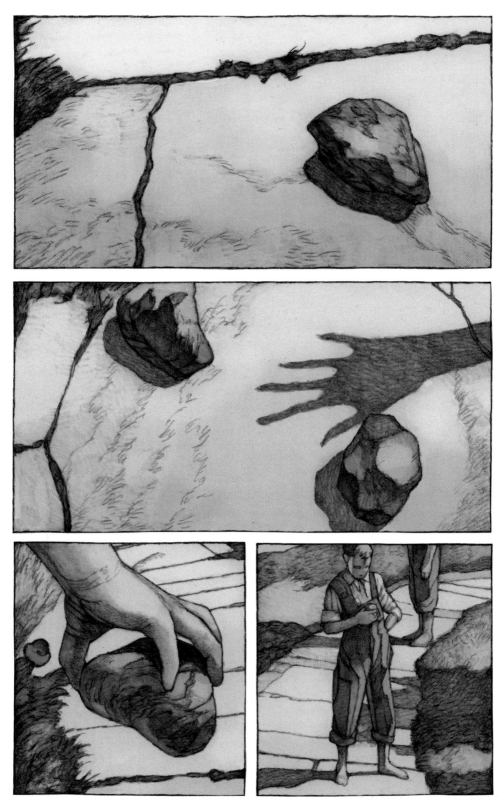

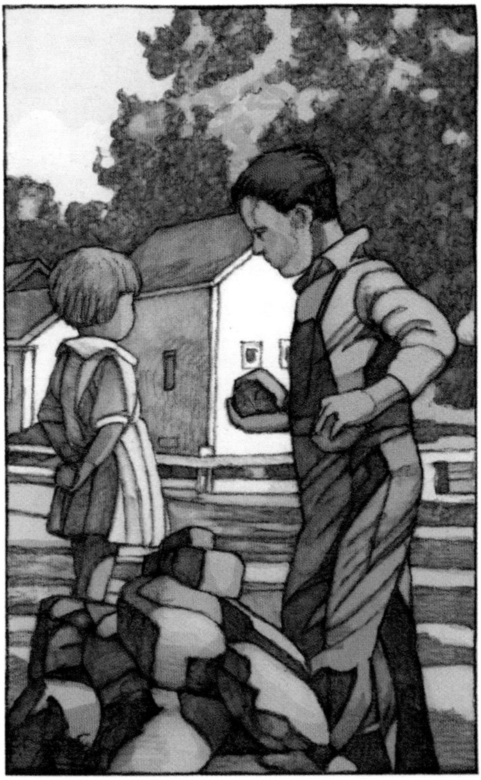
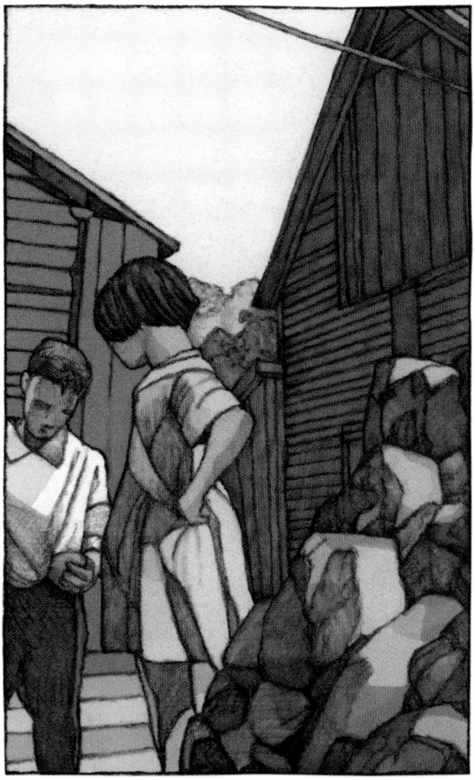
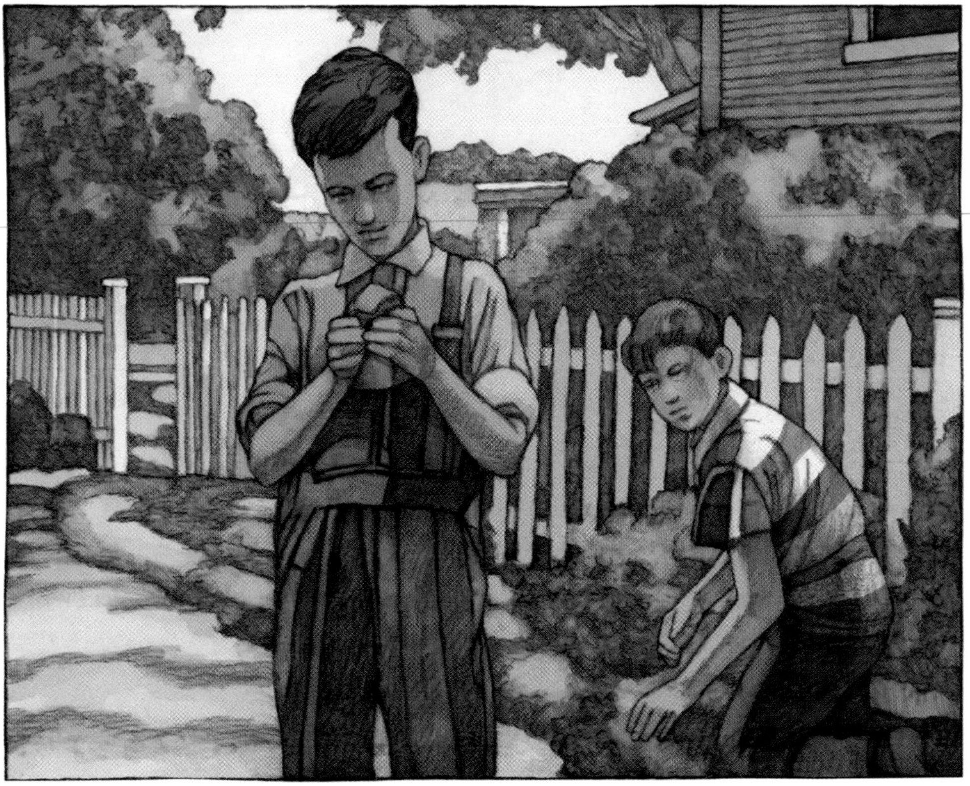

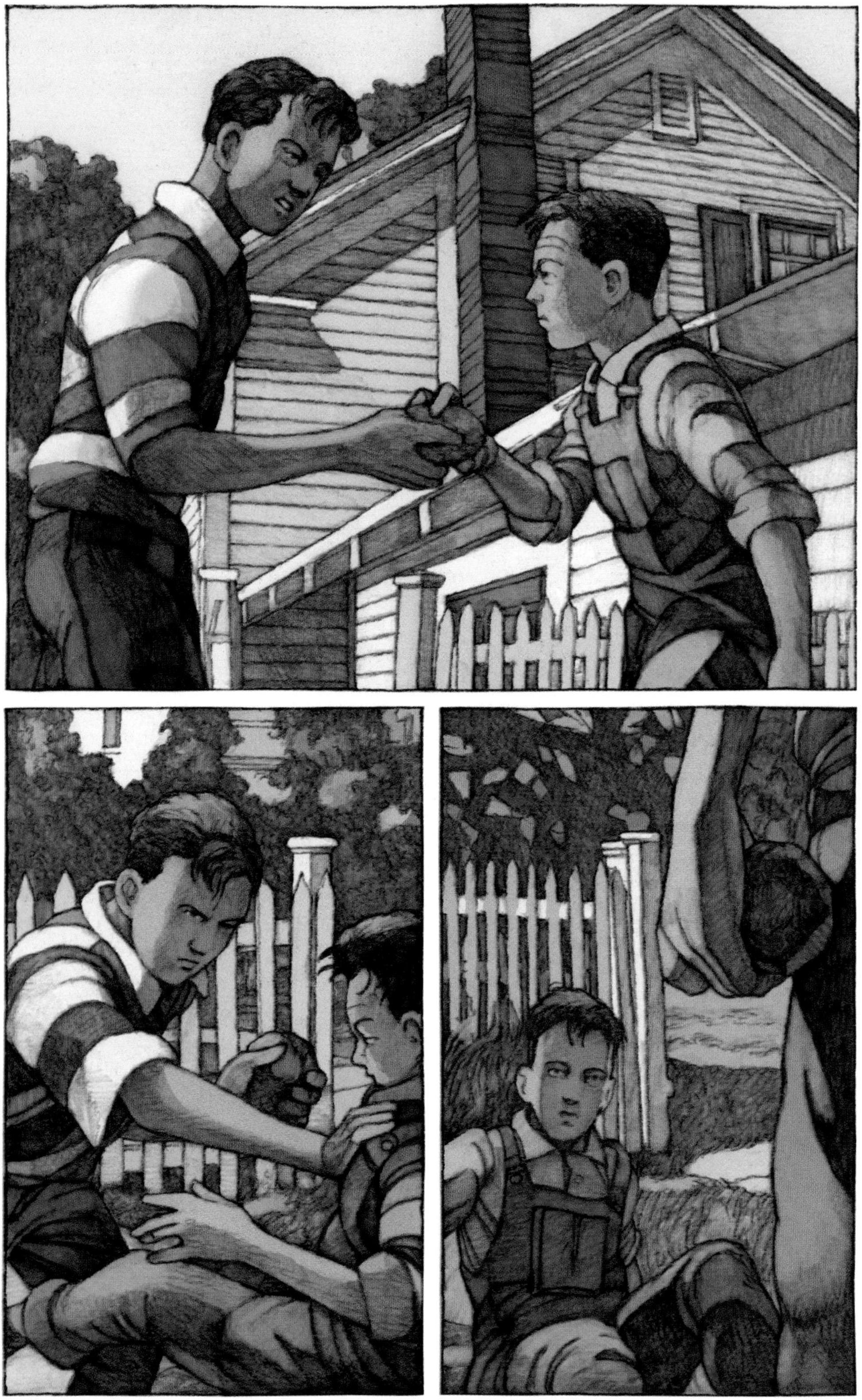

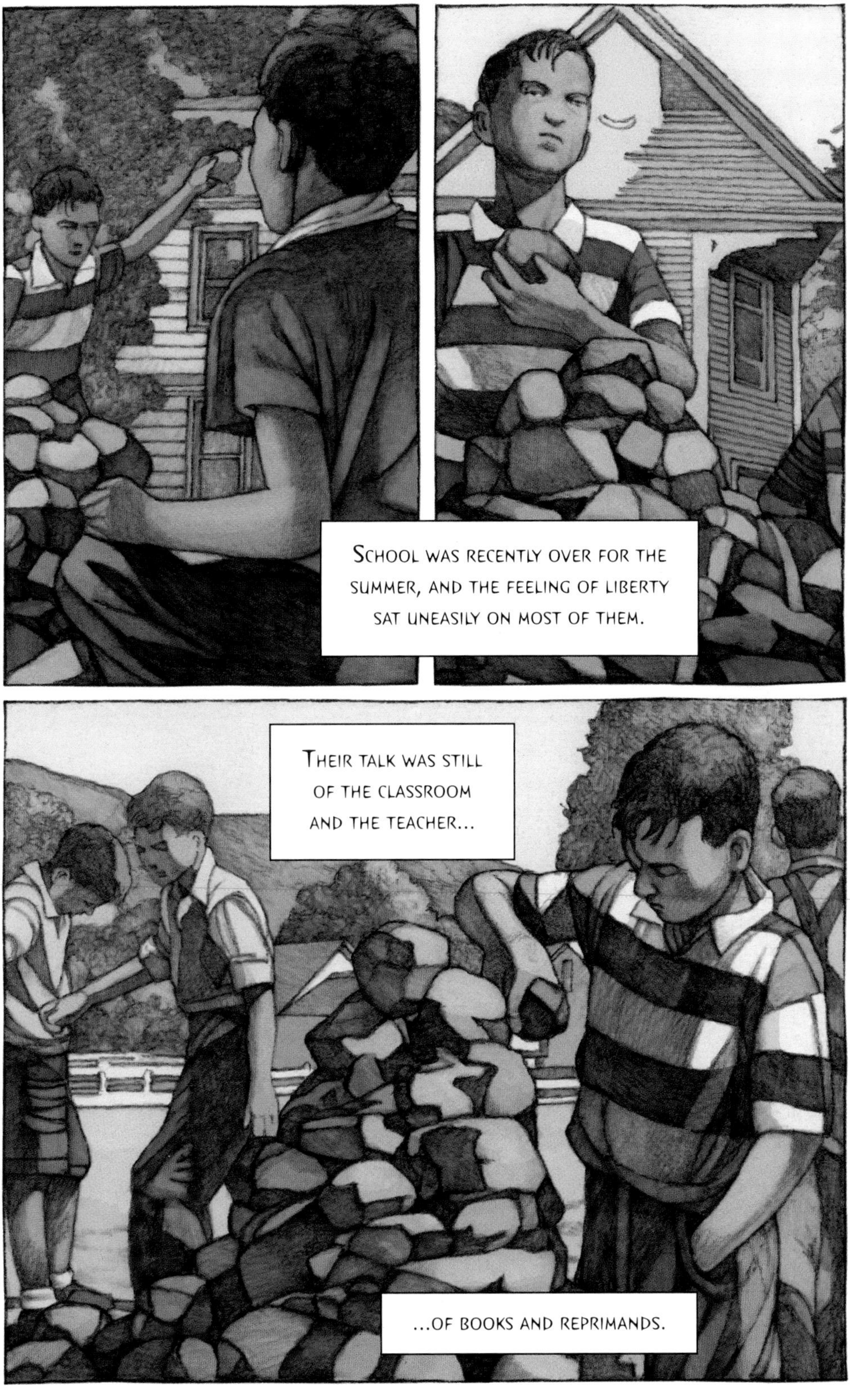
School was recently over for the summer, and the feeling of liberty sat uneasily on most of them.
Their talk was still of the classroom and the teacher...
...of books and reprimands.

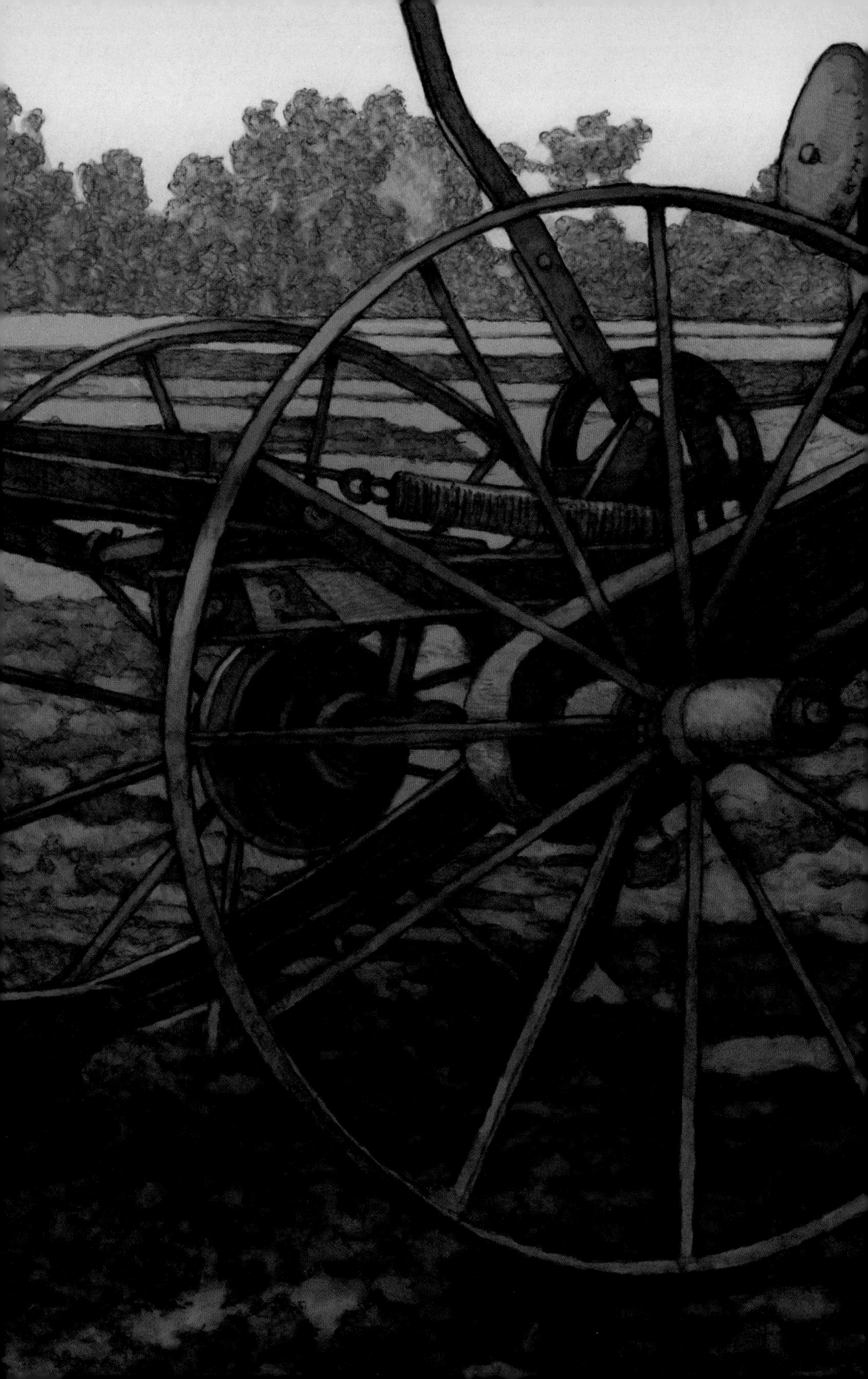

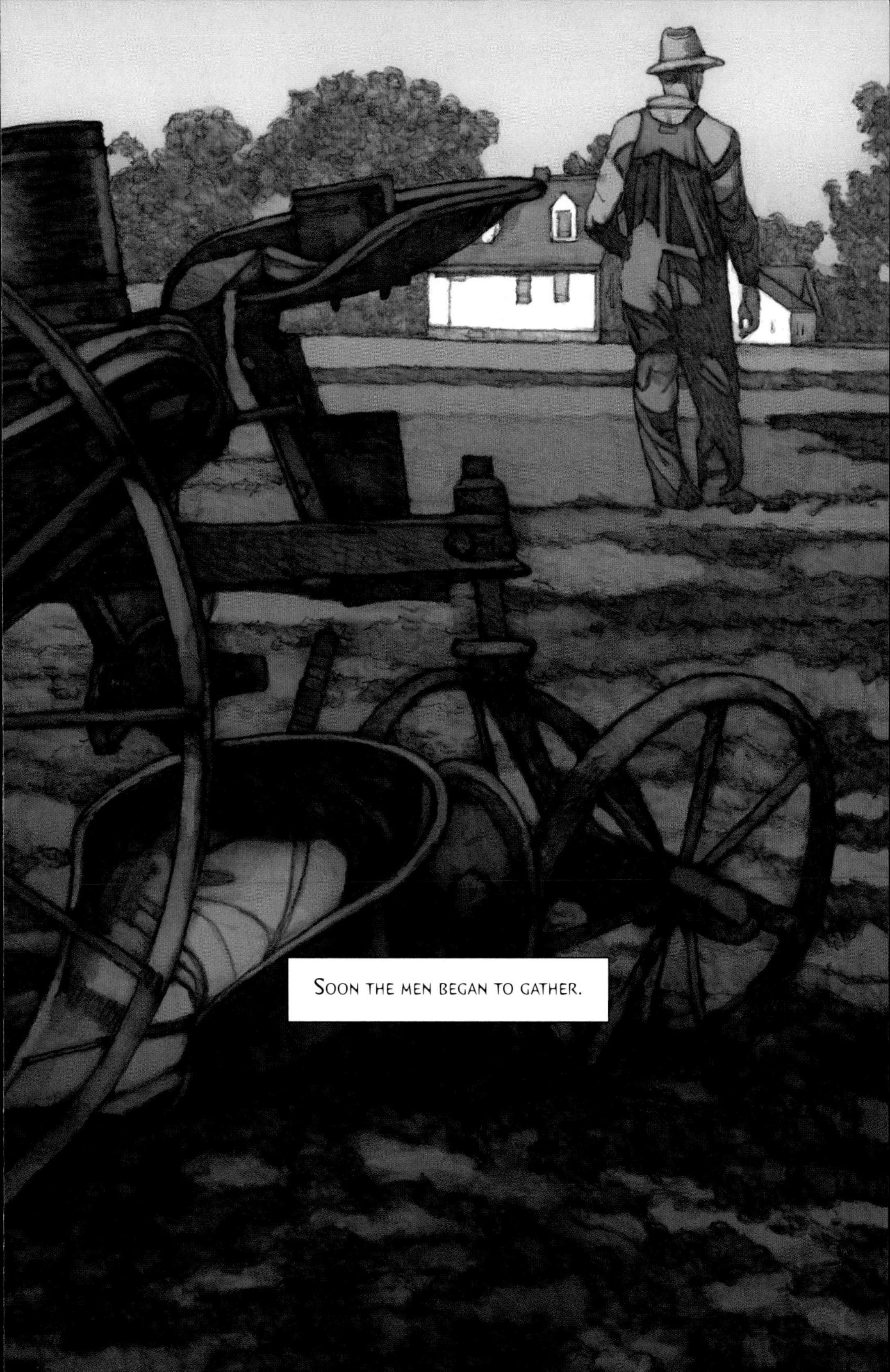
Soon the men began to gather.

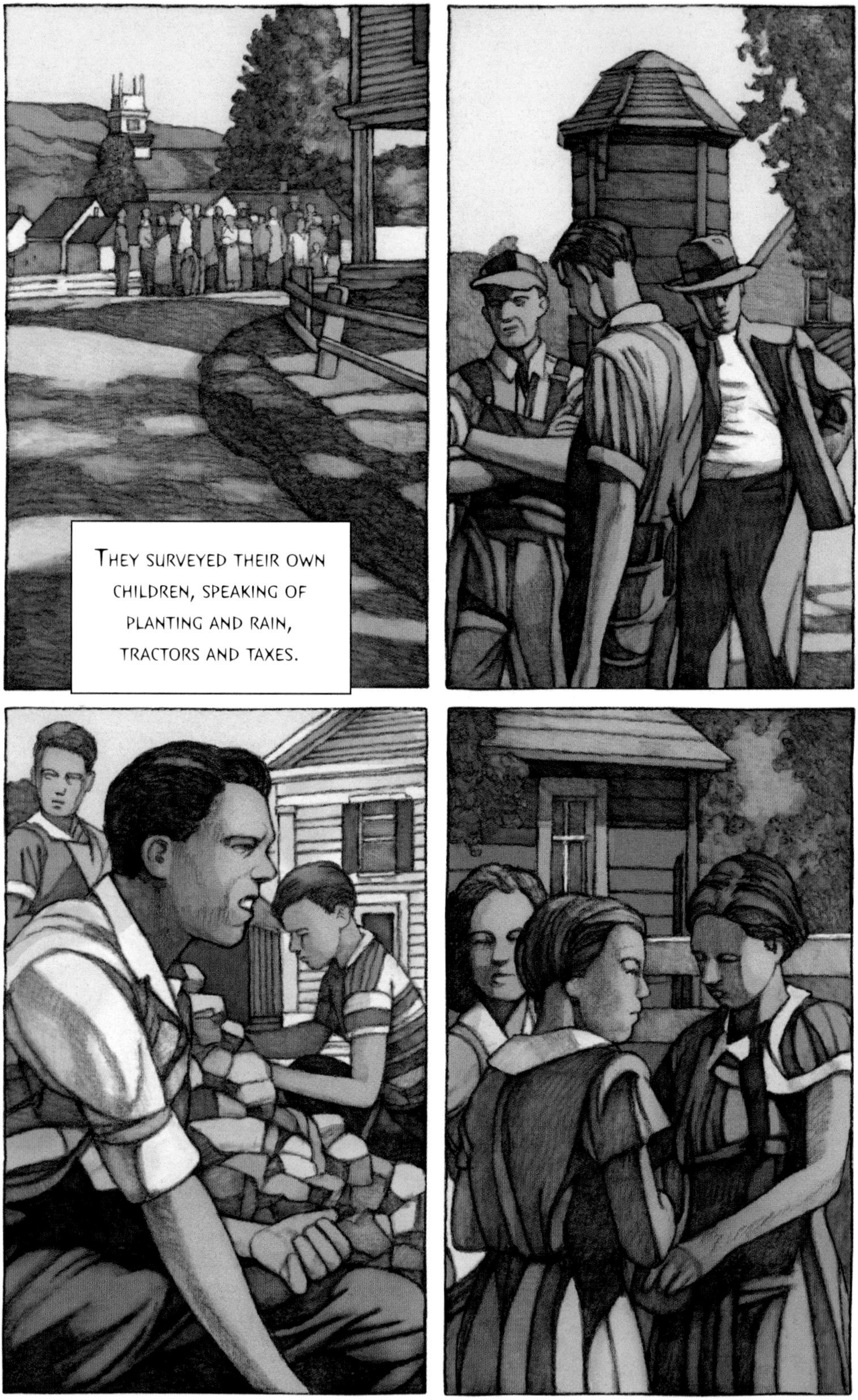
THEY SURVEYED THEIR OWN CHILDREN, SPEAKING OF PLANTING AND RAIN, TRACTORS AND TAXES.

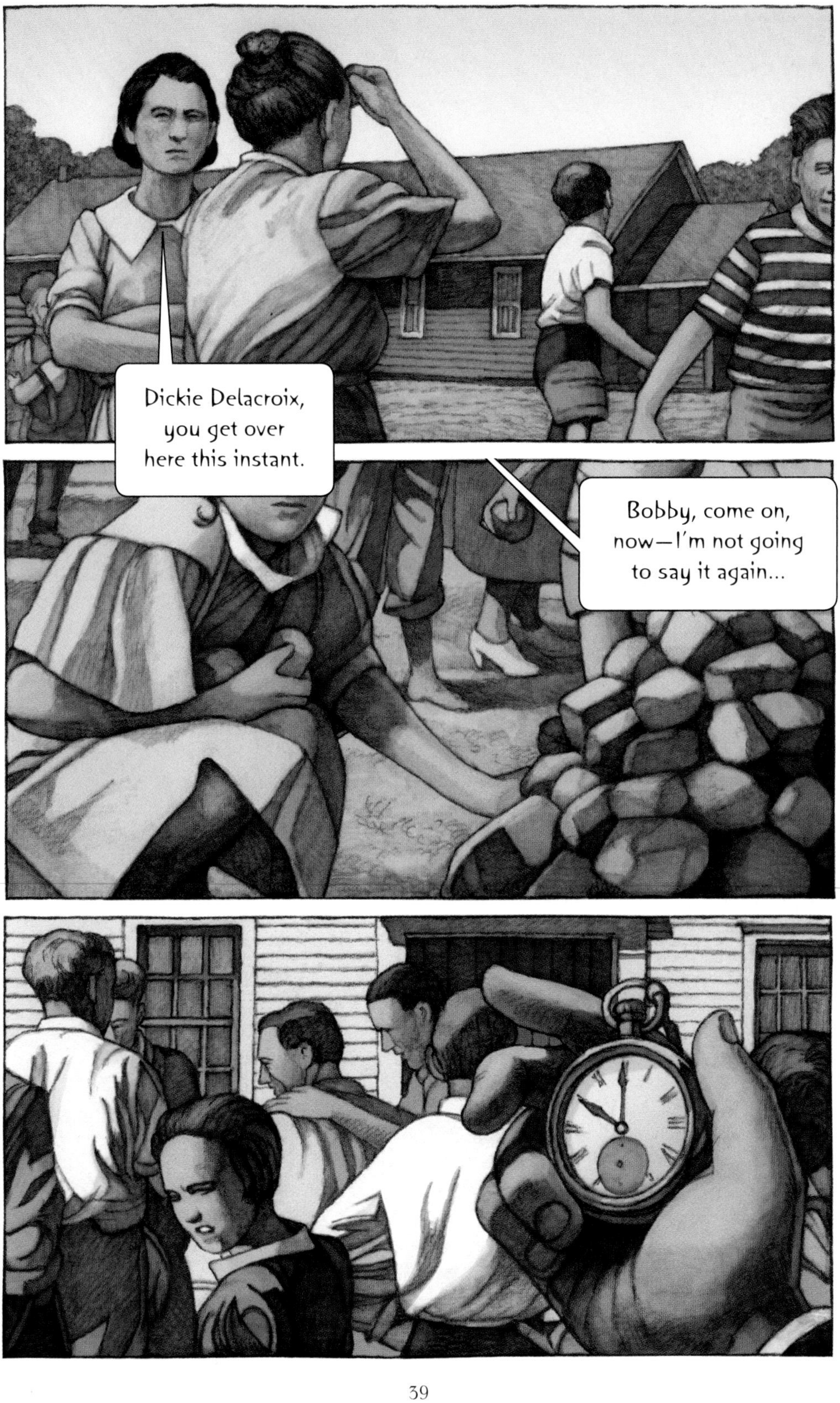
Dickie Delacroix, you get over here this instant.
Bobby, come on, now—I'm not going to say it again...

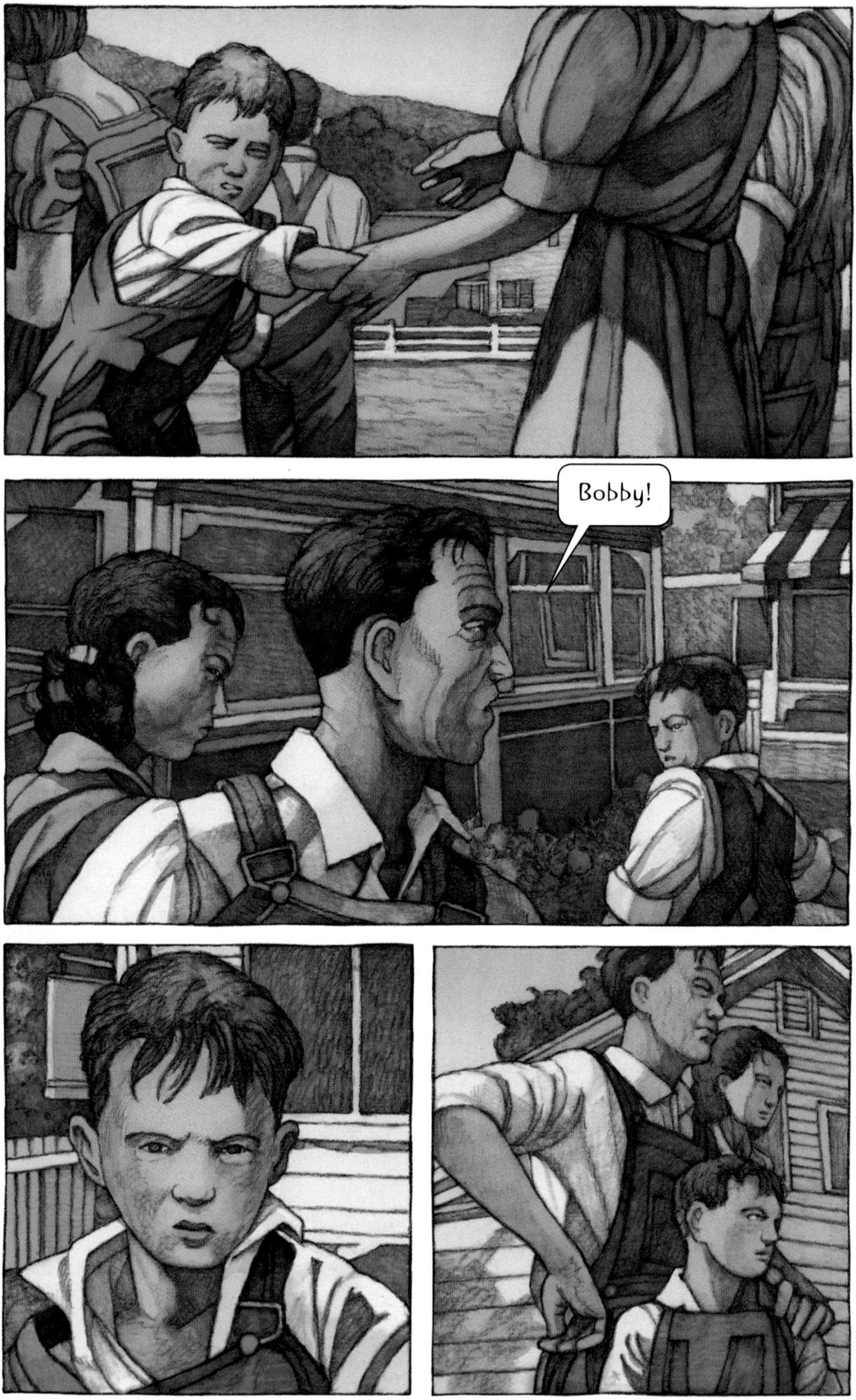
Bobby!

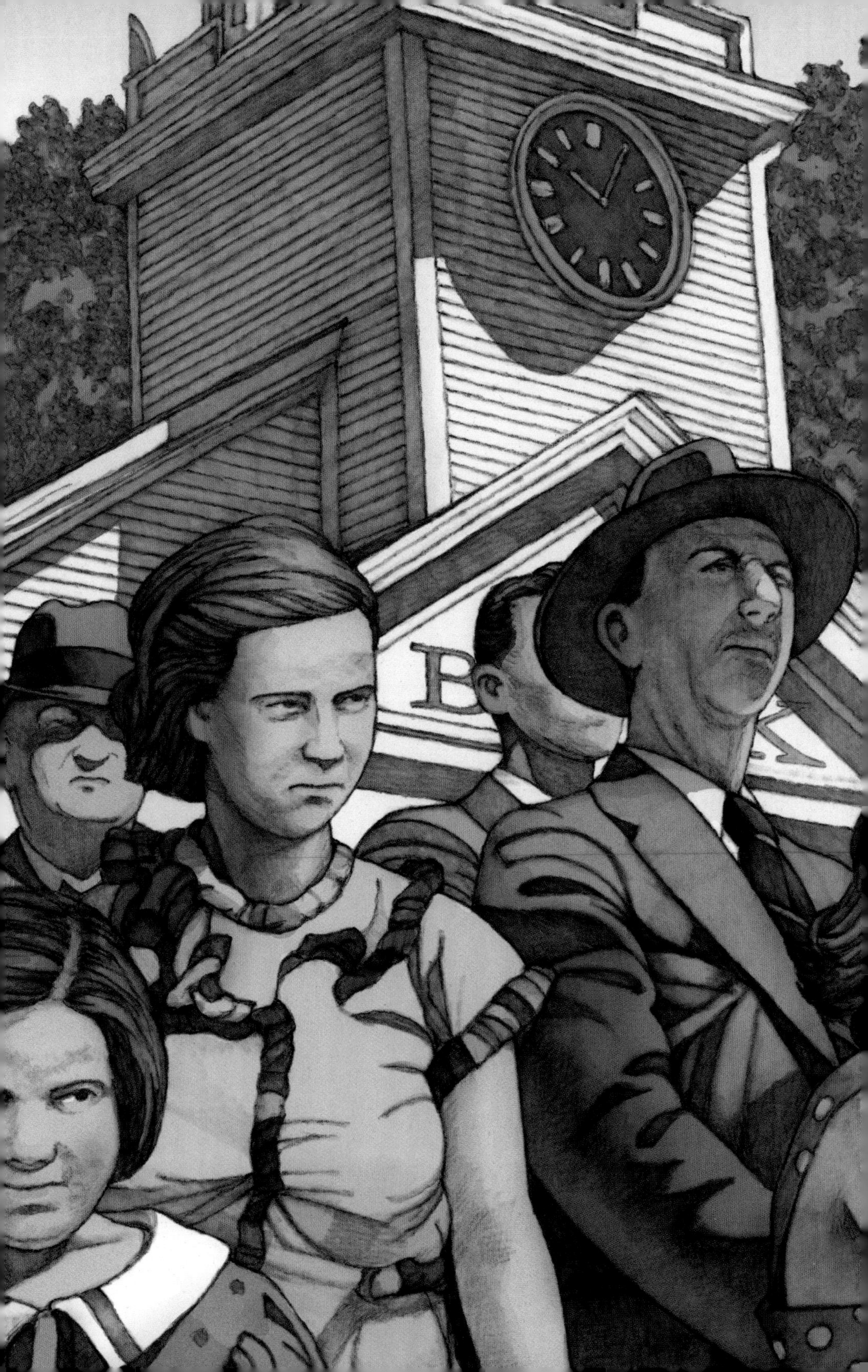

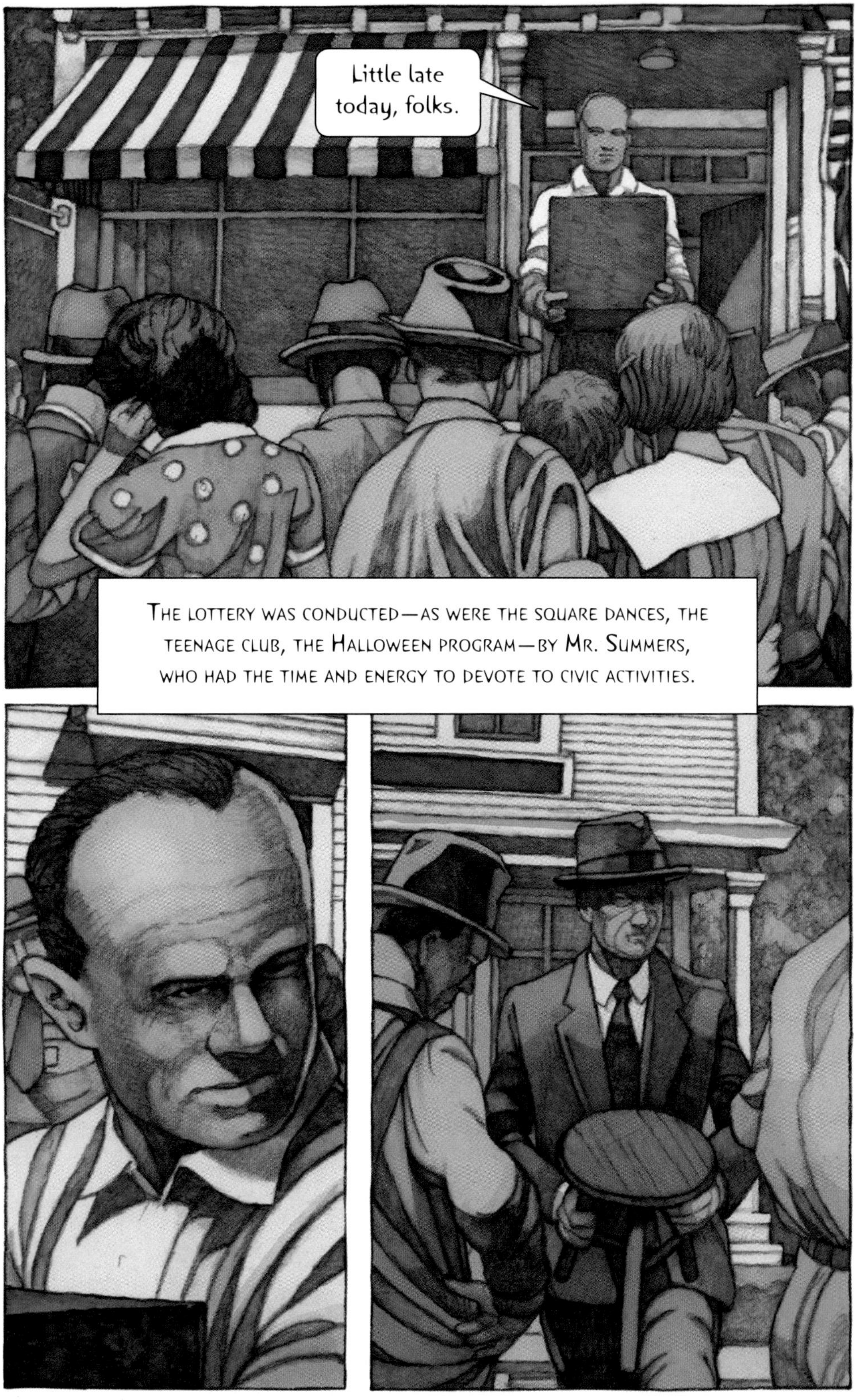
Little late today, folks.
The lottery was conducted—as were the square dances, the teenage club, the Halloween program—by Mr. Summers, who had the time and energy to devote to civic activities.

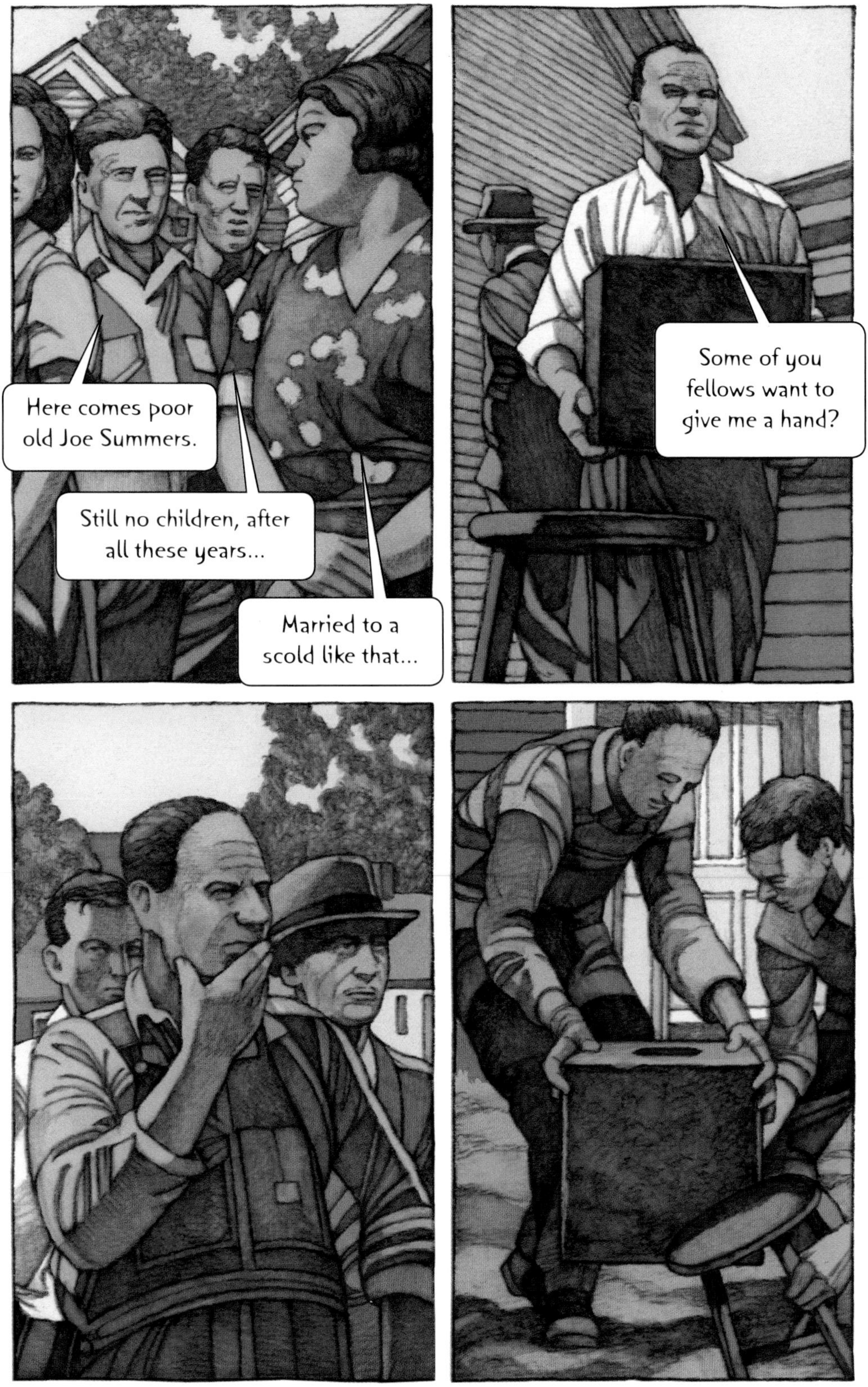
Here comes poor old Joe Summers.
Still no children, after all these years...
Married to a scold like that...
Some of you fellows want to give me a hand?

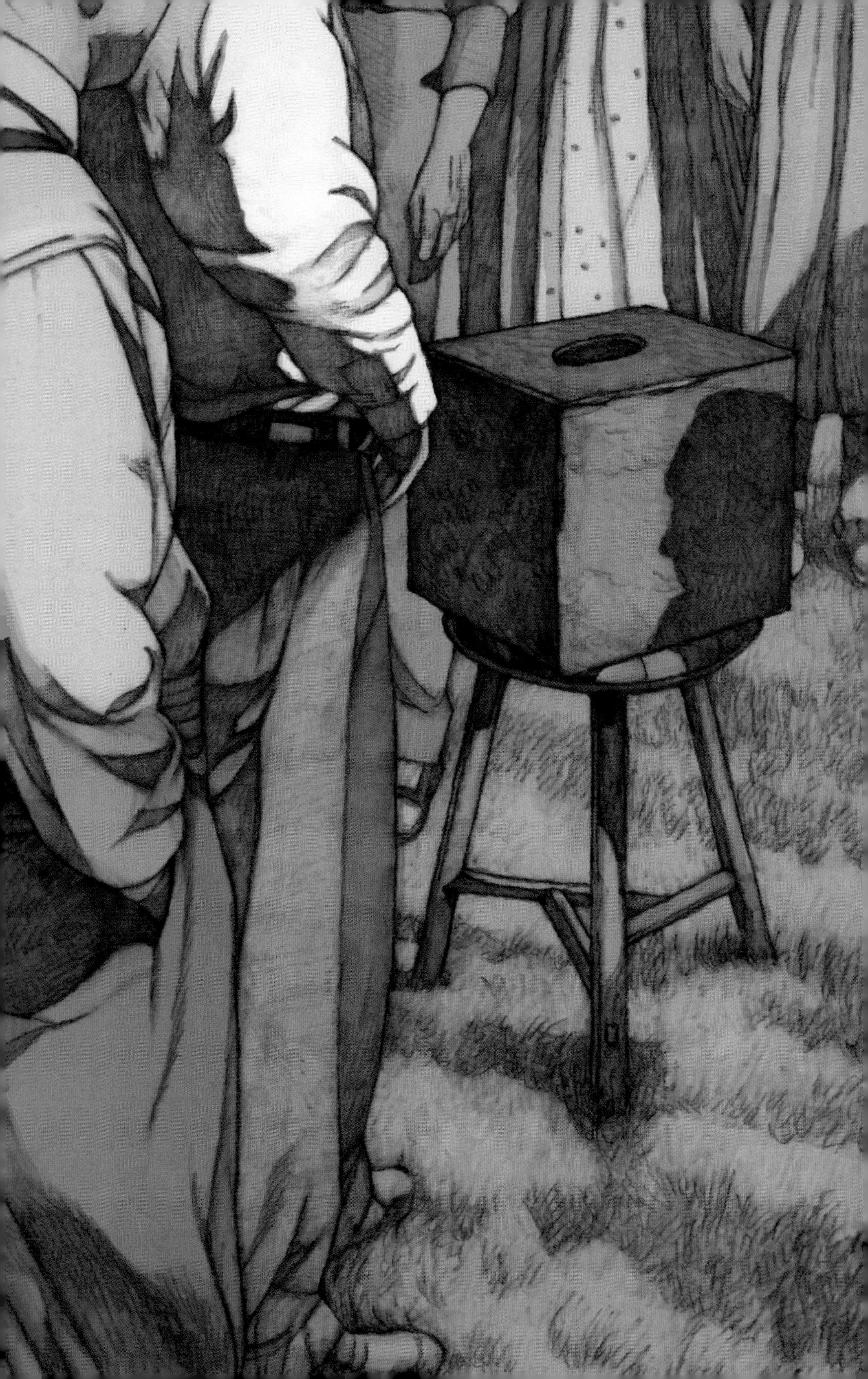

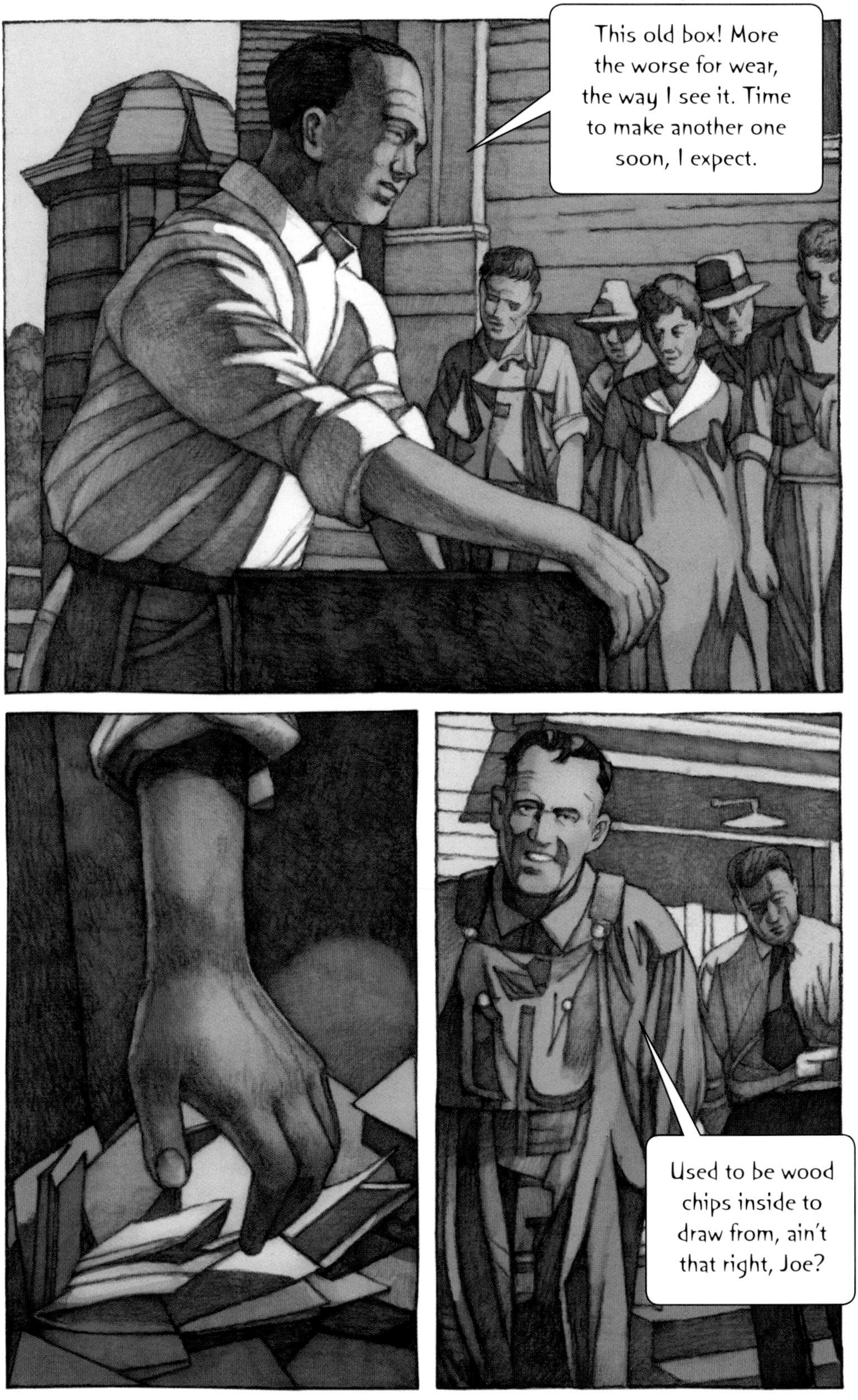
This old box! More the worse for wear, the way I see it. Time to make another one soon, I expect.
Used to be wood chips inside to draw from, ain't that right, Joe?

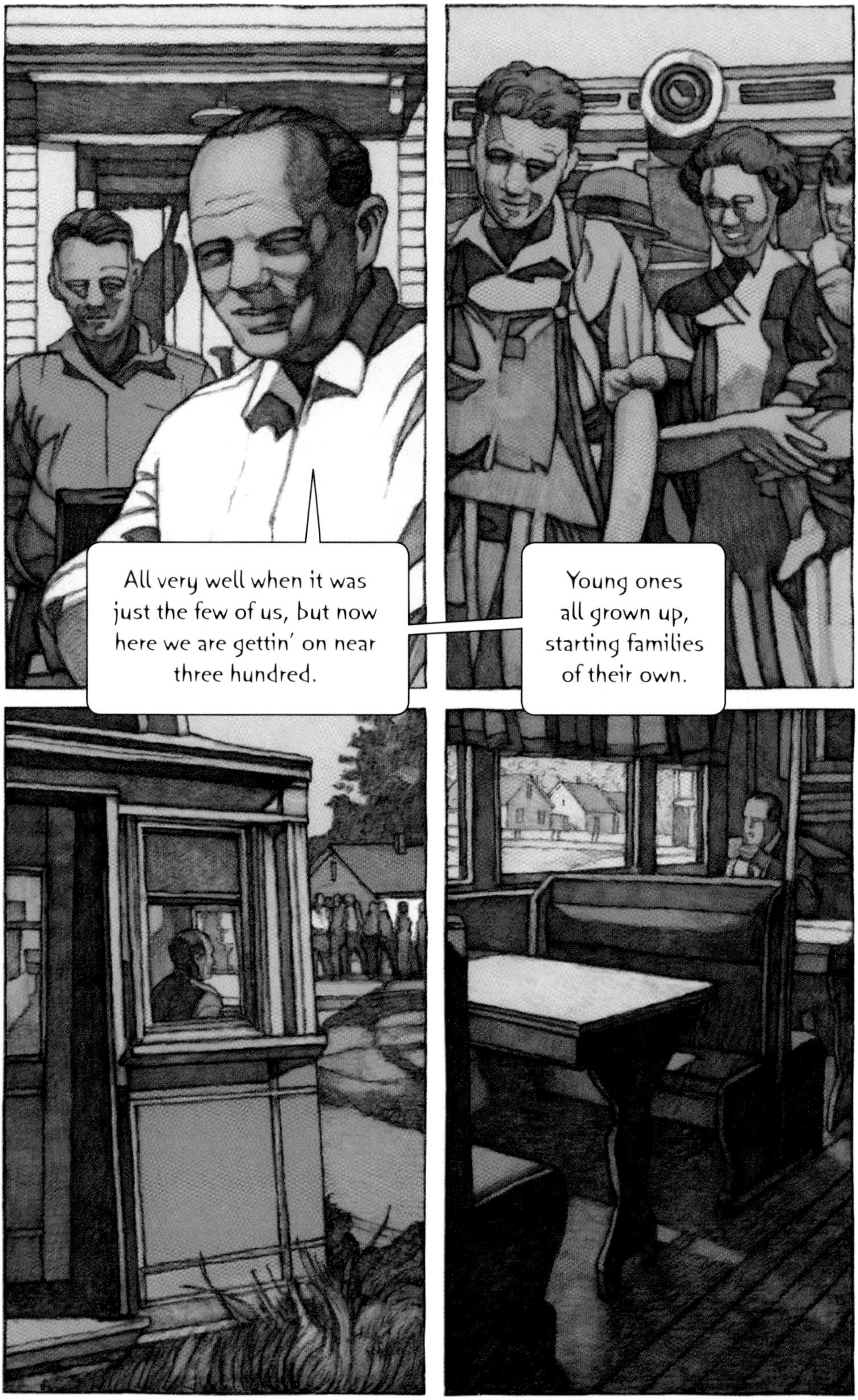
All very well when it was just the few of us, but now here we are gettin' on near three hundred.
Young ones all grown up, starting families of their own.

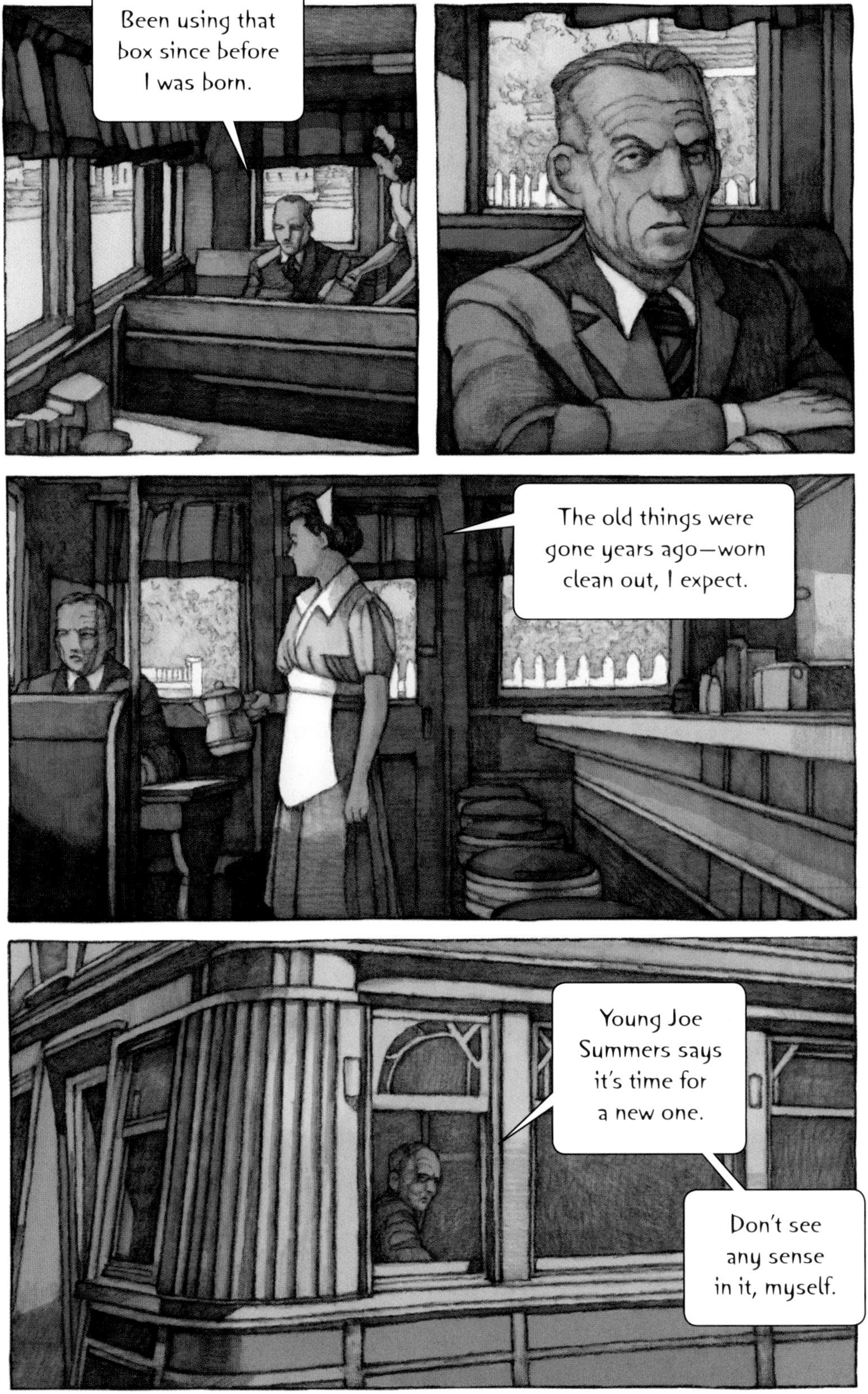
Been using that box since before I was born.
The old things were gone years ago—worn clean out, I expect.
Young Joe Summers says it's time for a new one.
Don't see any sense in it, myself.

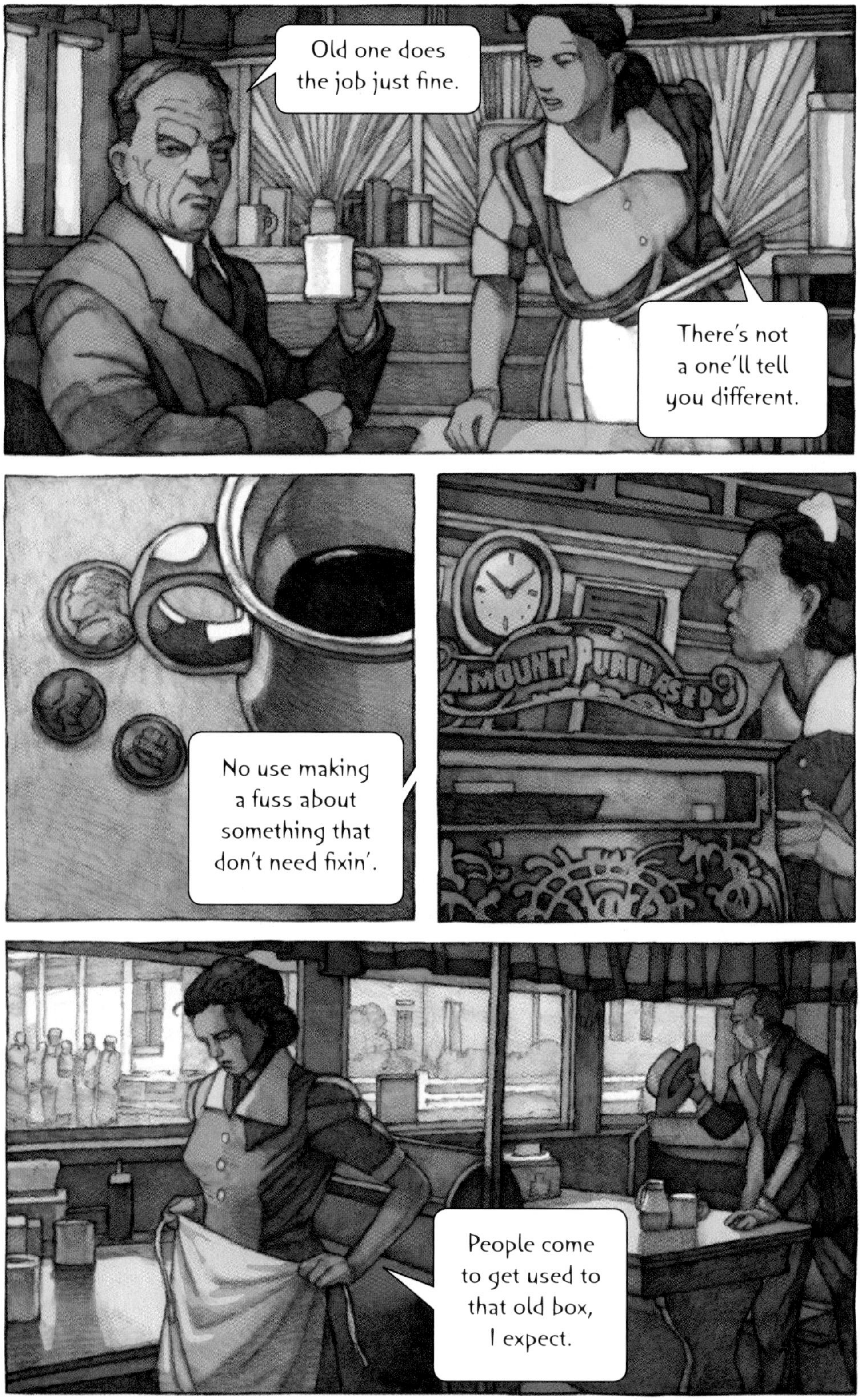
Old one does the job just fine.
There's not a one'll tell you different.
No use making a fuss about something that don't need fixin'.
AMOUNT PURCHASED
People come to get used to that old box, I expect.

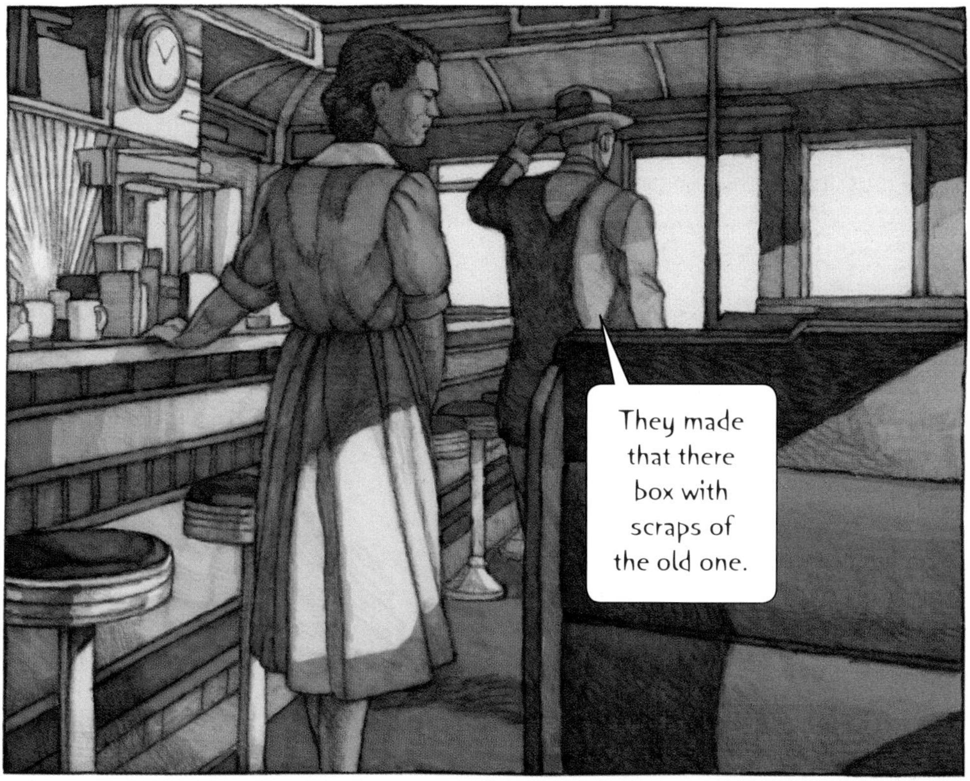
They made that there box with scraps of the old one.

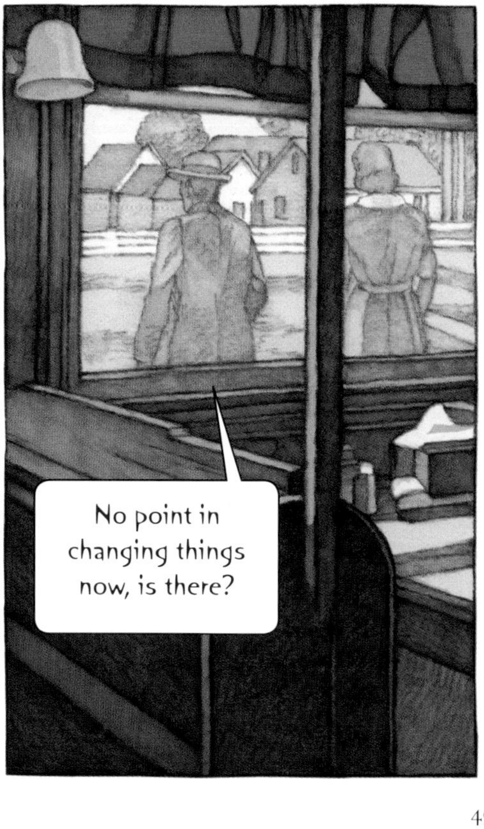
No point in changing things now, is there?

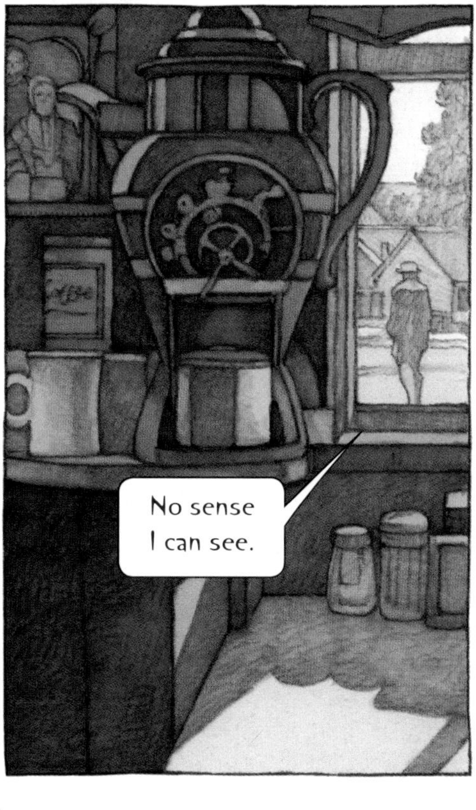
No sense I can see.

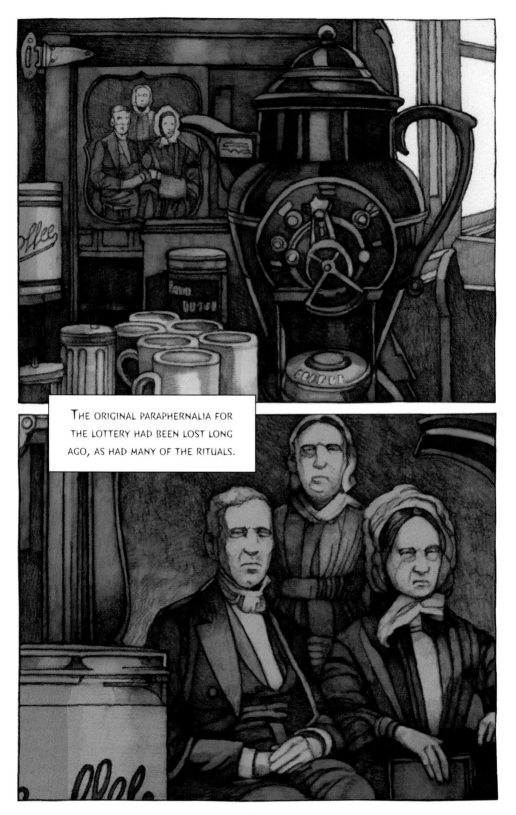

THE ORIGINAL PARAPHERNALIA FOR THE LOTTERY HAD BEEN LOST LONG AGO, AS HAD MANY OF THE RITUALS.

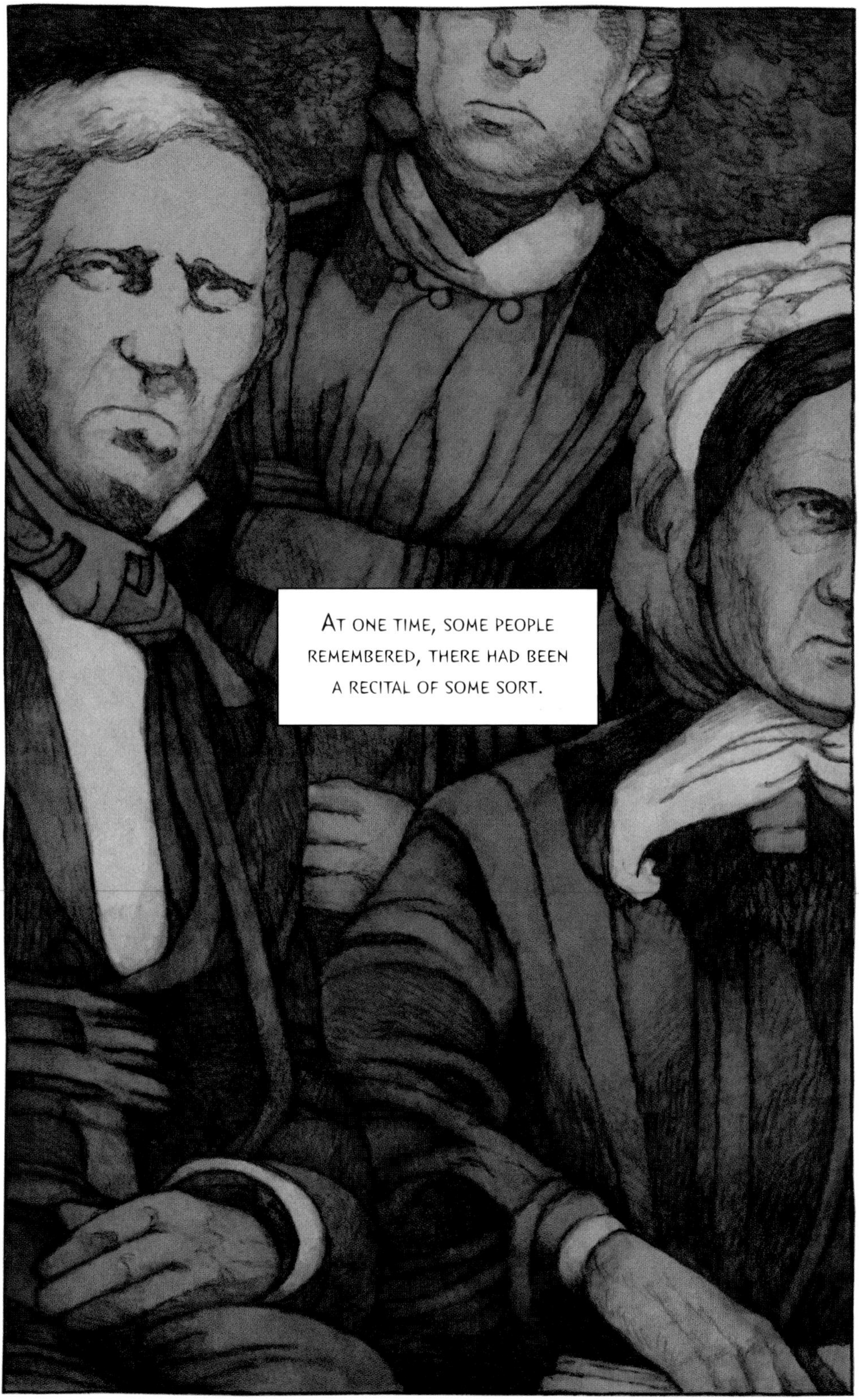
AT ONE TIME, SOME PEOPLE REMEMBERED, THERE HAD BEEN A RECITAL OF SOME SORT.

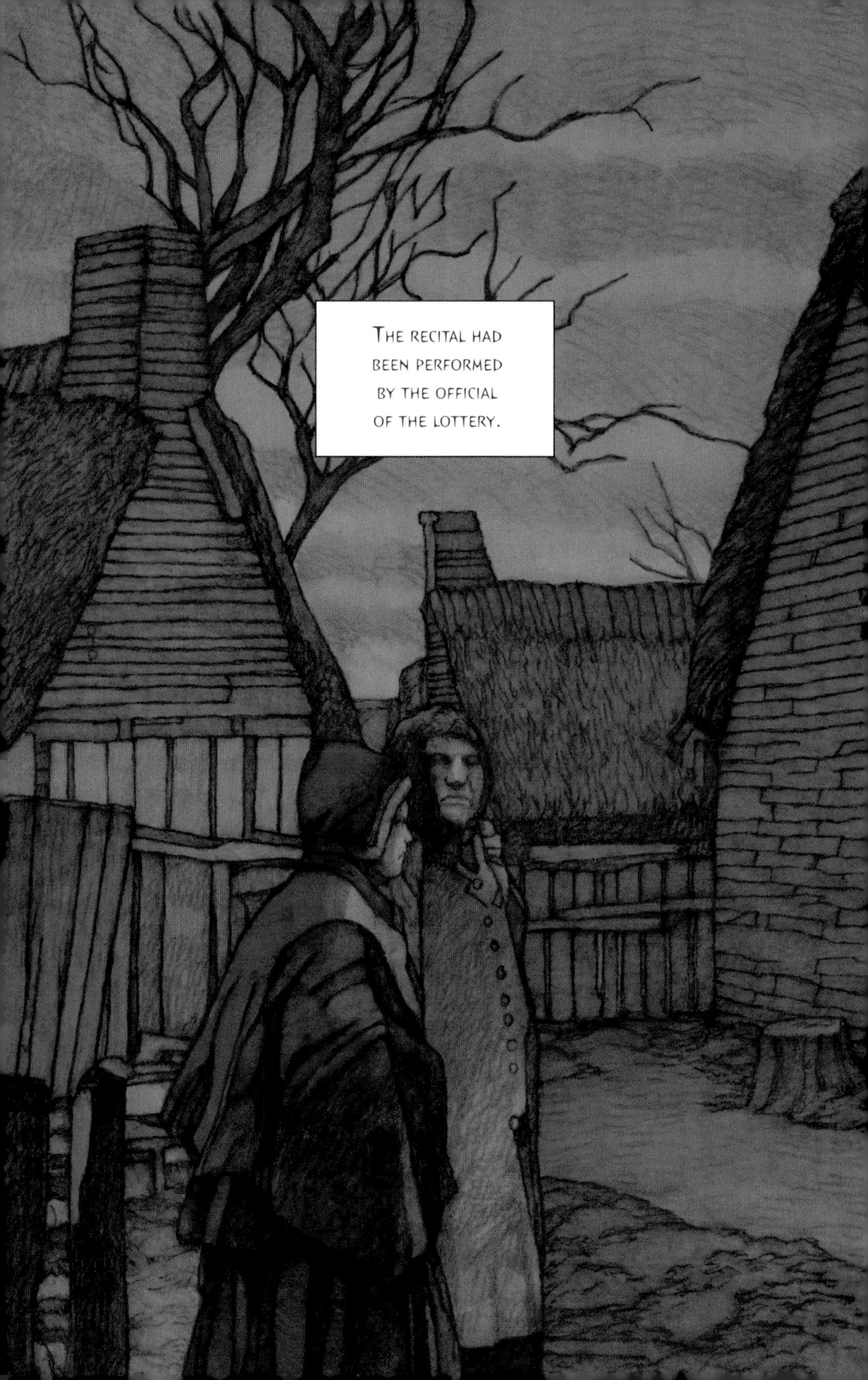
The recital had been performed by the official of the lottery.

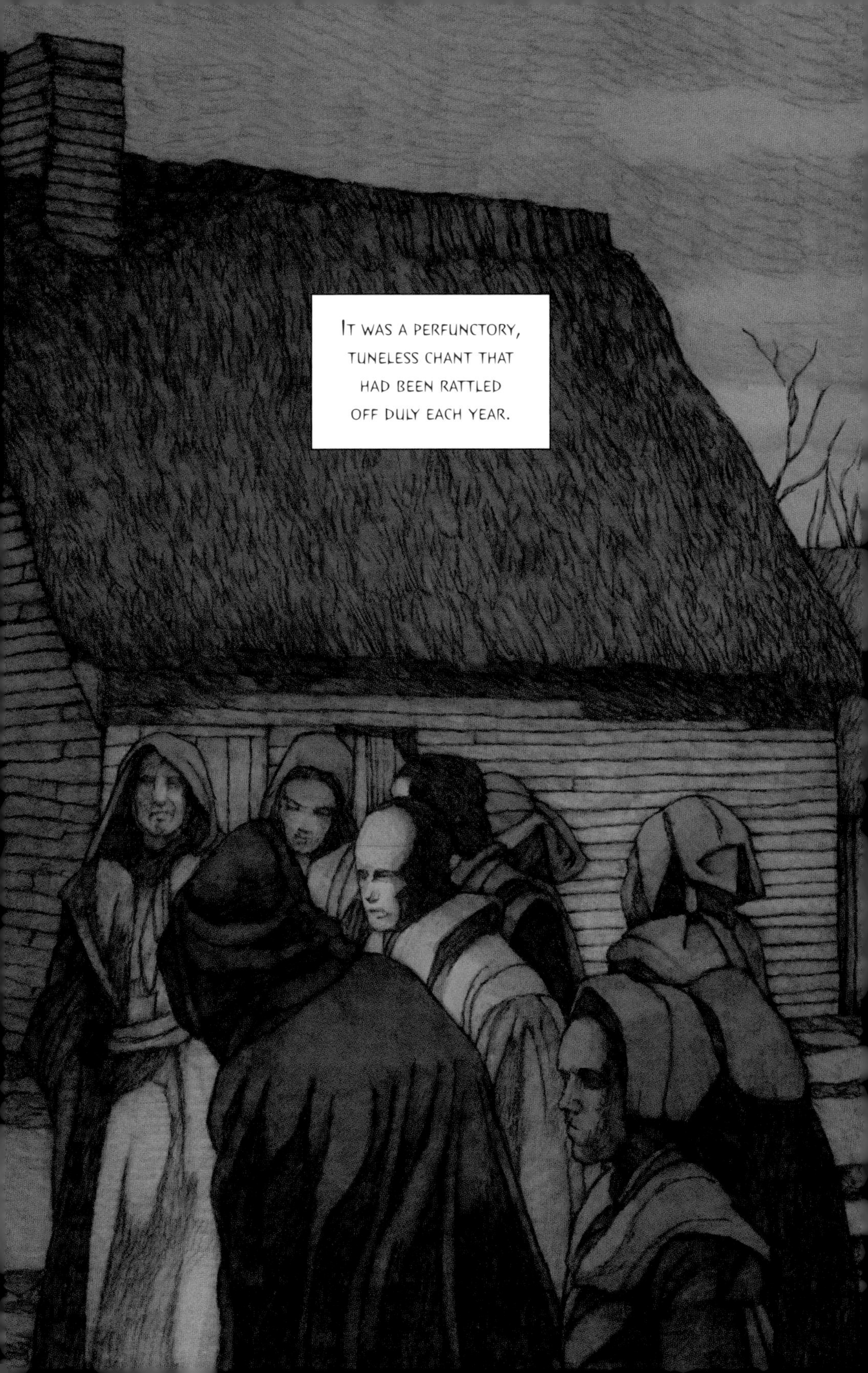
IT WAS A PERFUNCTORY, TUNELESS CHANT THAT HAD BEEN RATTLED OFF DULY EACH YEAR.

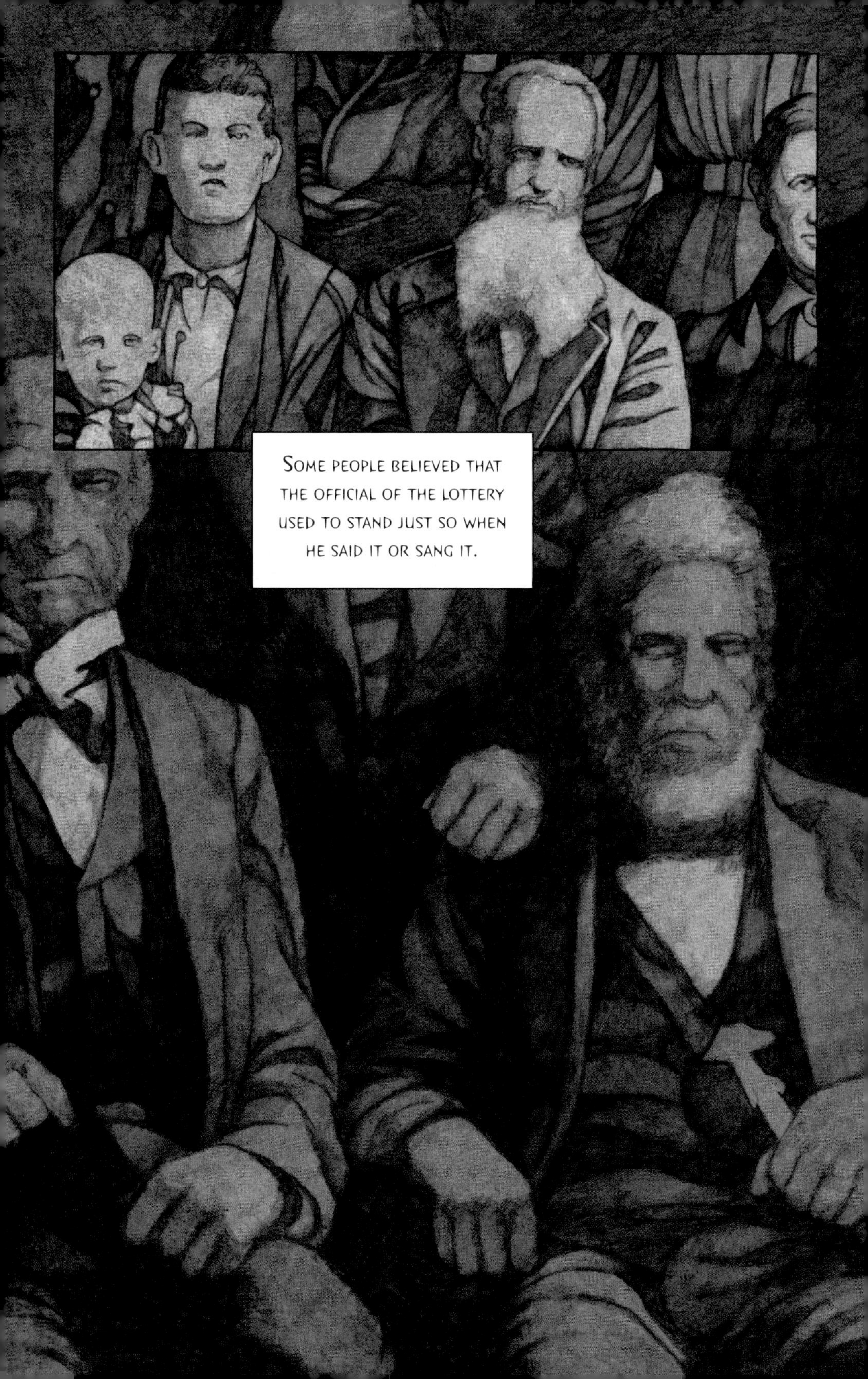
Some people believed that the official of the lottery used to stand just so when he said it or sang it.

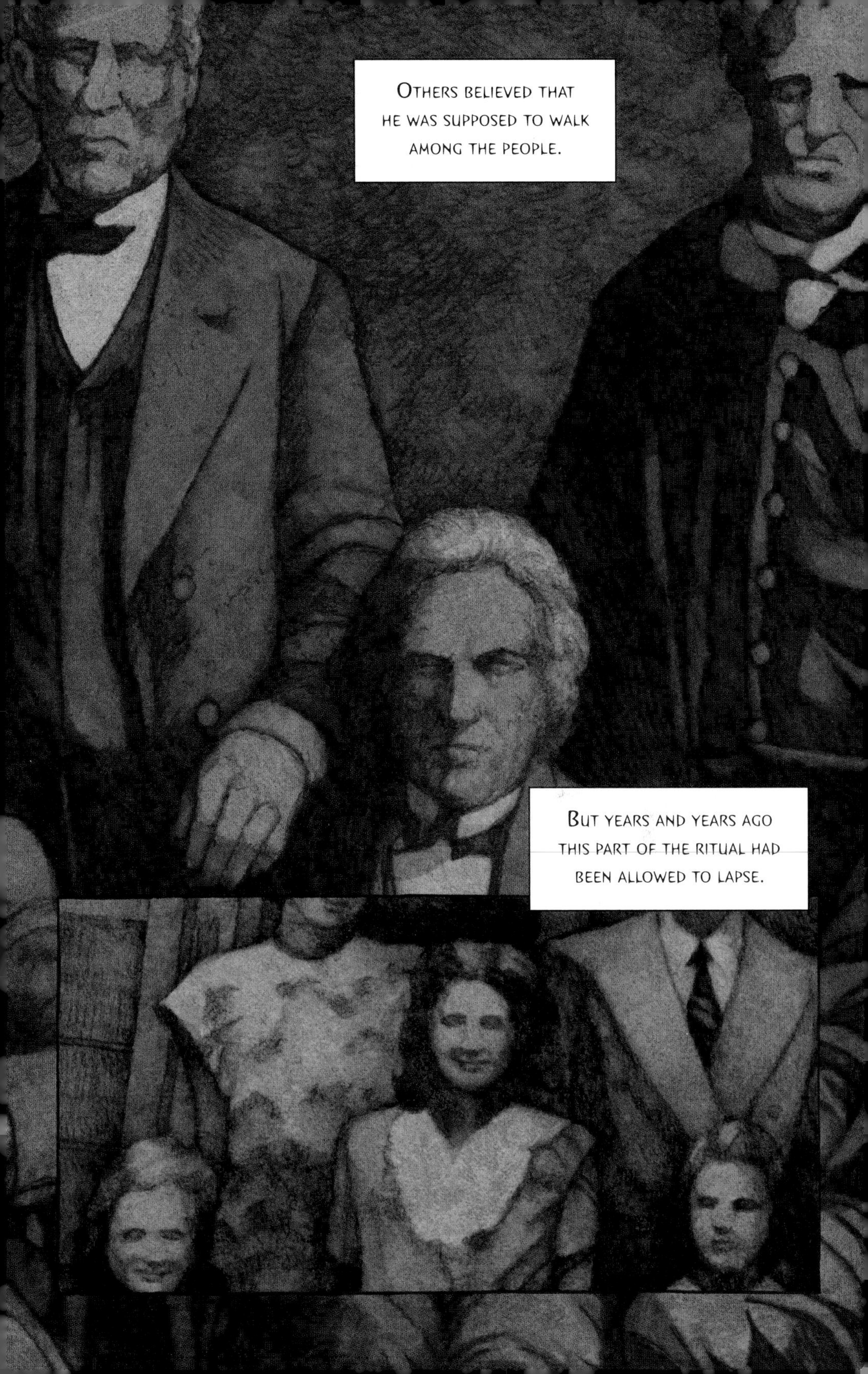
Others believed that he was supposed to walk among the people.
But years and years ago this part of the ritual had been allowed to lapse.

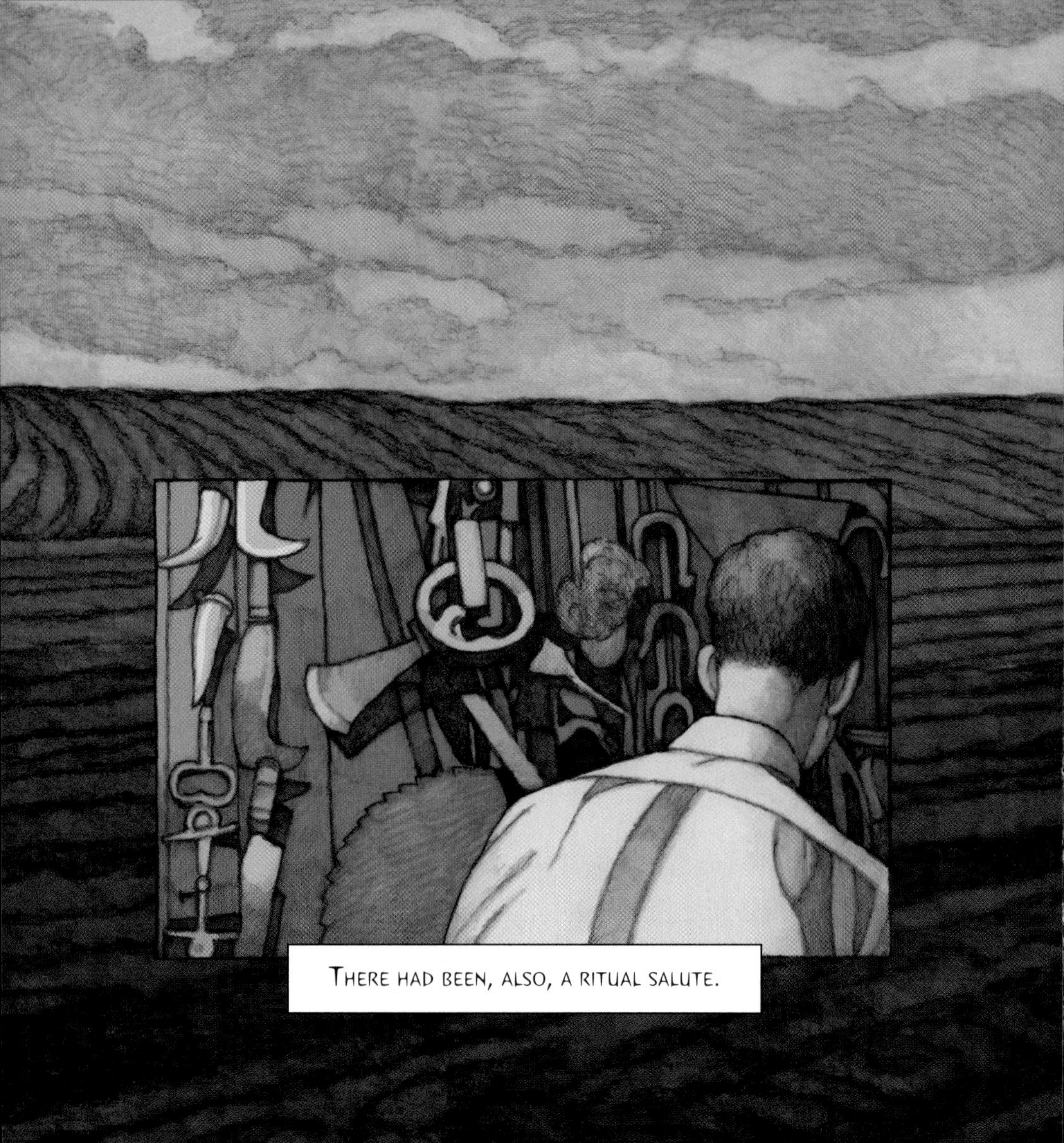
THERE HAD BEEN, ALSO, A RITUAL SALUTE.

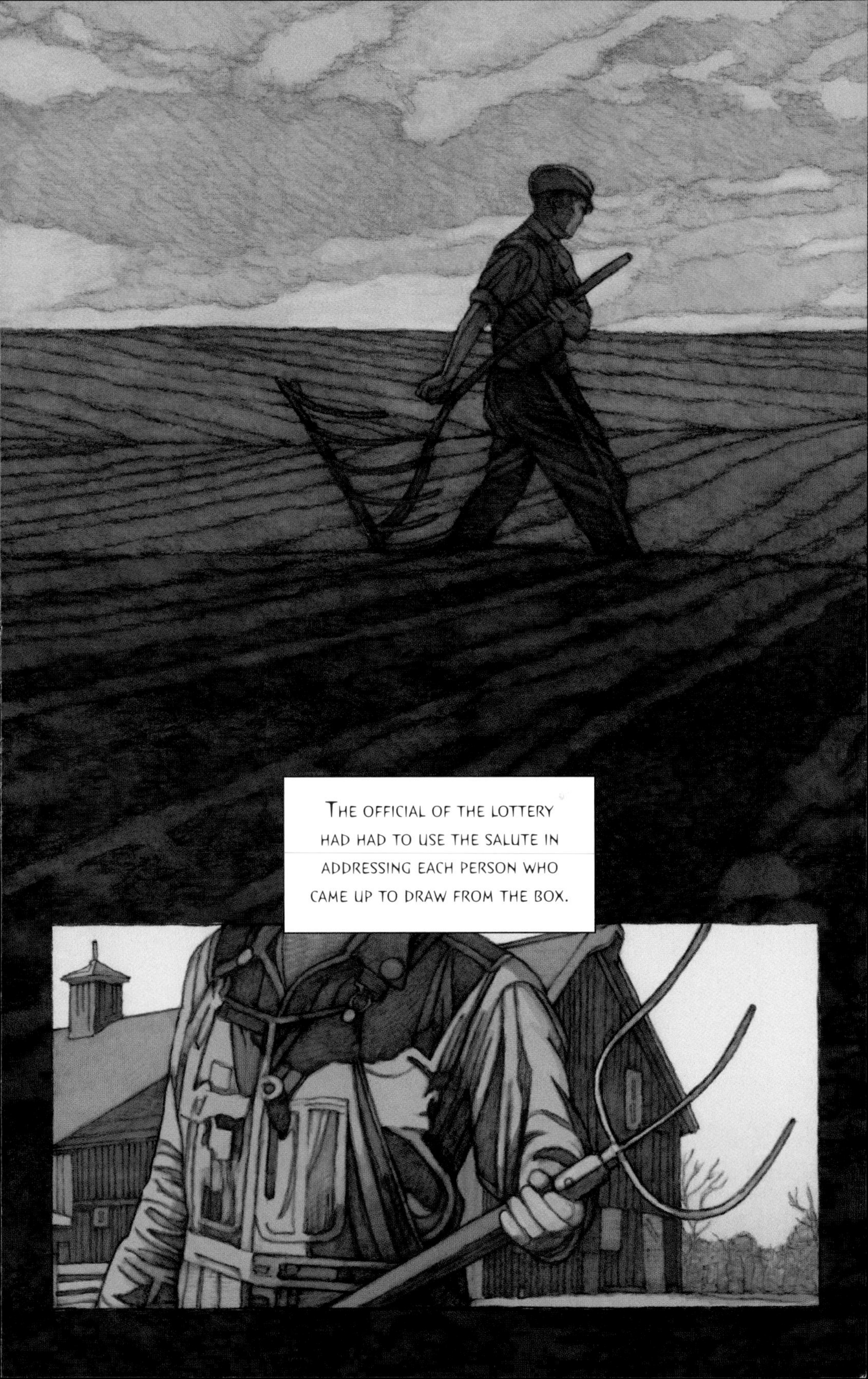
THE OFFICIAL OF THE LOTTERY HAD HAD TO USE THE SALUTE IN ADDRESSING EACH PERSON WHO CAME UP TO DRAW FROM THE BOX.

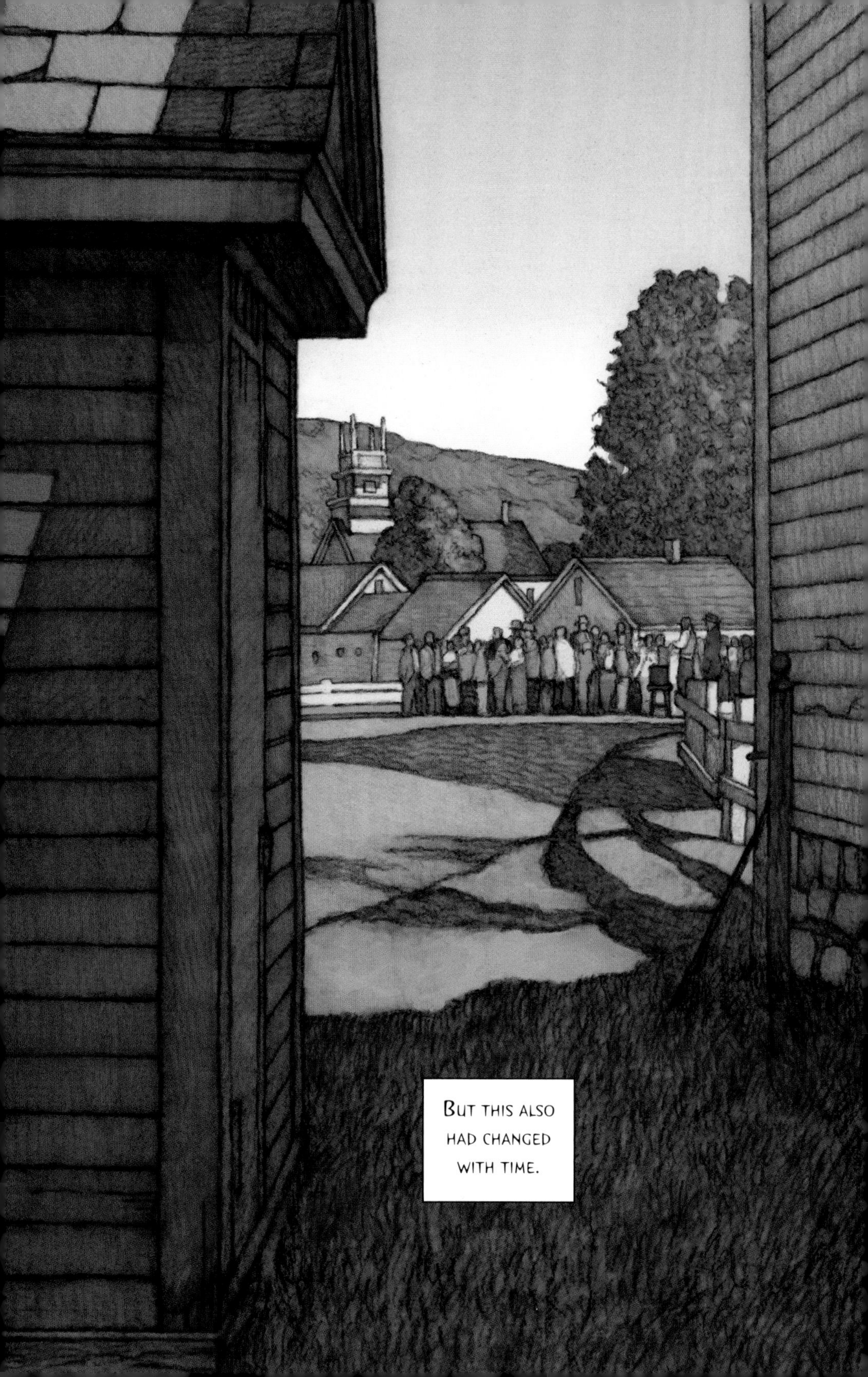
BUT THIS ALSO HAD CHANGED WITH TIME.

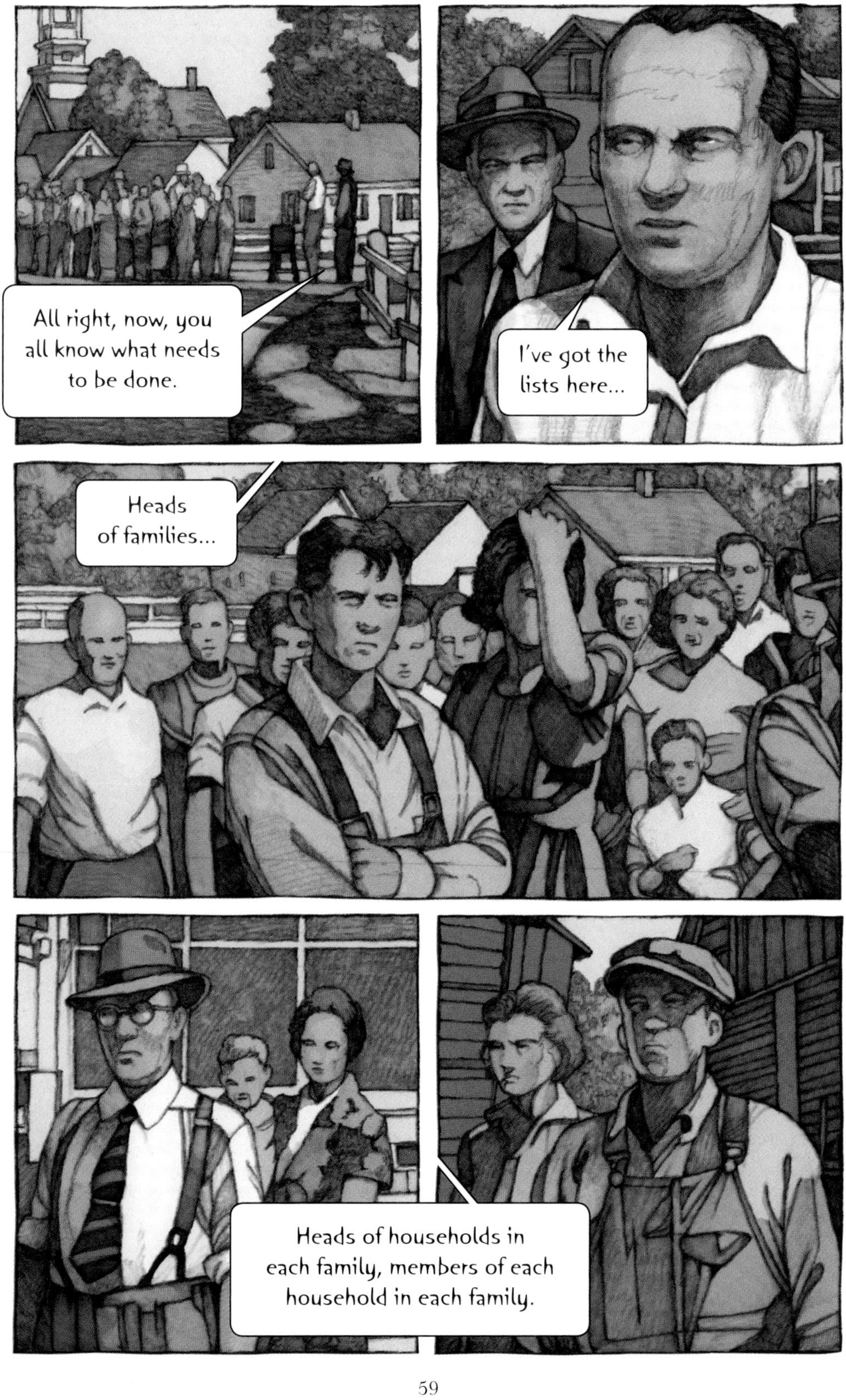
All right, now, you all know what needs to be done.
I've got the lists here...
Heads of families...
Heads of households in each family, members of each household in each family.

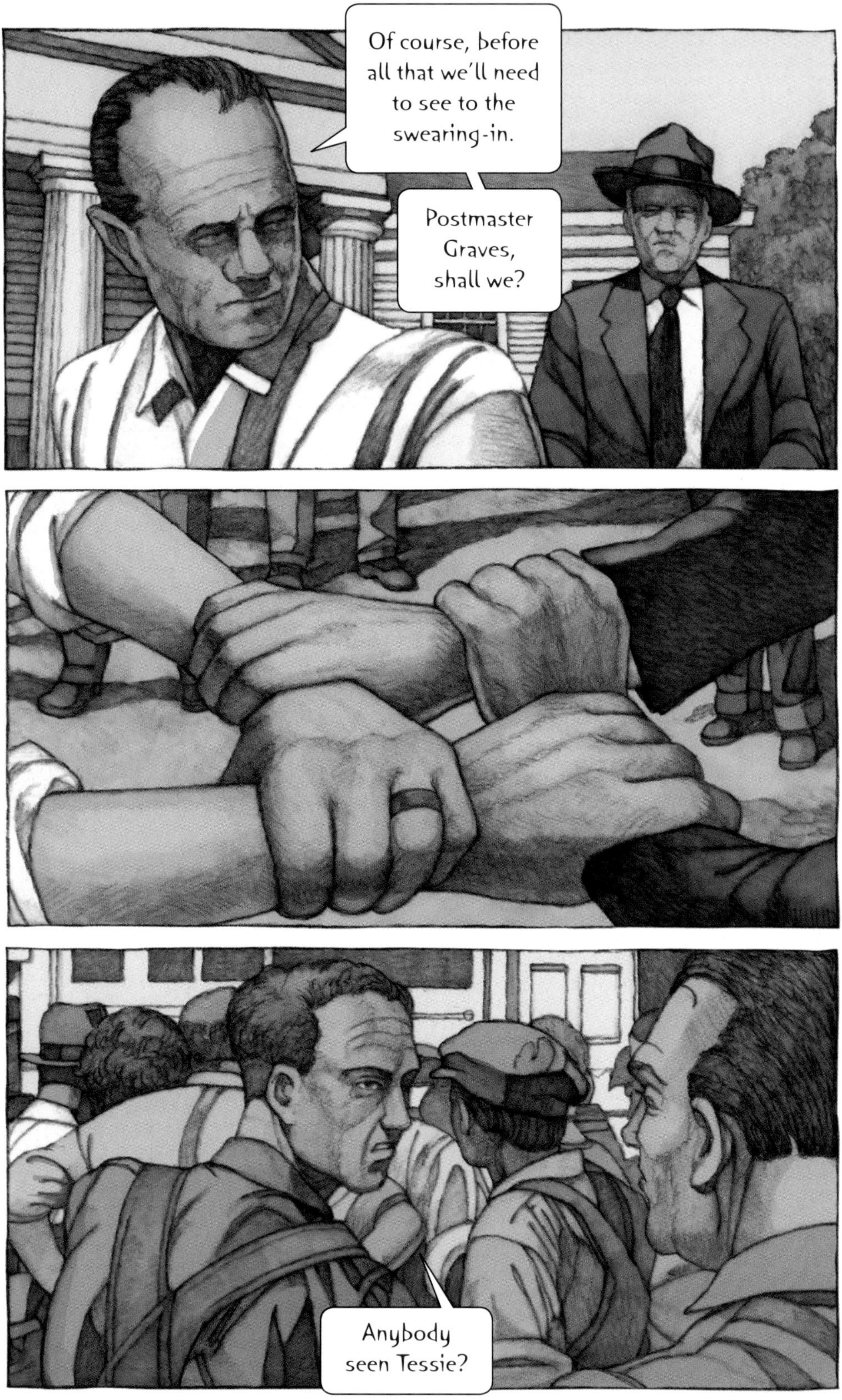
Of course, before all that we'll need to see to the swearing-in.
Postmaster Graves, shall we?
Anybody seen Tessie?

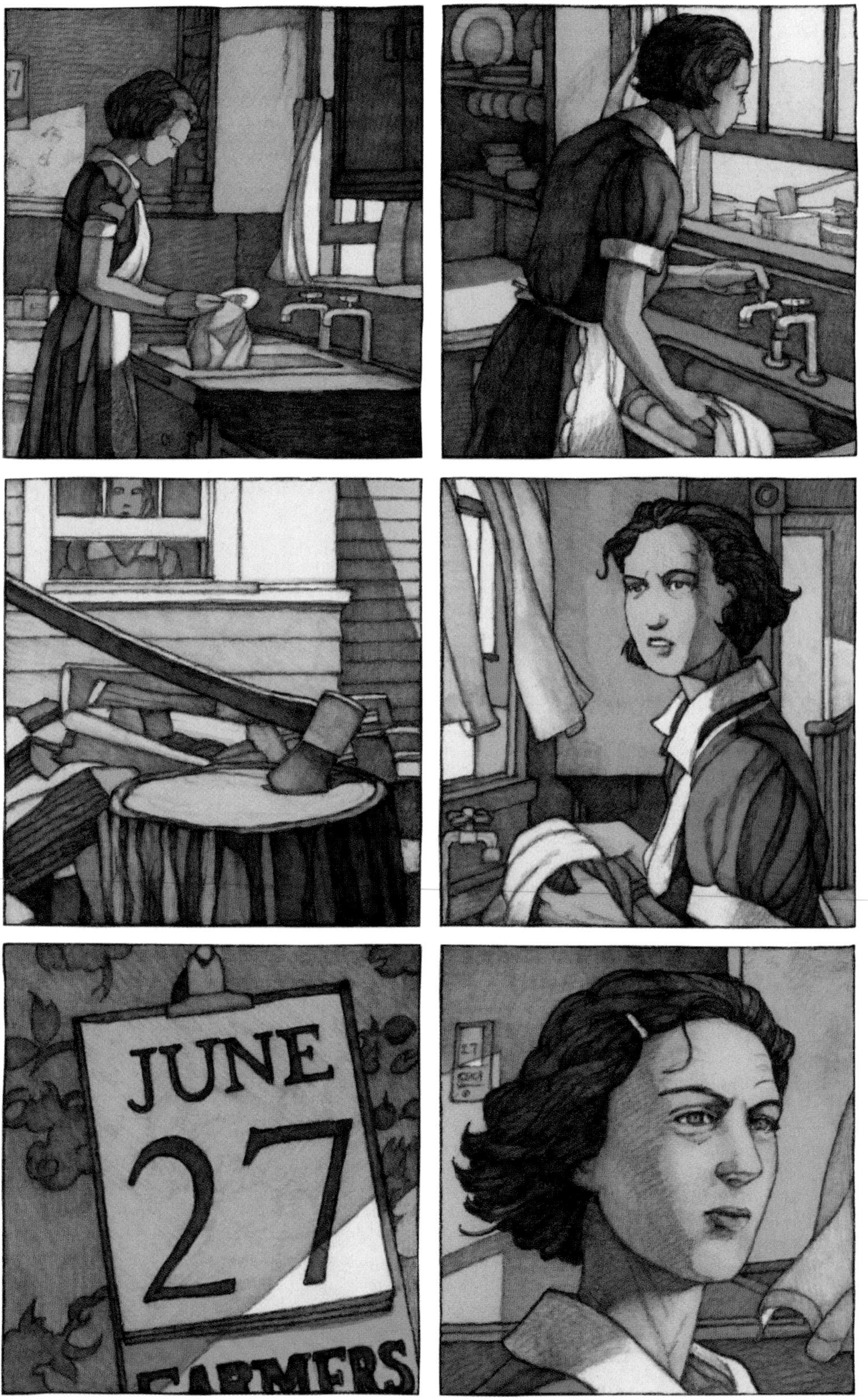
JUNE
27

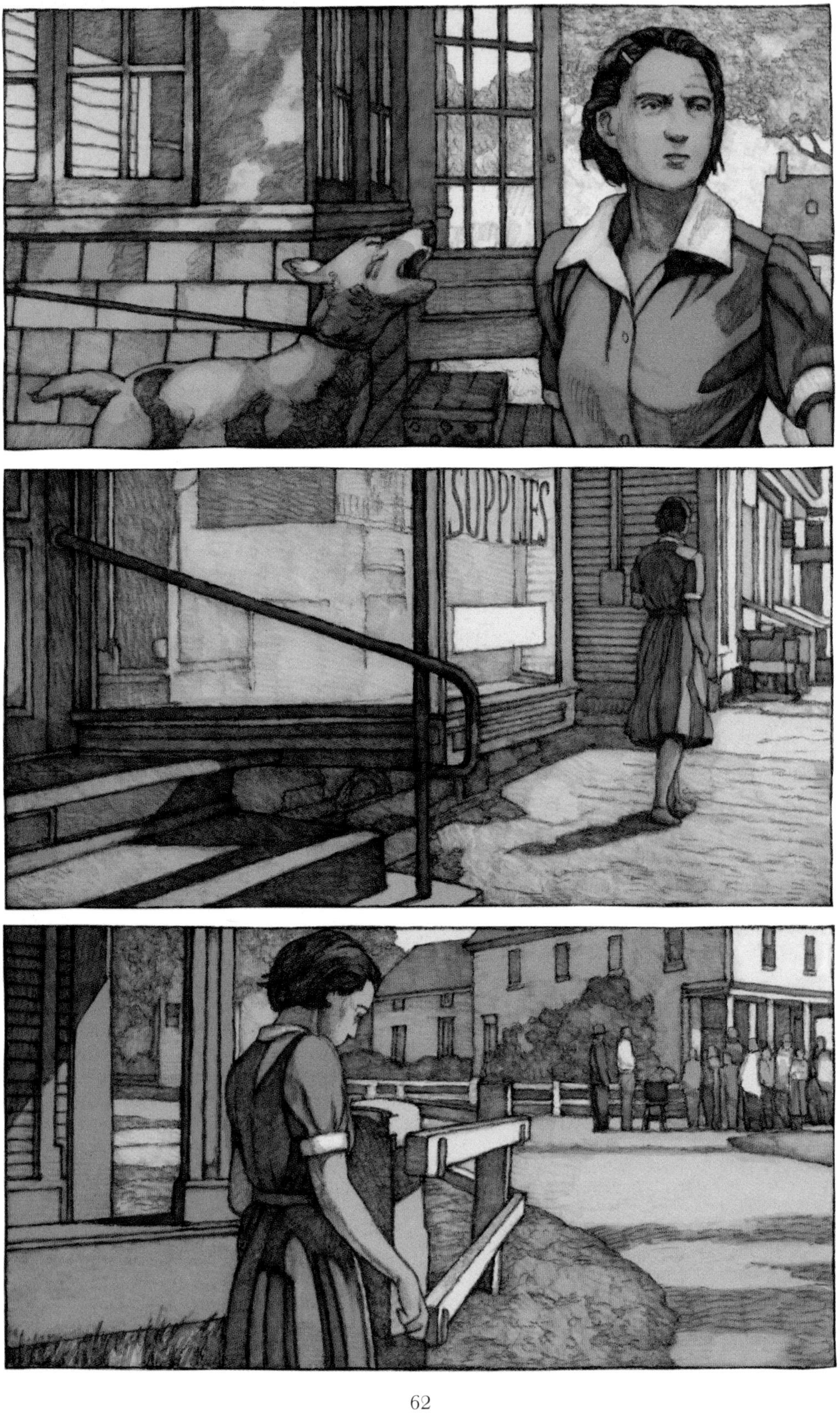
SUPPLIES

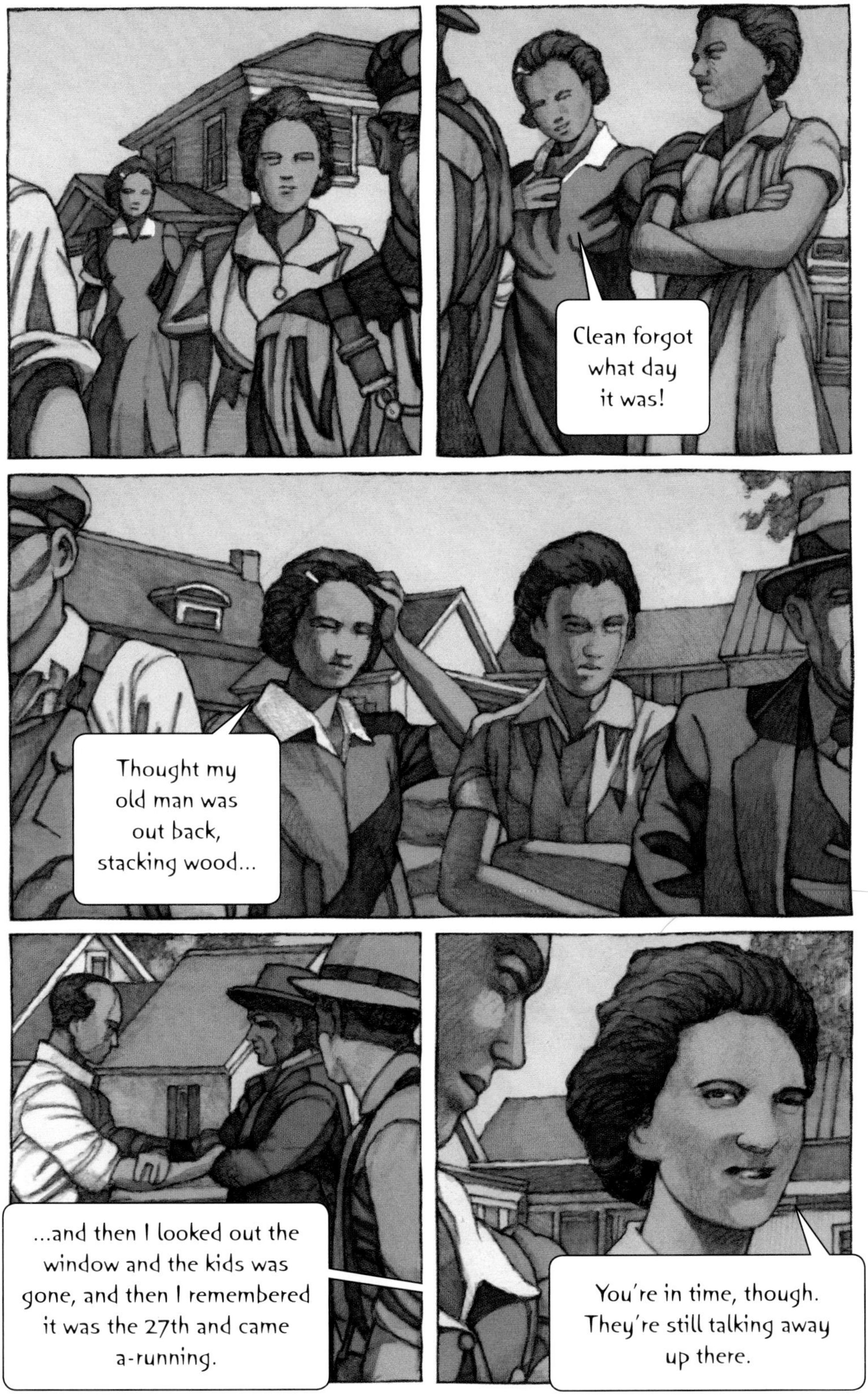
Clean forgot what day it was!
Thought my old man was out back, stacking wood...
...and then I looked out the window and the kids was gone, and then I remembered it was the 27th and came a-running.
You're in time, though. They're still talking away up there.

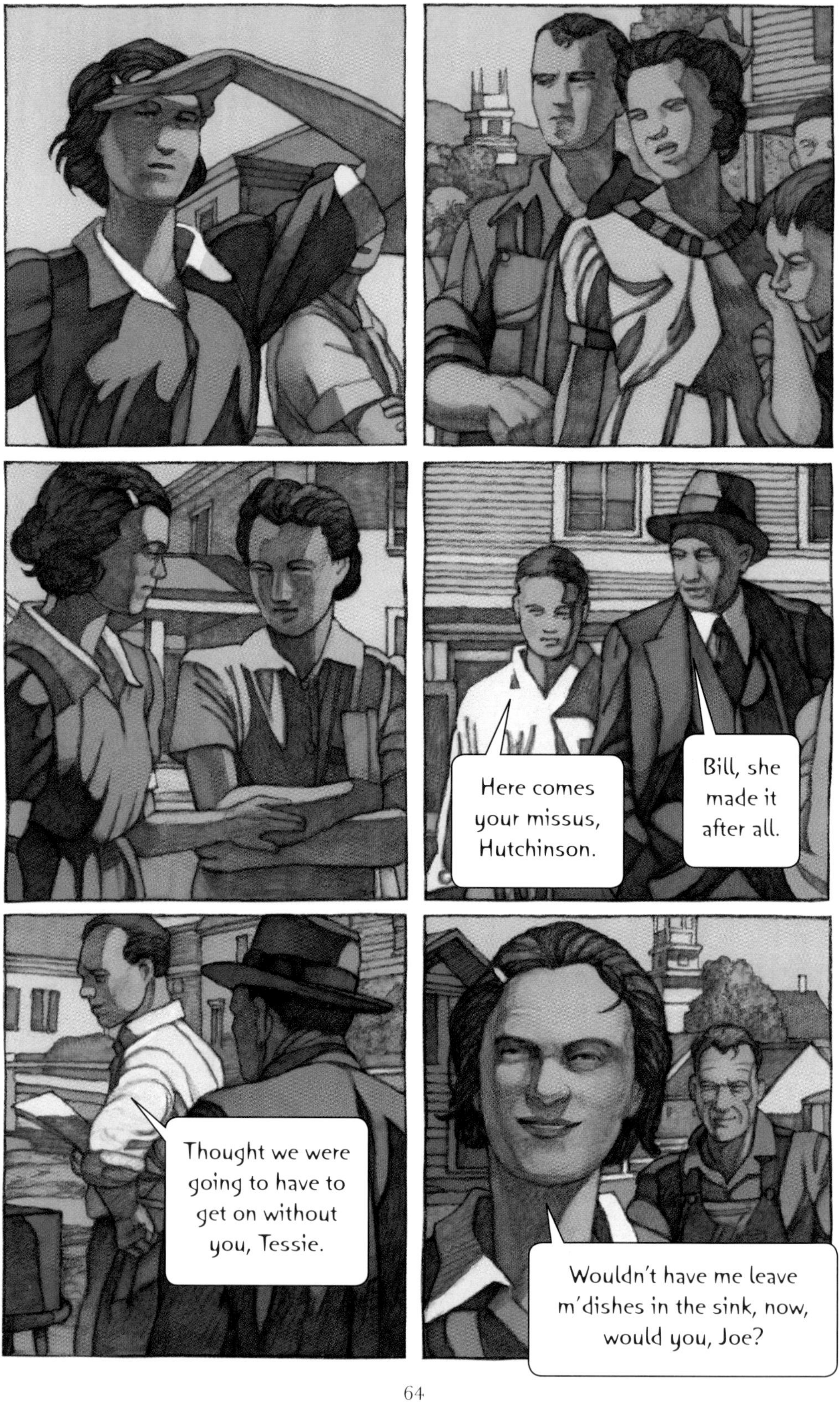
Here comes your missus, Hutchinson.
Bill, she made it after all.
Thought we were going to have to get on without you, Tessie.
Wouldn't have me leave m'dishes in the sink, now, would you, Joe?

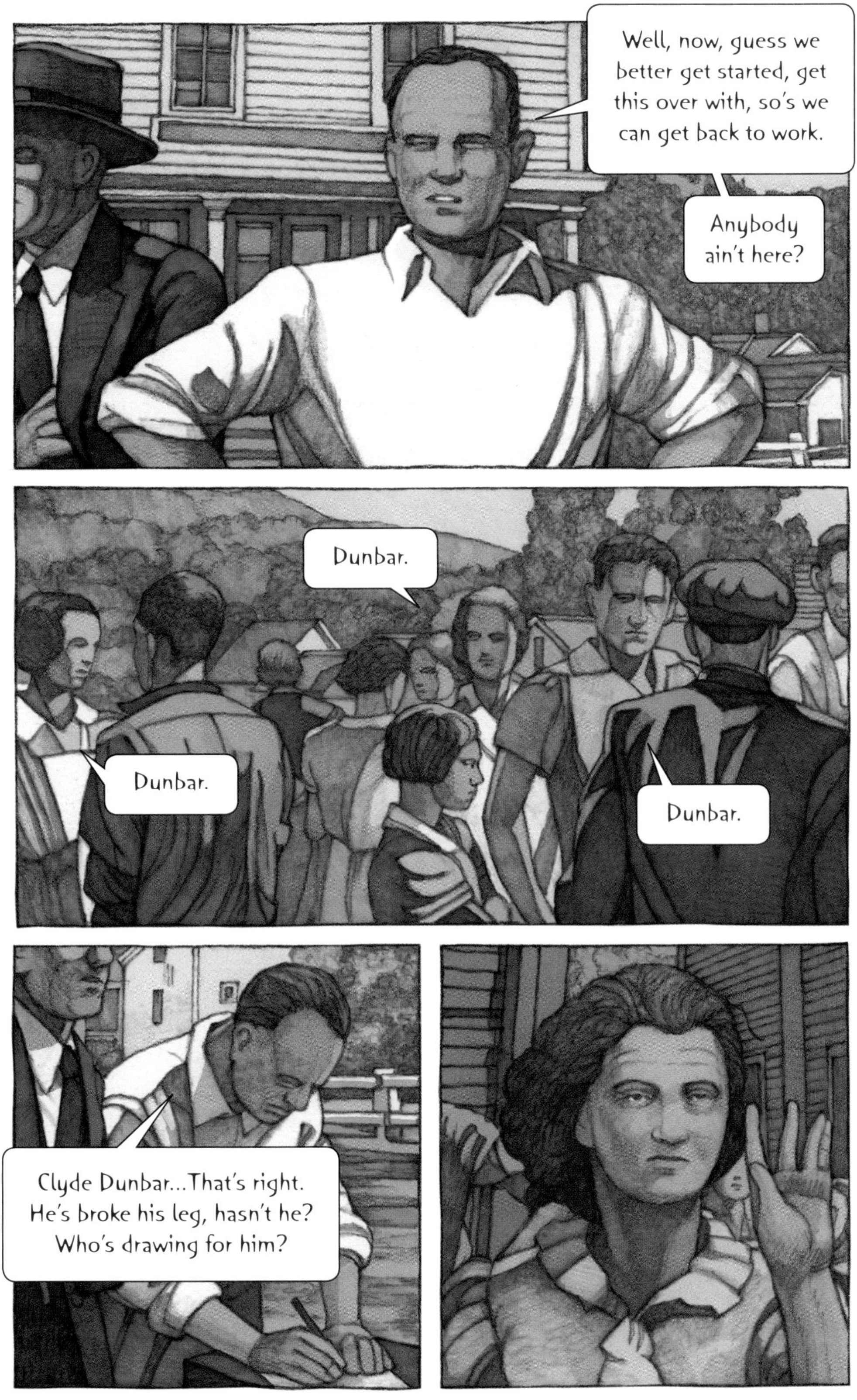
Well, now, guess we better get started, get this over with, so's we can get back to work.
Anybody ain't here?
Dunbar.
Dunbar.
Dunbar.
Clyde Dunbar...That's right. He's broke his leg, hasn't he? Who's drawing for him?

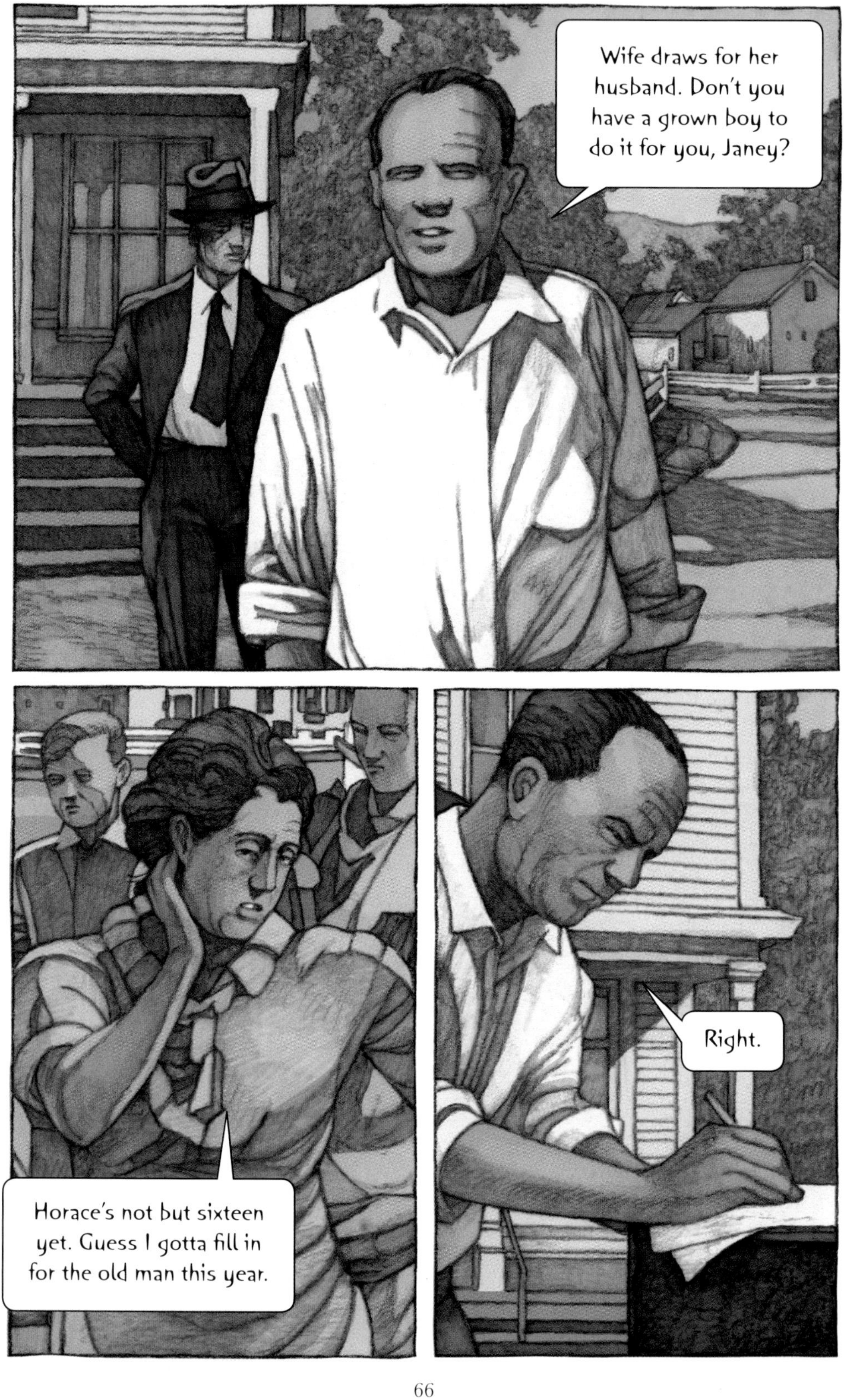
Wife draws for her husband. Don't you have a grown boy to do it for you, Janey?
Horace's not but sixteen yet. Guess I gotta fill in for the old man this year.
Right.

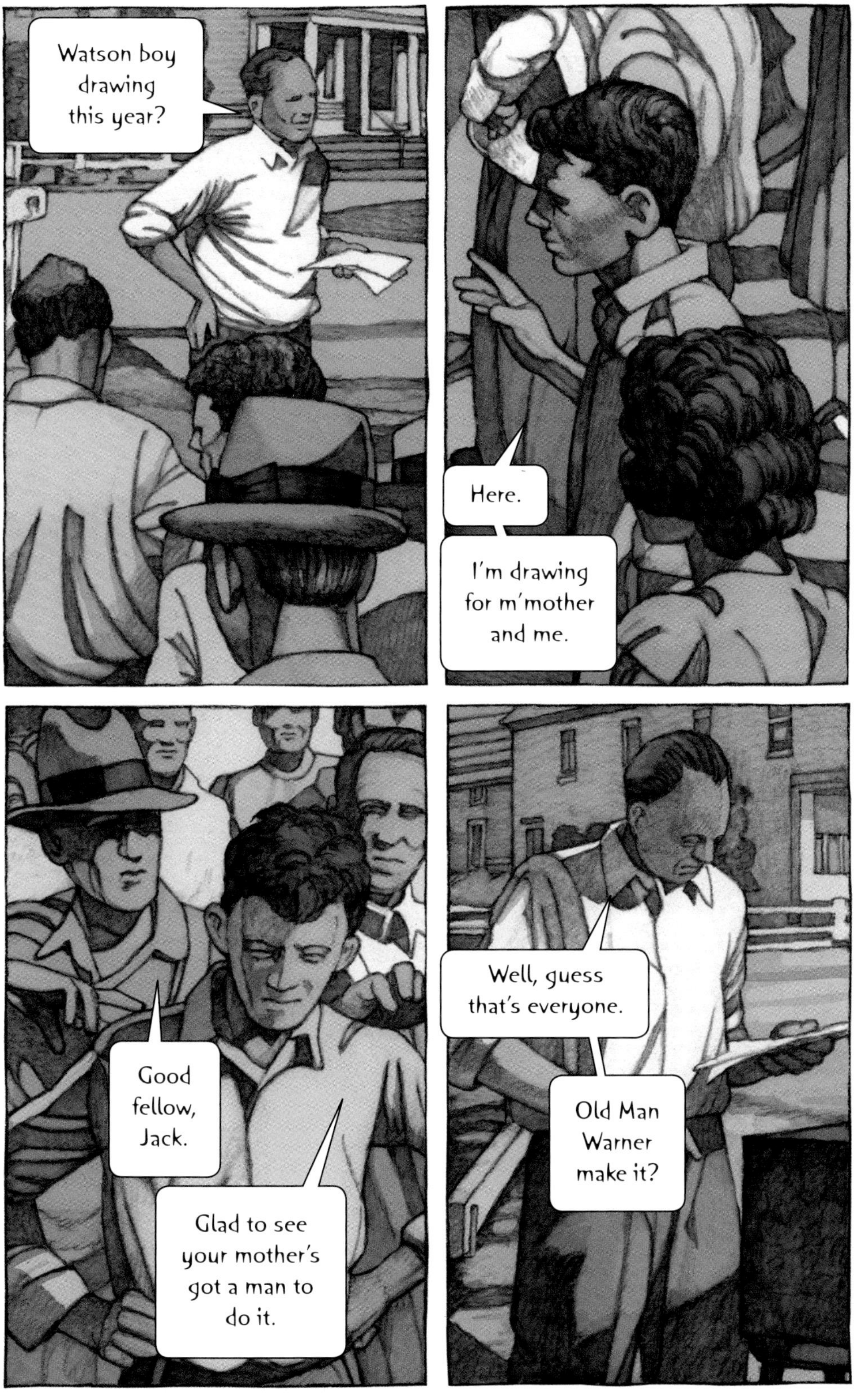
Watson boy drawing this year?
Here.
I'm drawing for m'mother and me.
Good fellow, Jack.
Glad to see your mother's got a man to do it.
Well, guess that's everyone.
Old Man Warner make it?

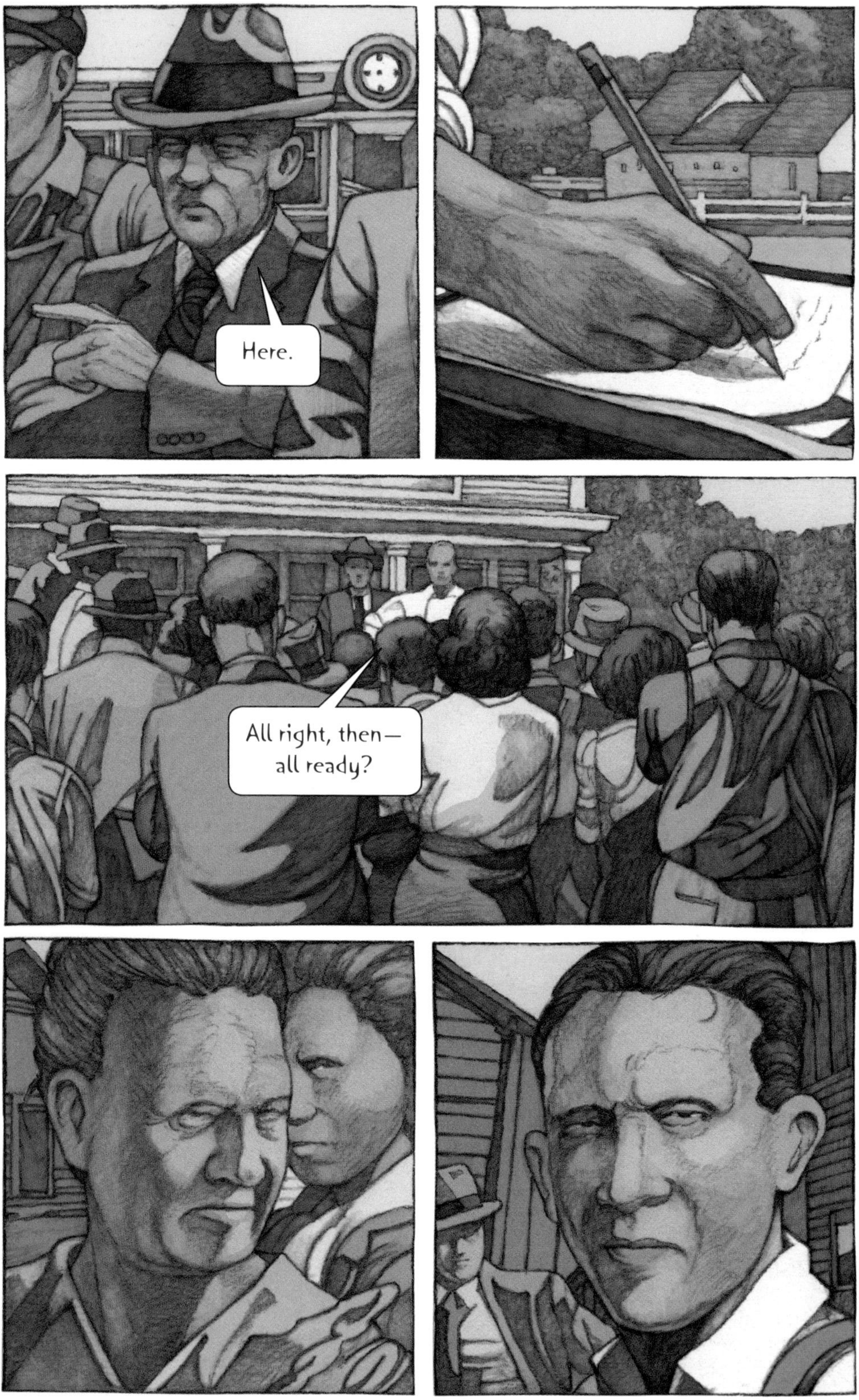
Here.
All right, then—
all ready?

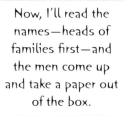

Now, I'll read the names—heads of families first—and the men come up and take a paper out of the box.

Keep the paper folded in your hand without looking at it until everyone has had a turn.

Everything clear?

Adams.

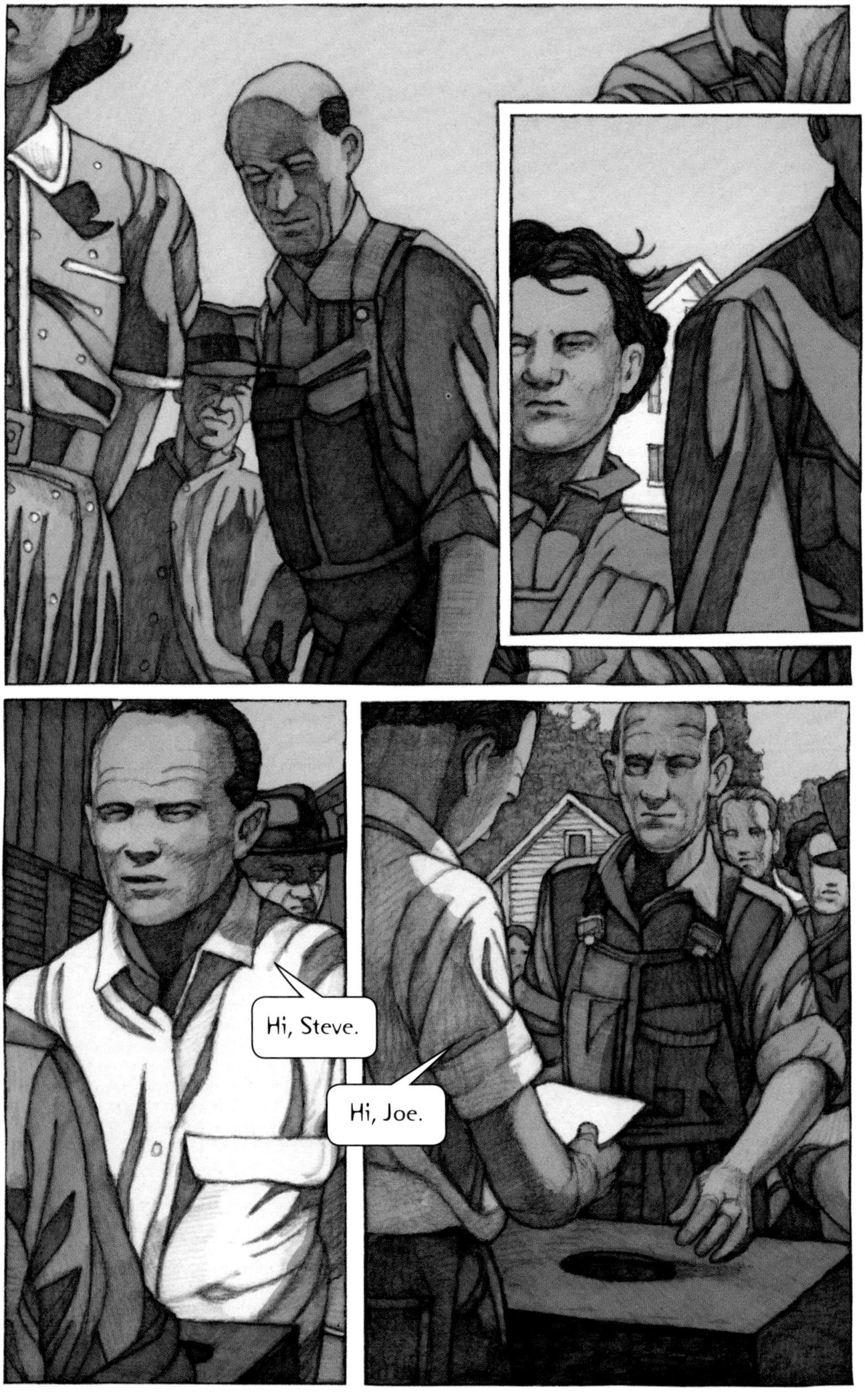
Hi, Steve.
Hi, Joe.

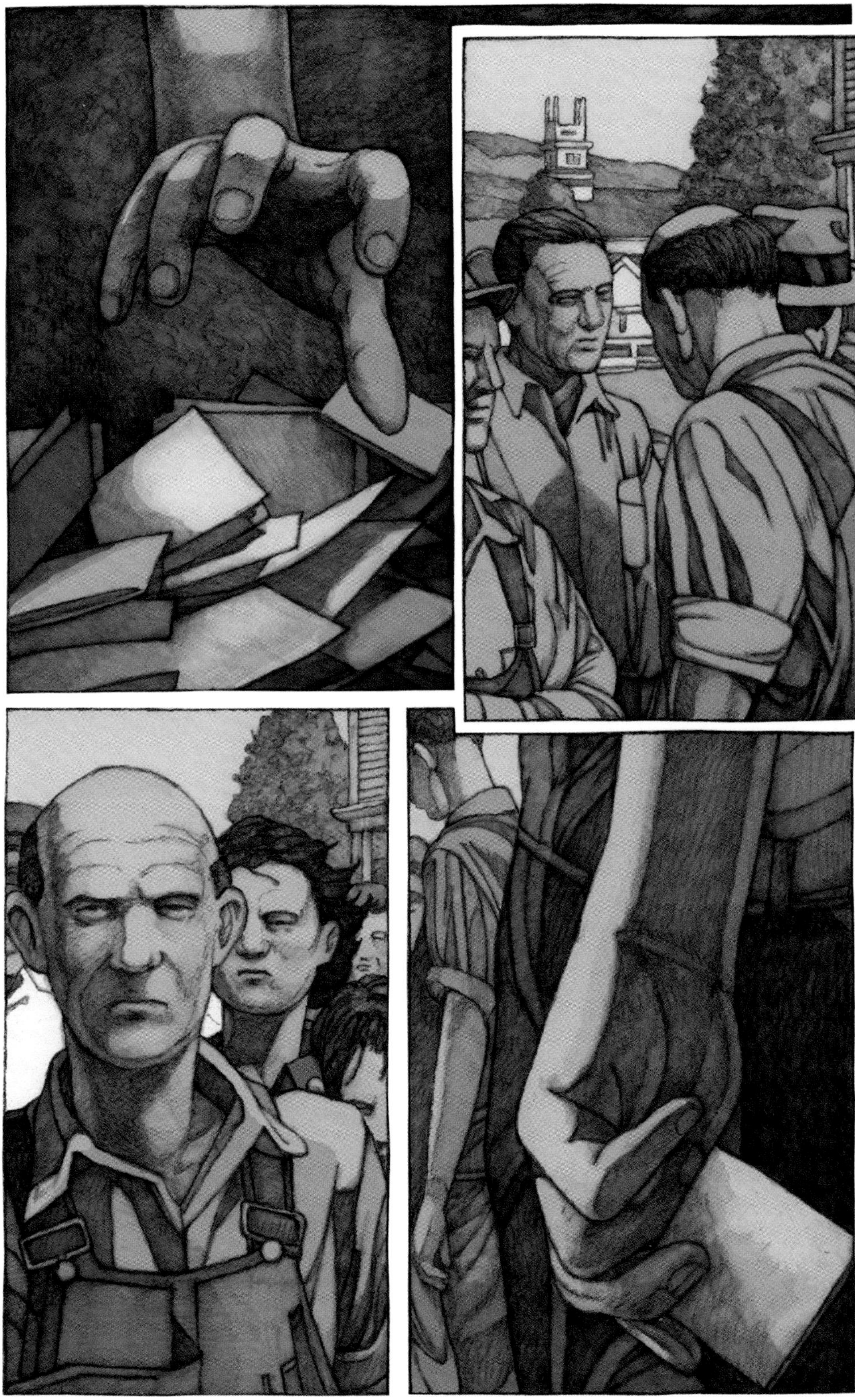

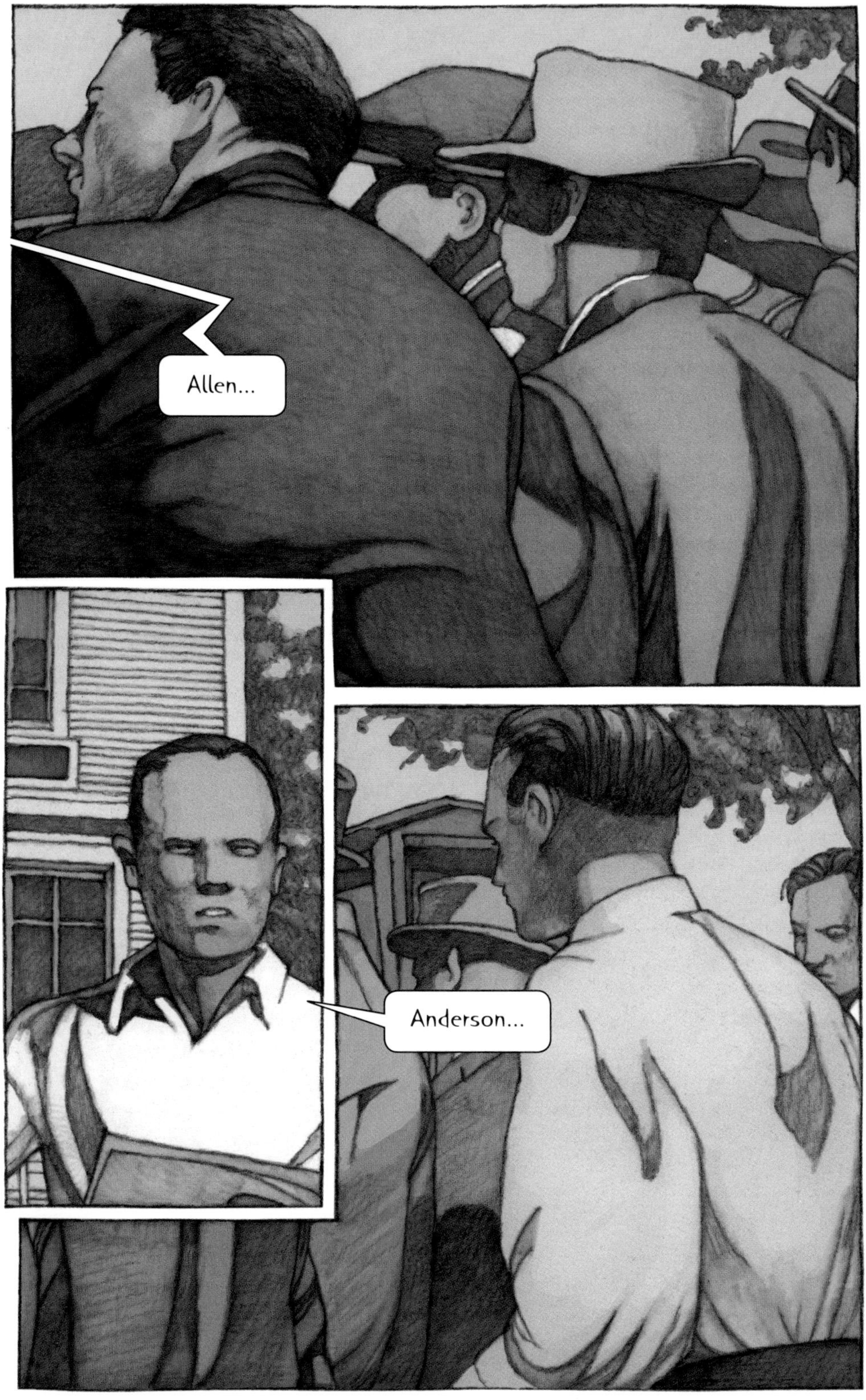
Allen...
Anderson...

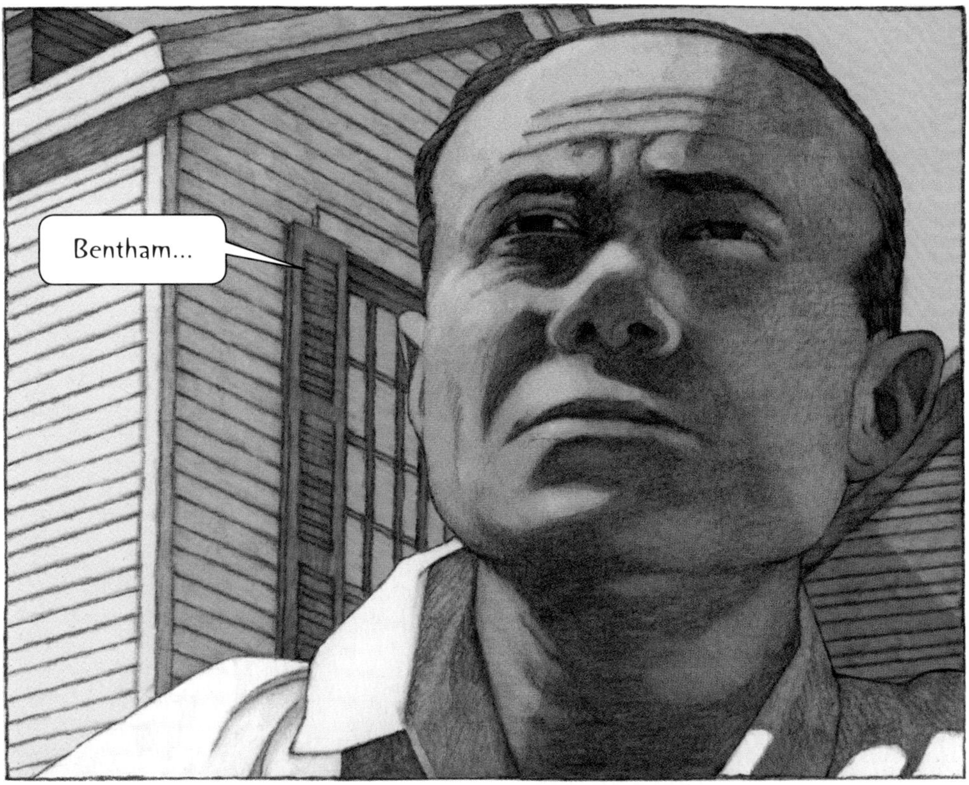
Bentham...

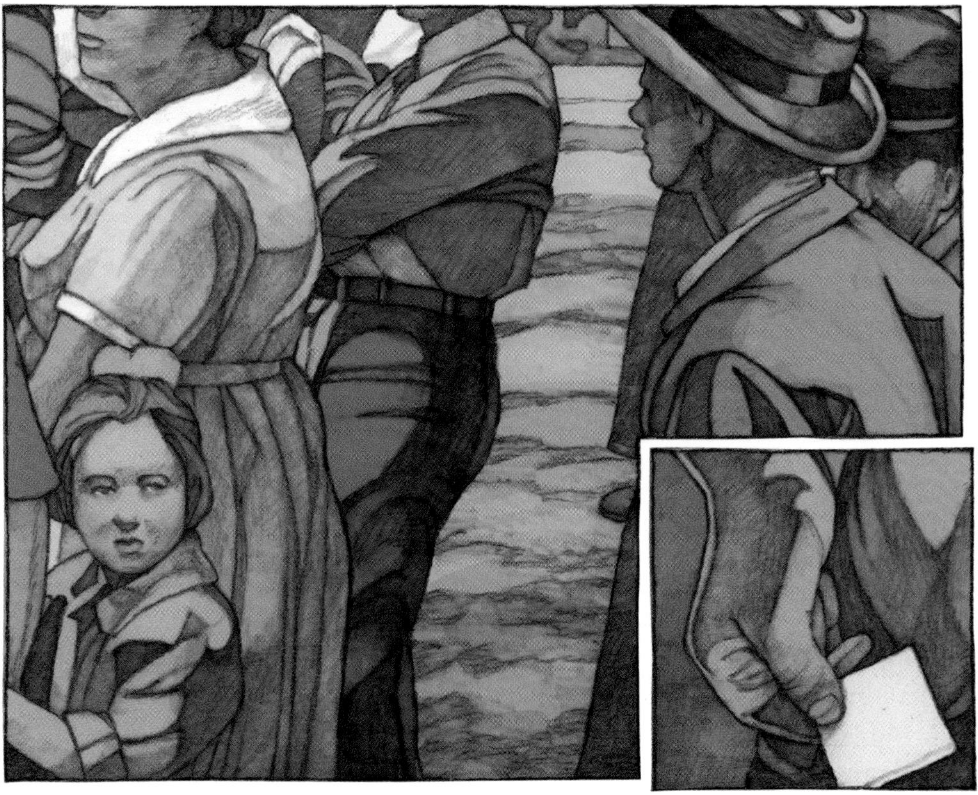

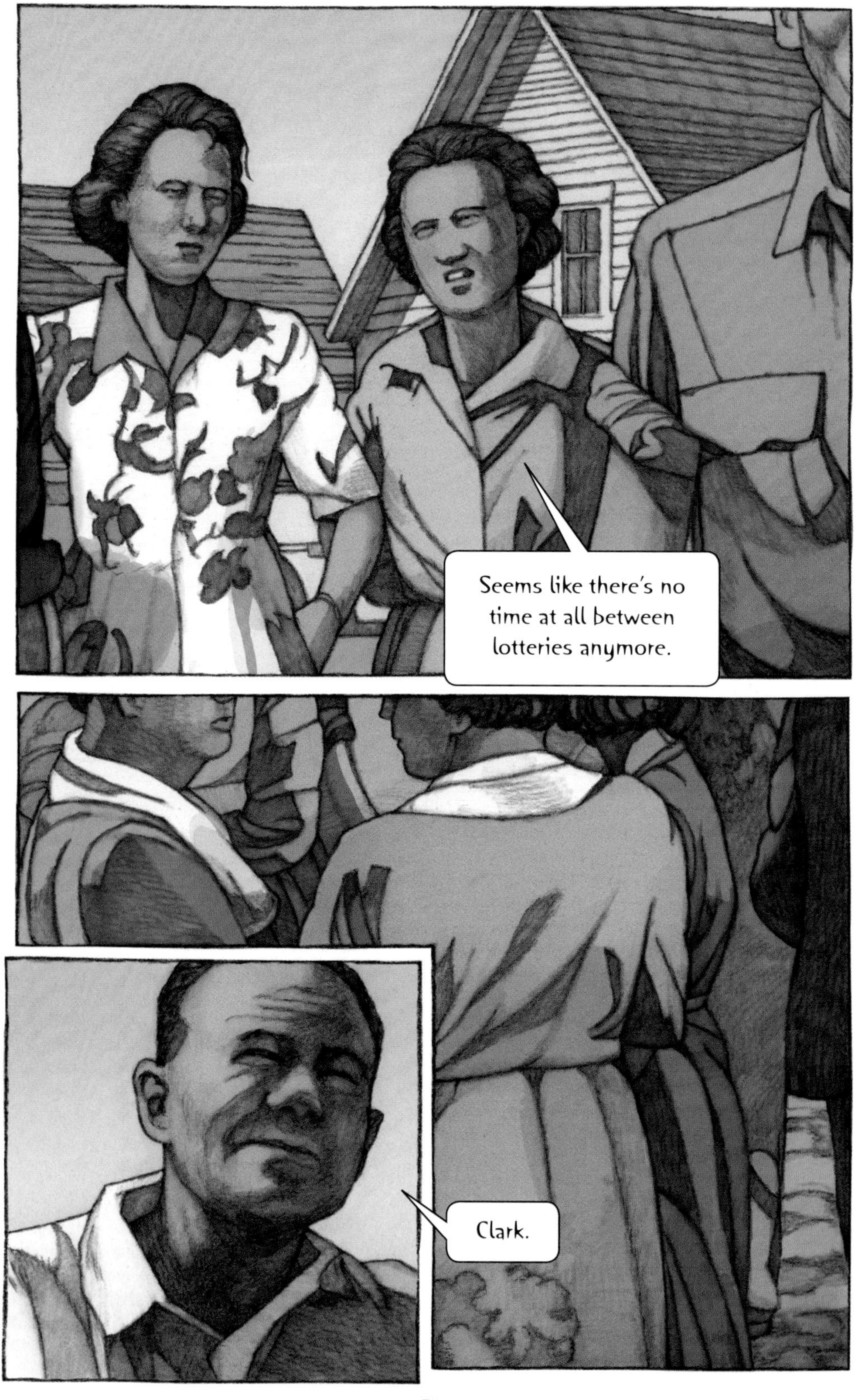
Seems like there's no time at all between lotteries anymore.
Clark.

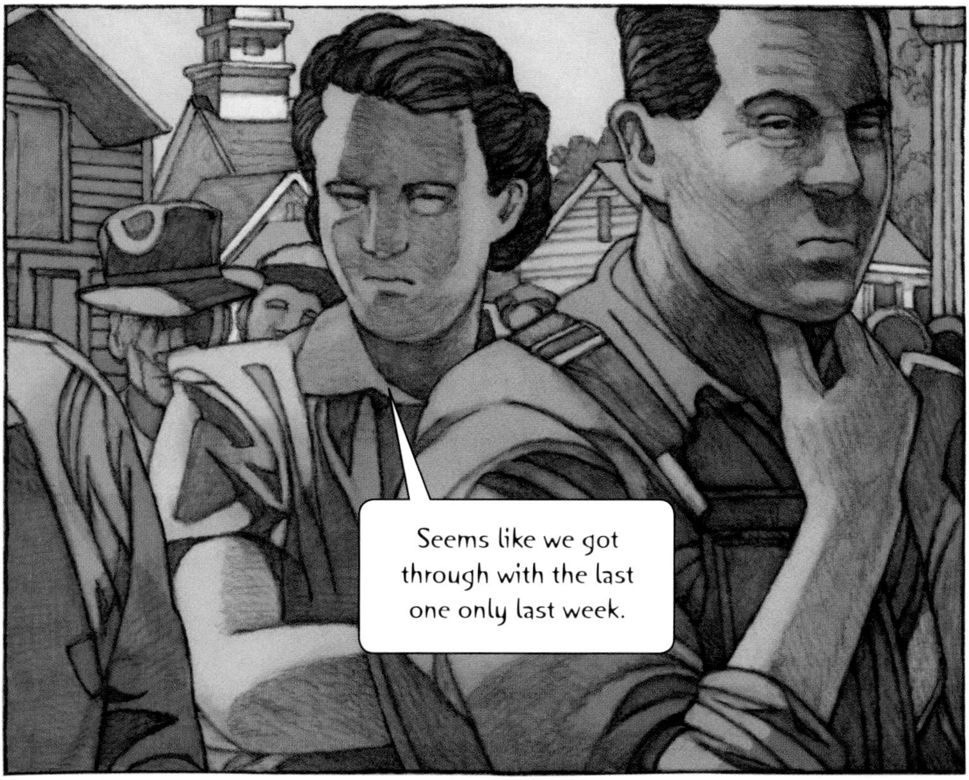
Seems like we got through with the last one only last week.

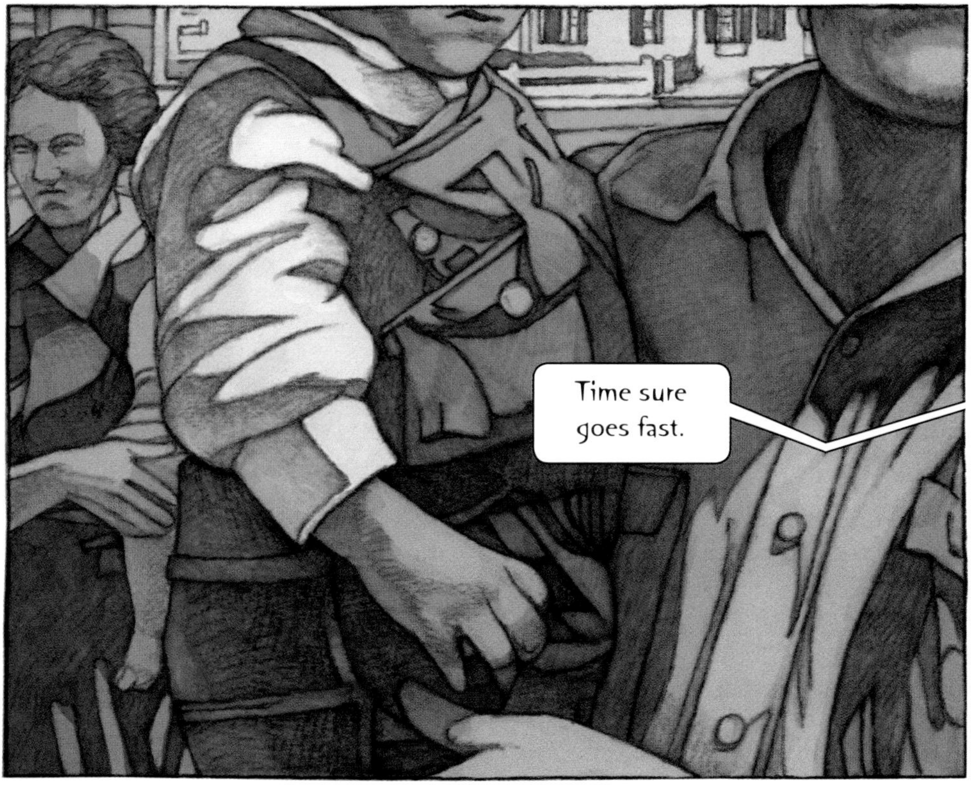
Time sure goes fast.

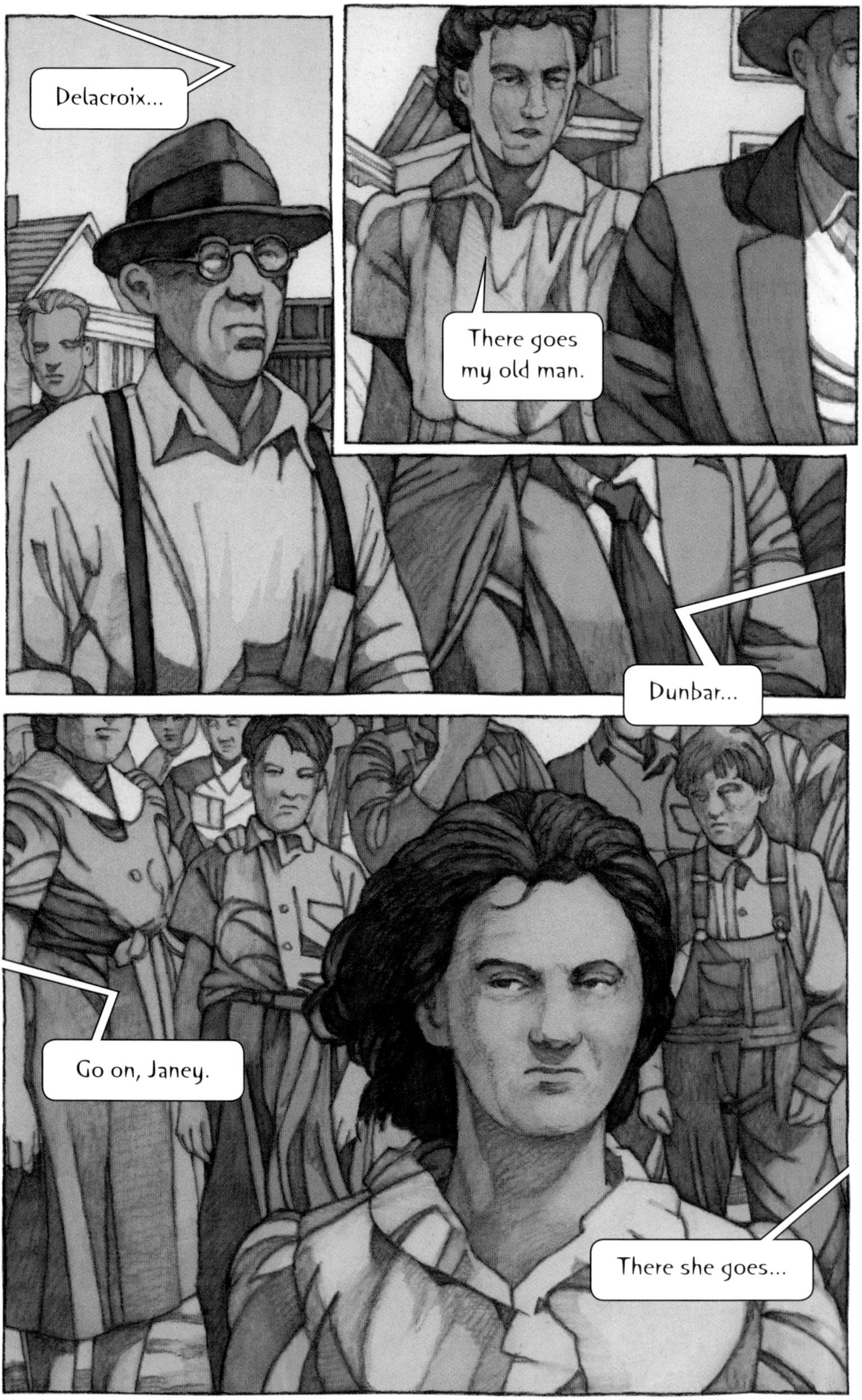
Delacroix...
There goes my old man.
Dunbar...
Go on, Janey.
There she goes...

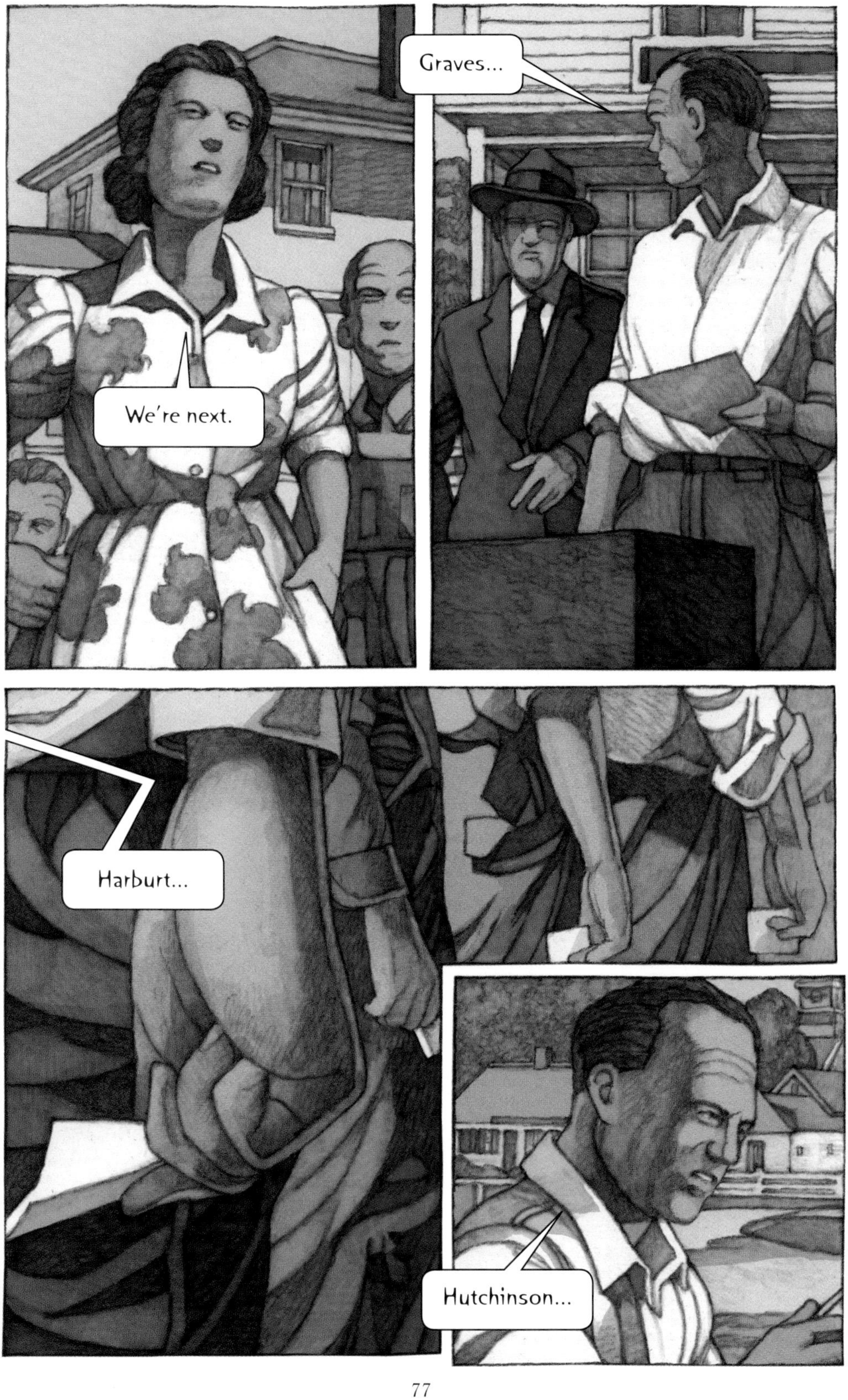
We're next.
Graves...
Harburt...
Hutchinson...

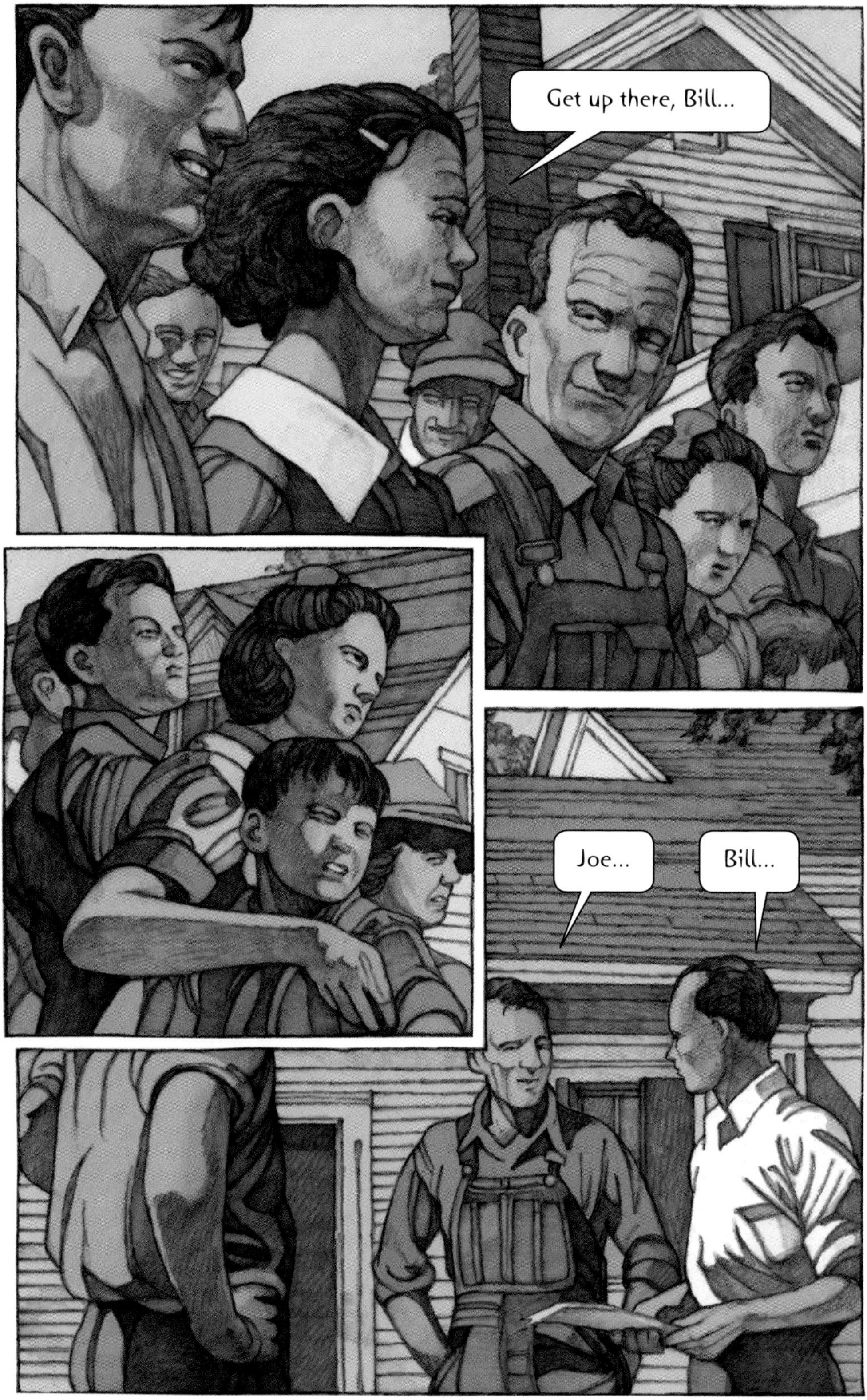
Get up there, Bill...
Joe...
Bill...

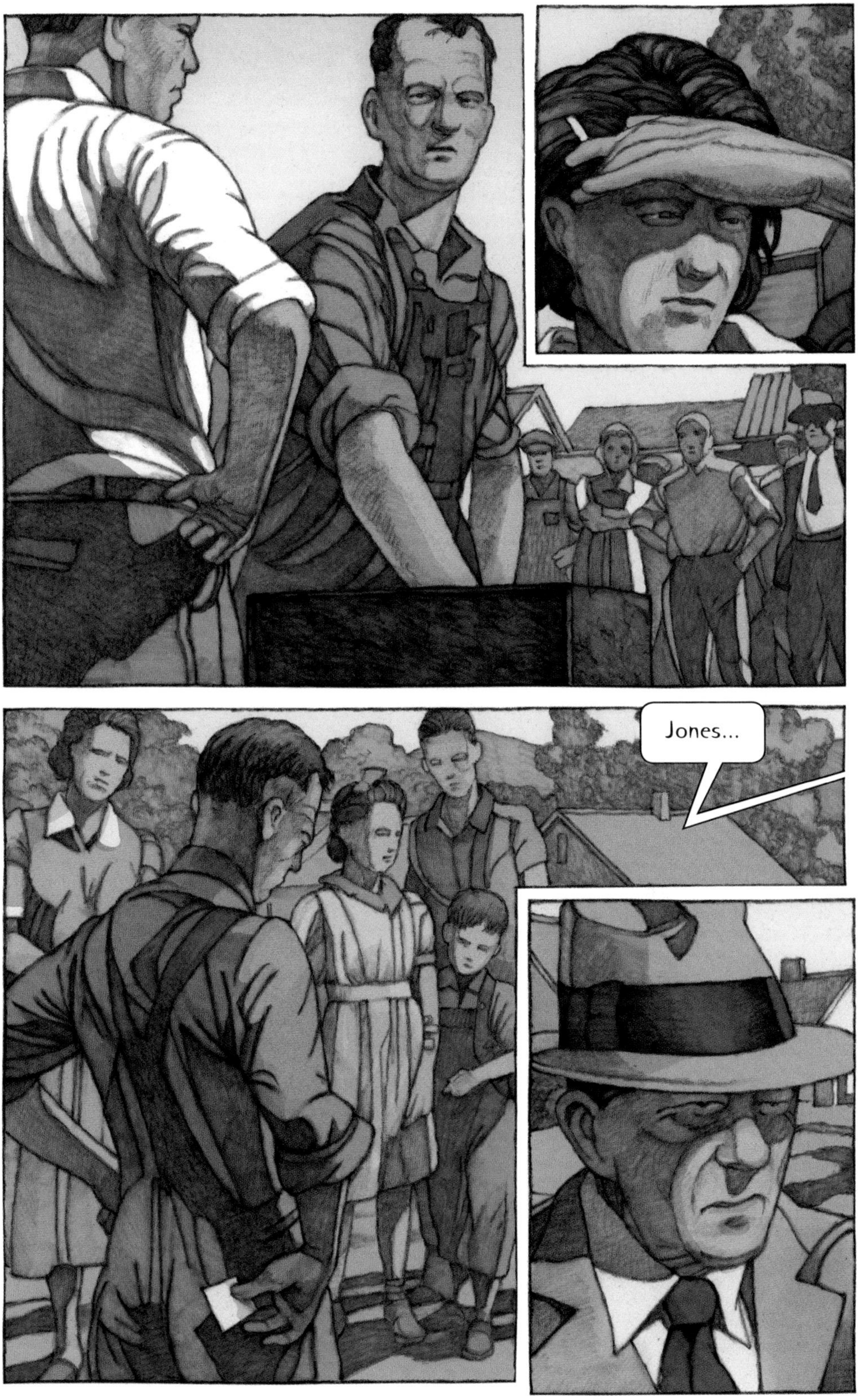
Jones...

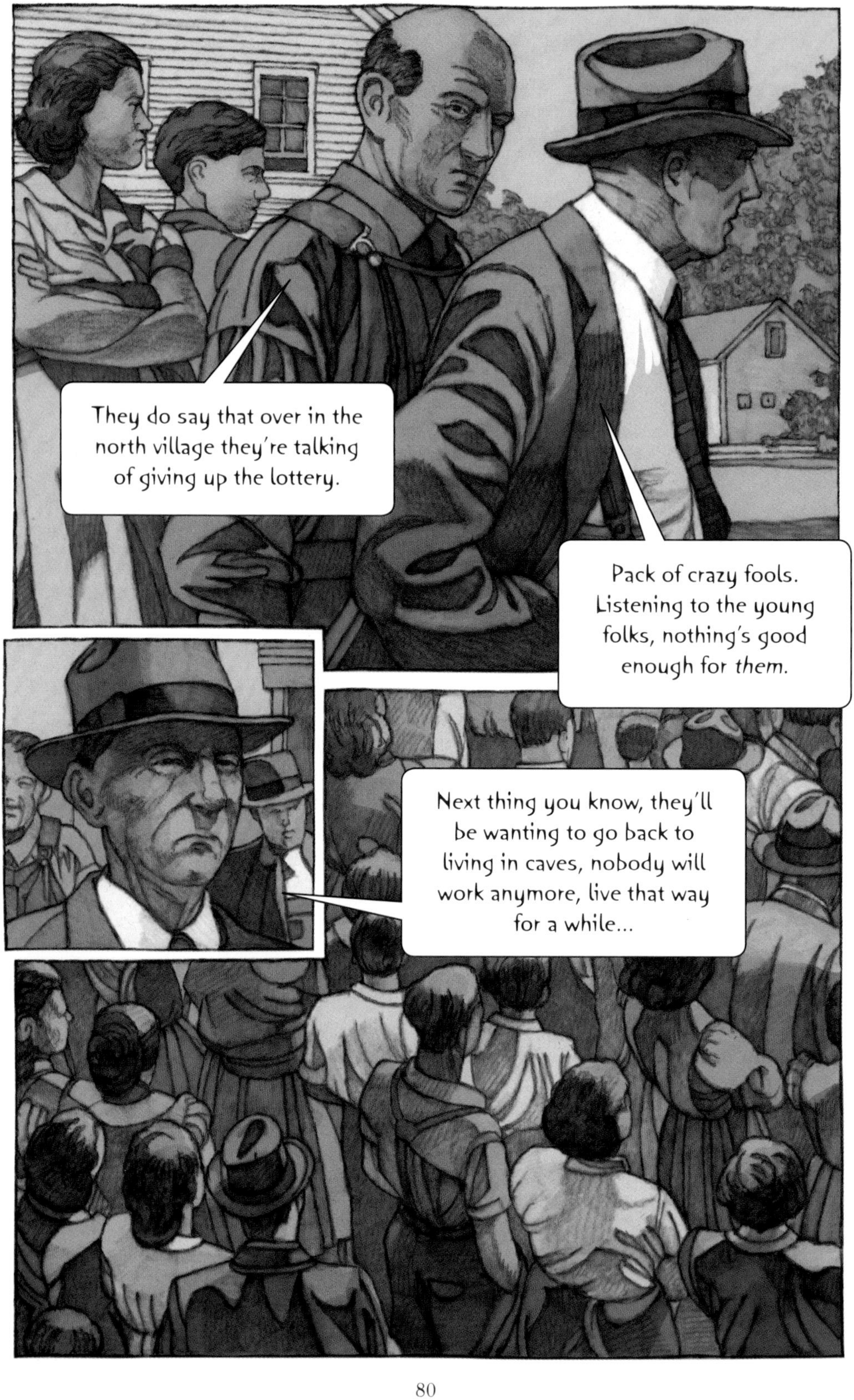
They do say that over in the north village they're talking of giving up the lottery.
Pack of crazy fools. Listening to the young folks, nothing's good enough for *them*.
Next thing you know, they'll be wanting to go back to living in caves, nobody will work anymore, live that way for a while...

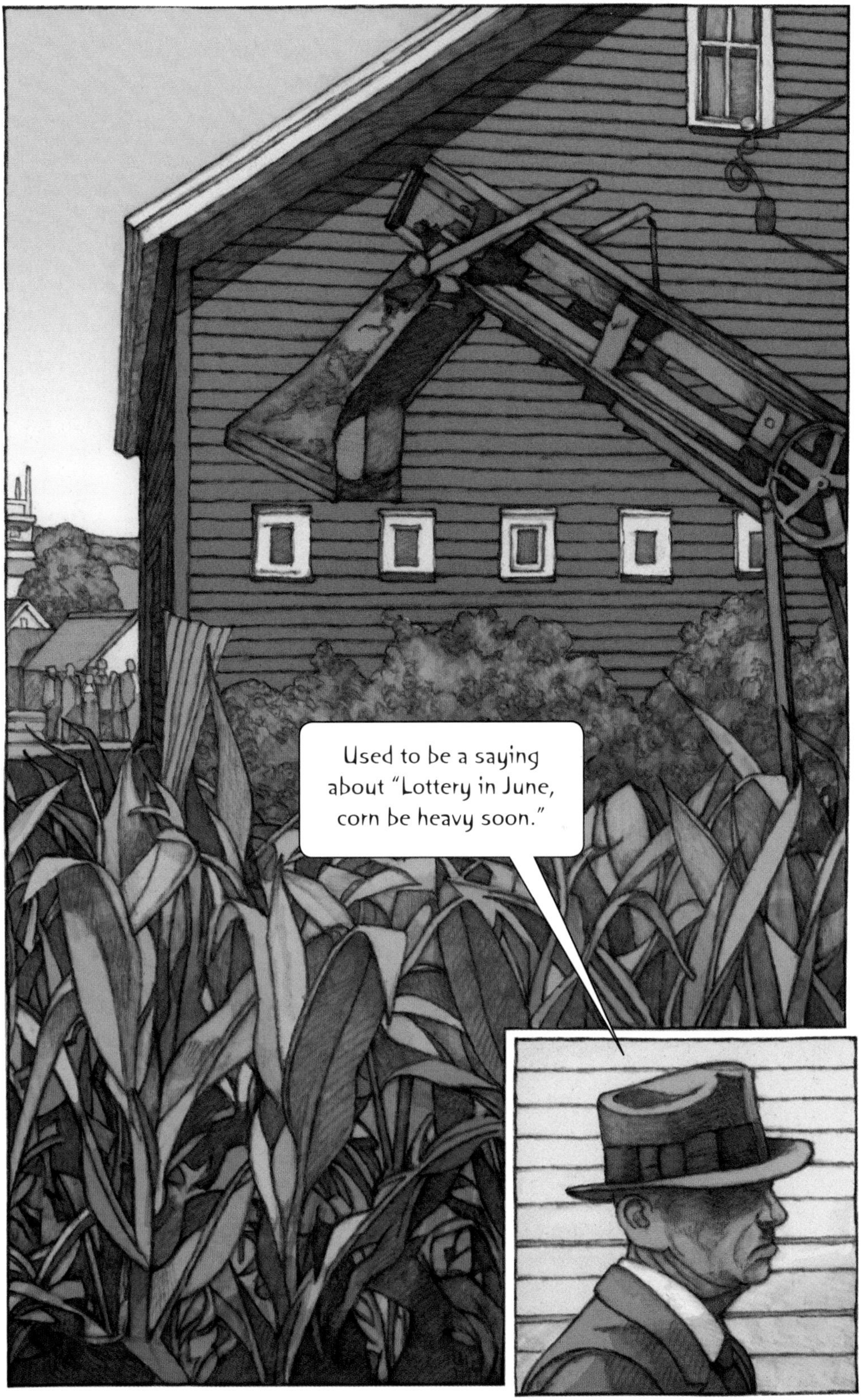
Used to be a saying about "Lottery in June, corn be heavy soon."

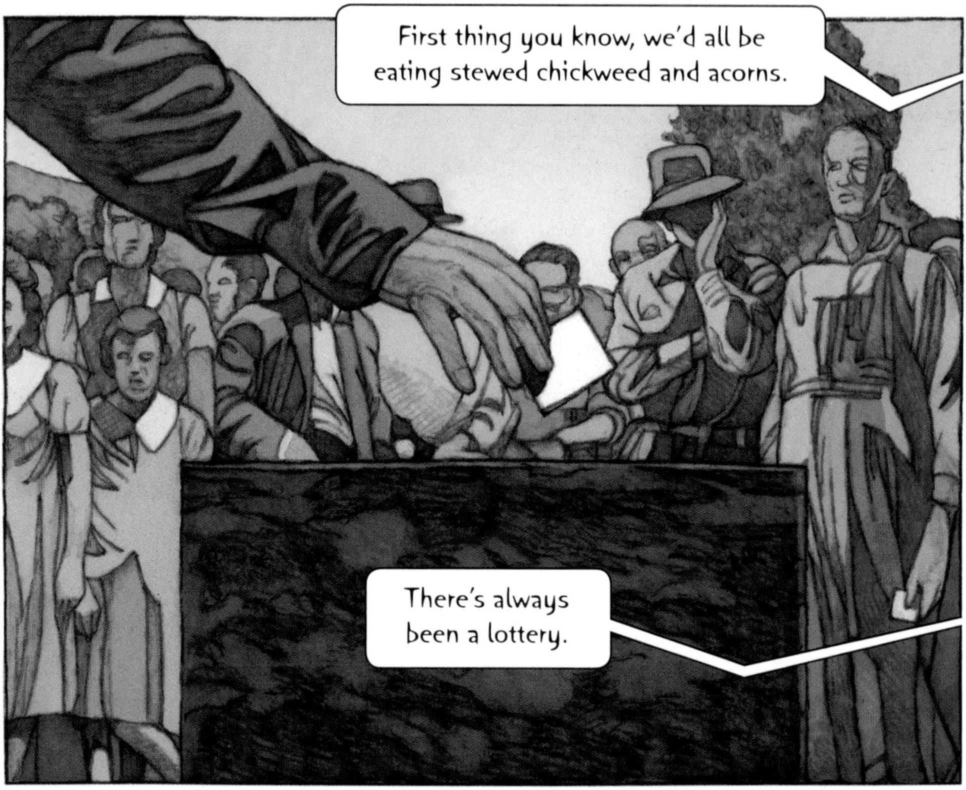
First thing you know, we'd all be eating stewed chickweed and acorns.
There's always been a lottery.

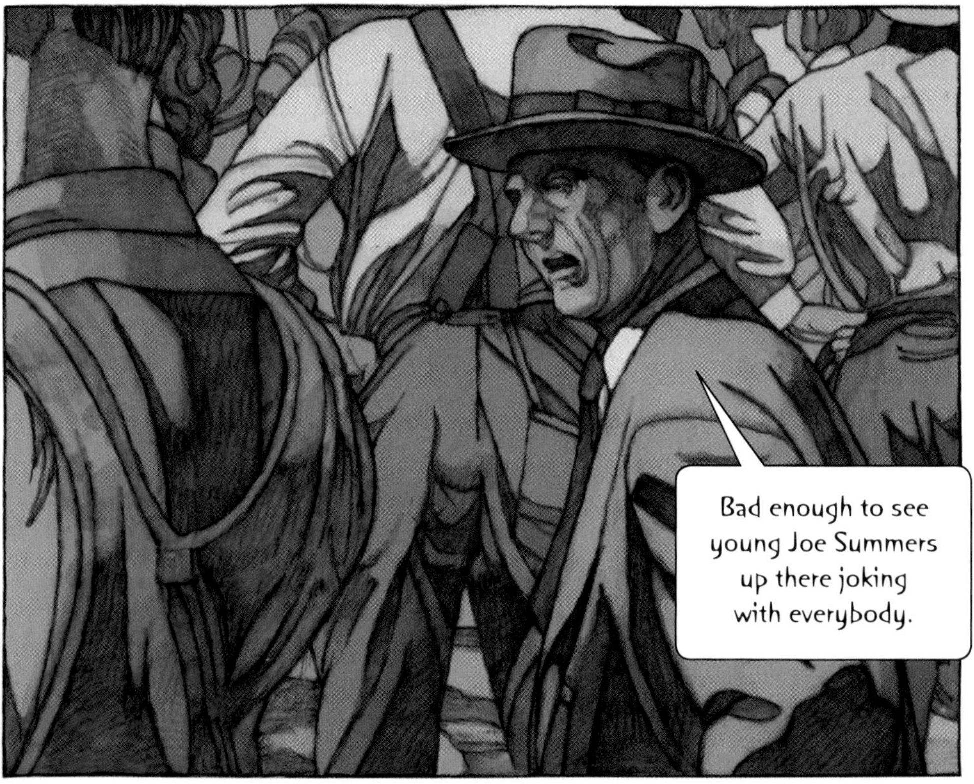
Bad enough to see young Joe Summers up there joking with everybody.

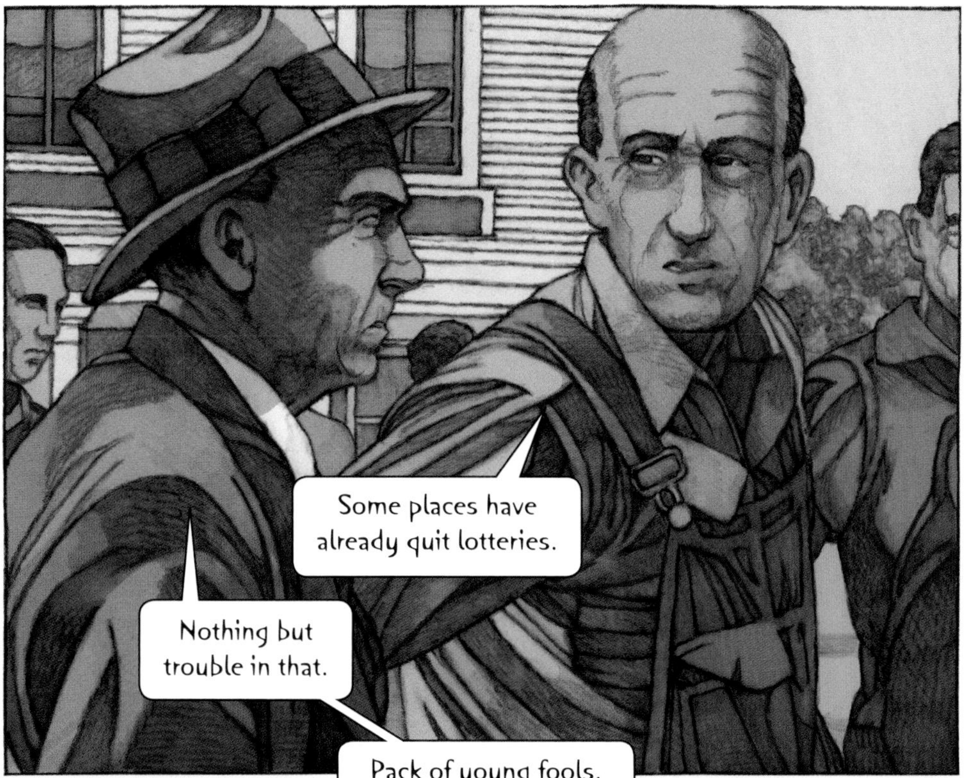
Some places have already quit lotteries.
Nothing but trouble in that.
Pack of young fools.

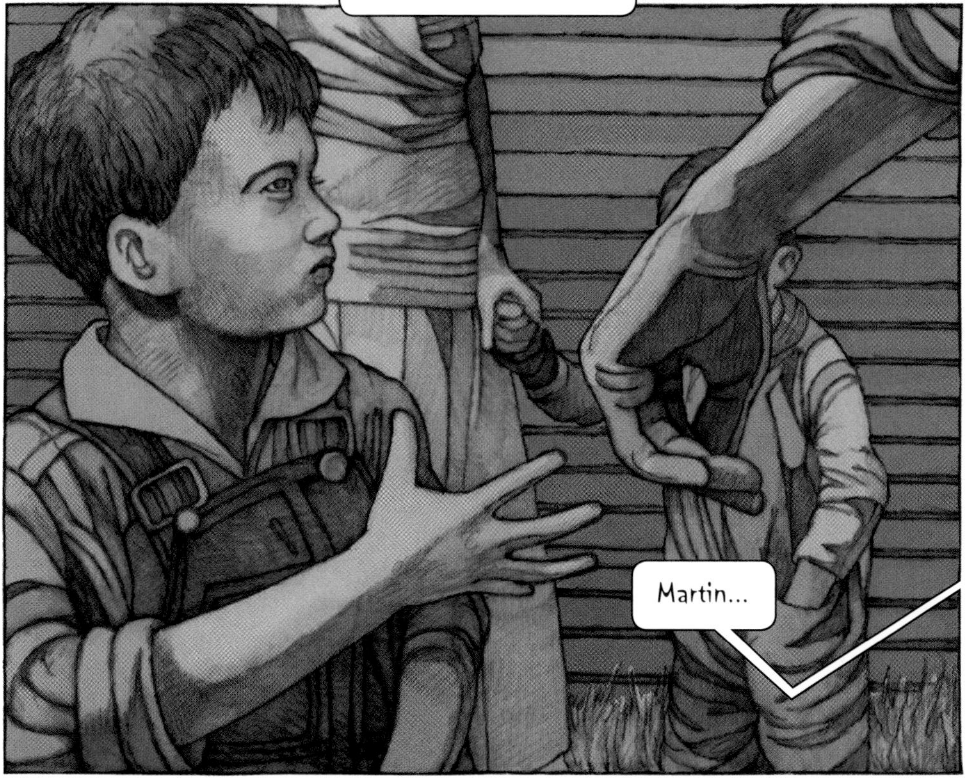
Martin...

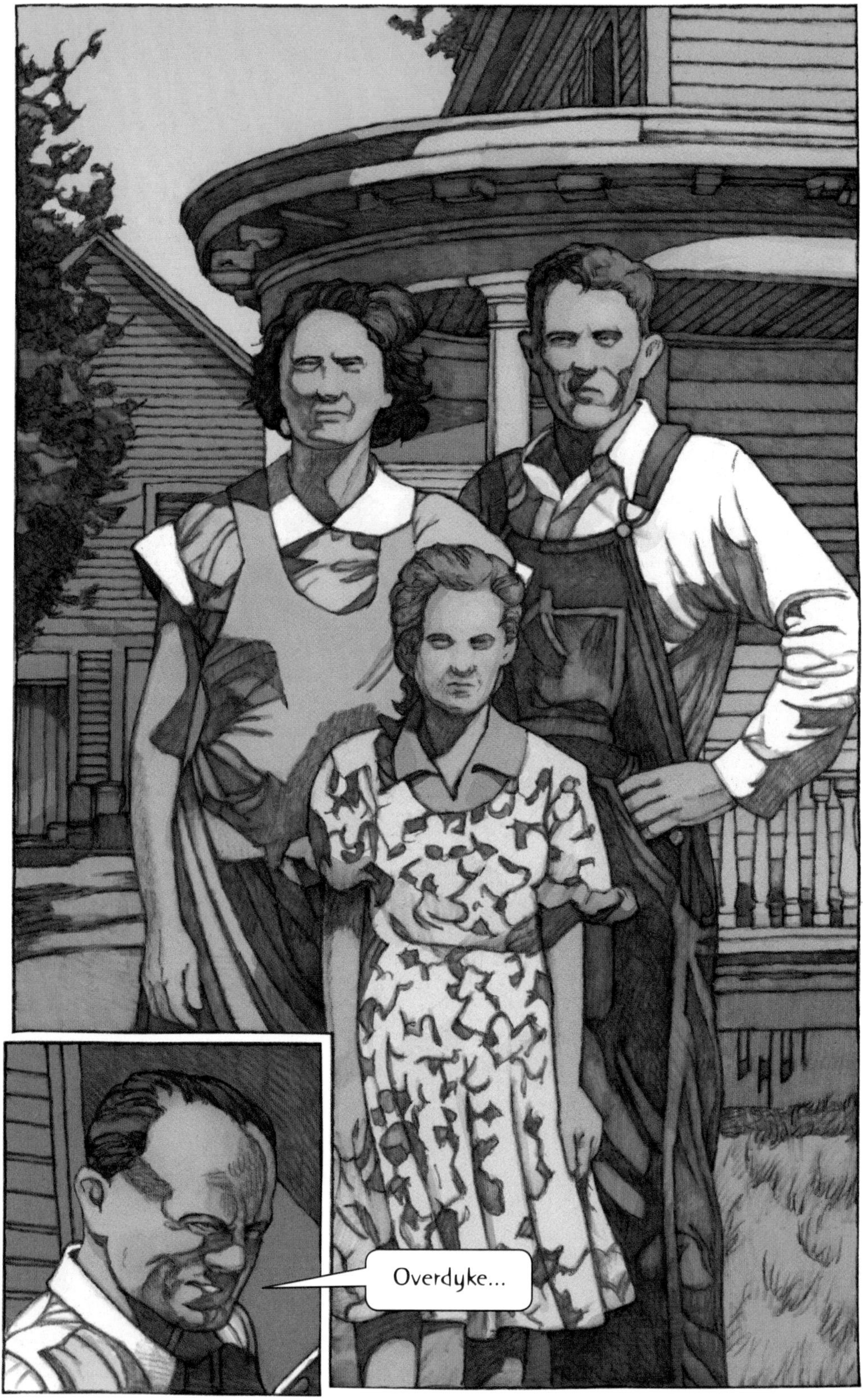
Overdyke...

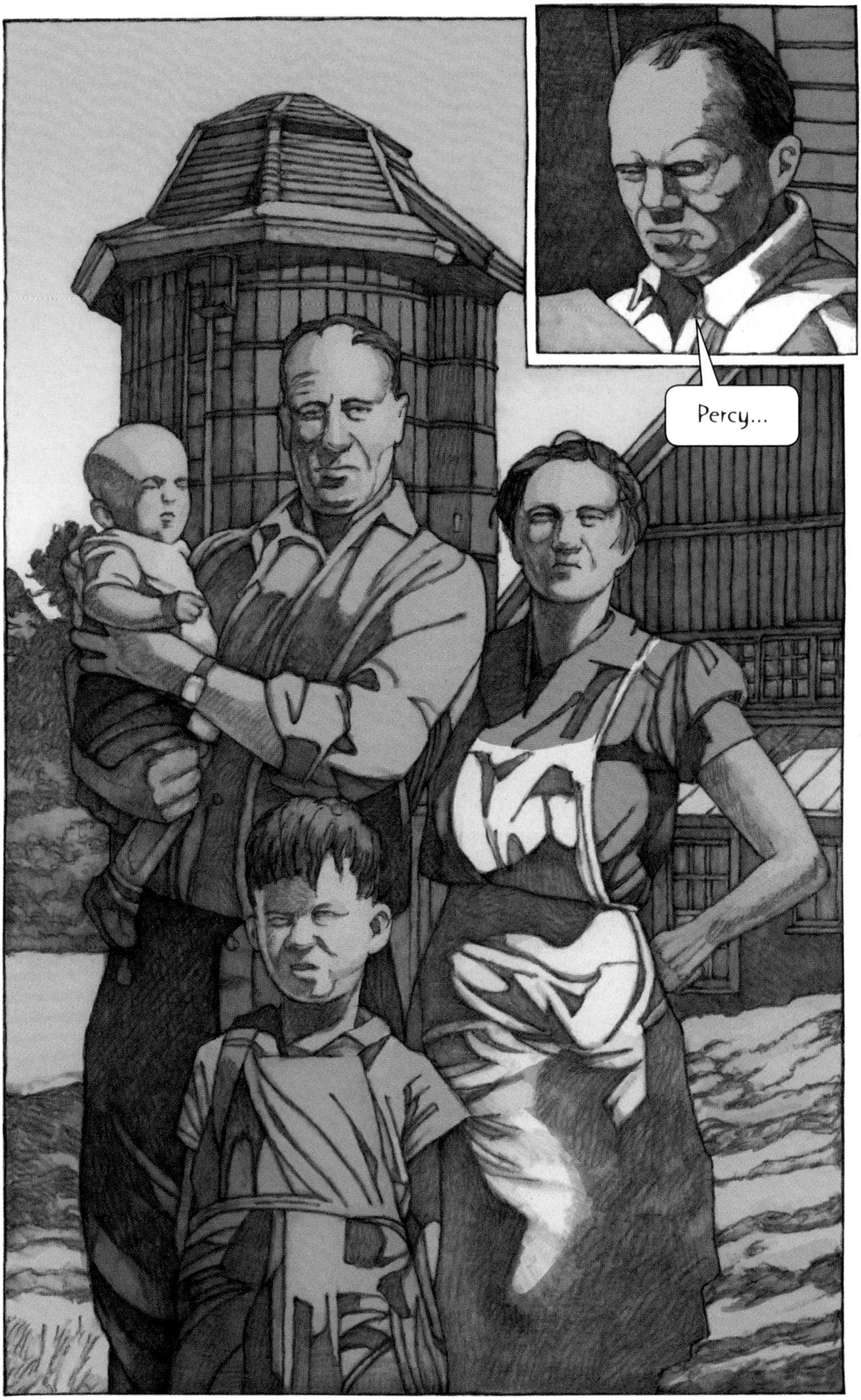
Percy...

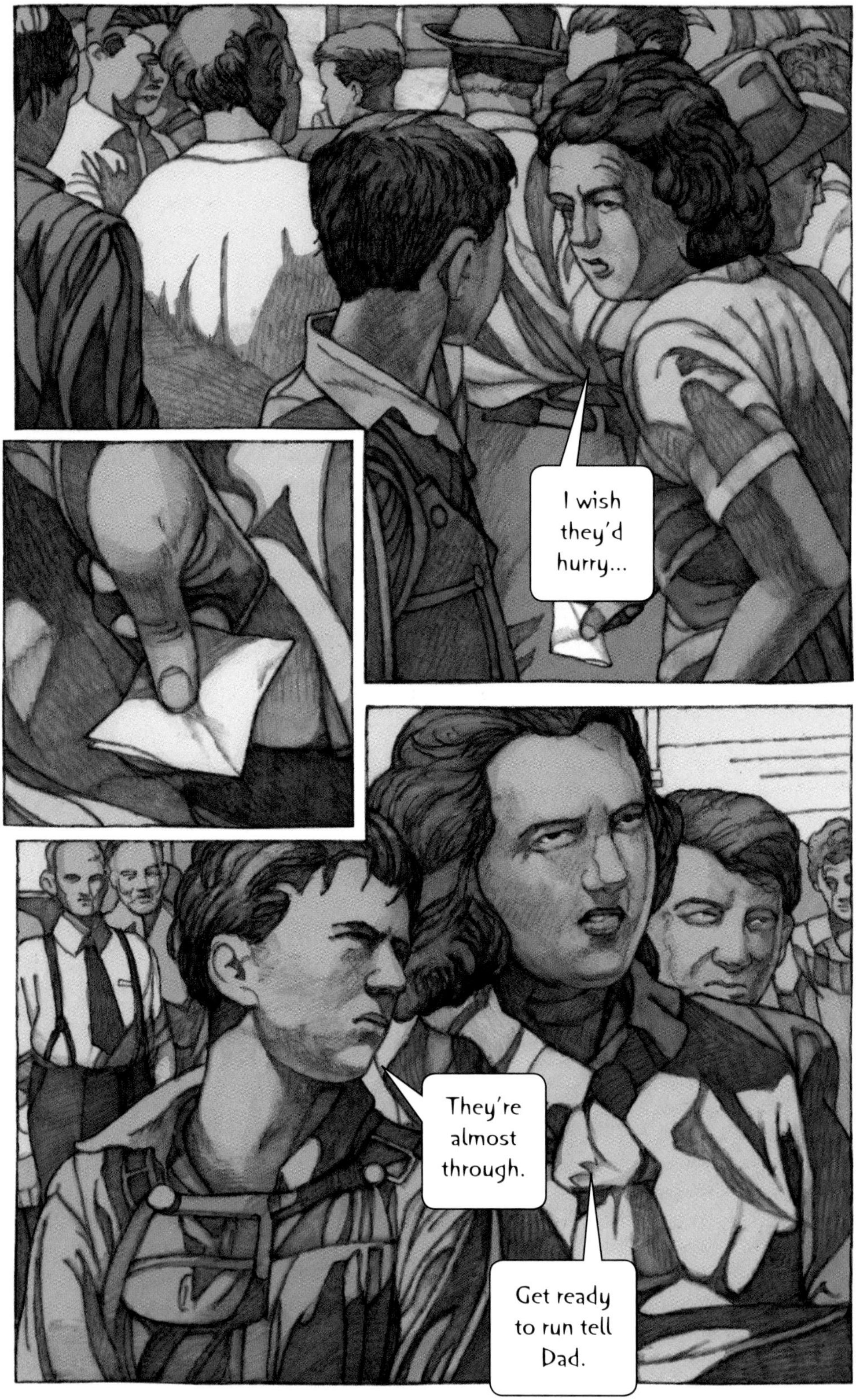
I wish they'd hurry...
They're almost through.
Get ready to run tell Dad.

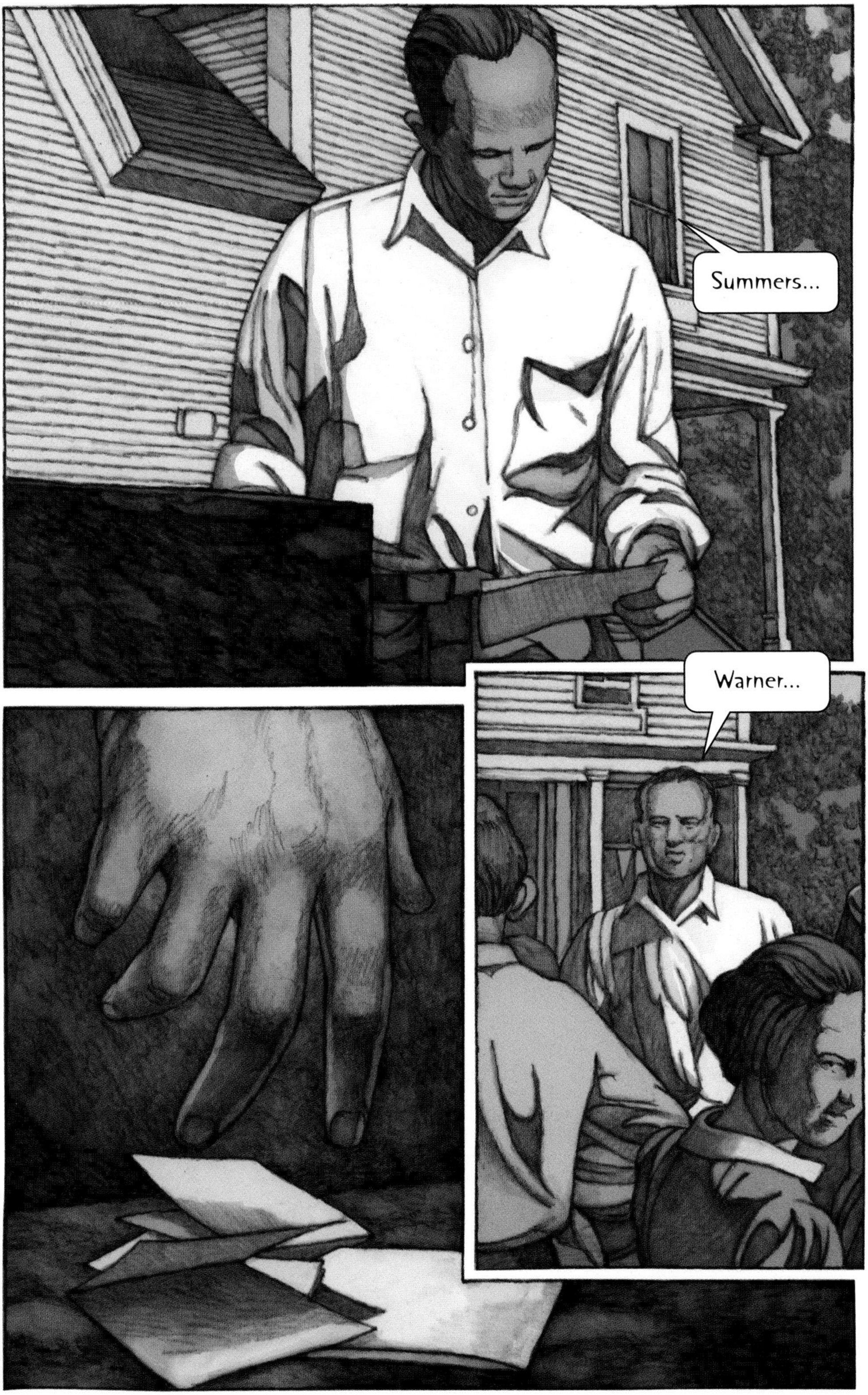
Summers...
Warner...

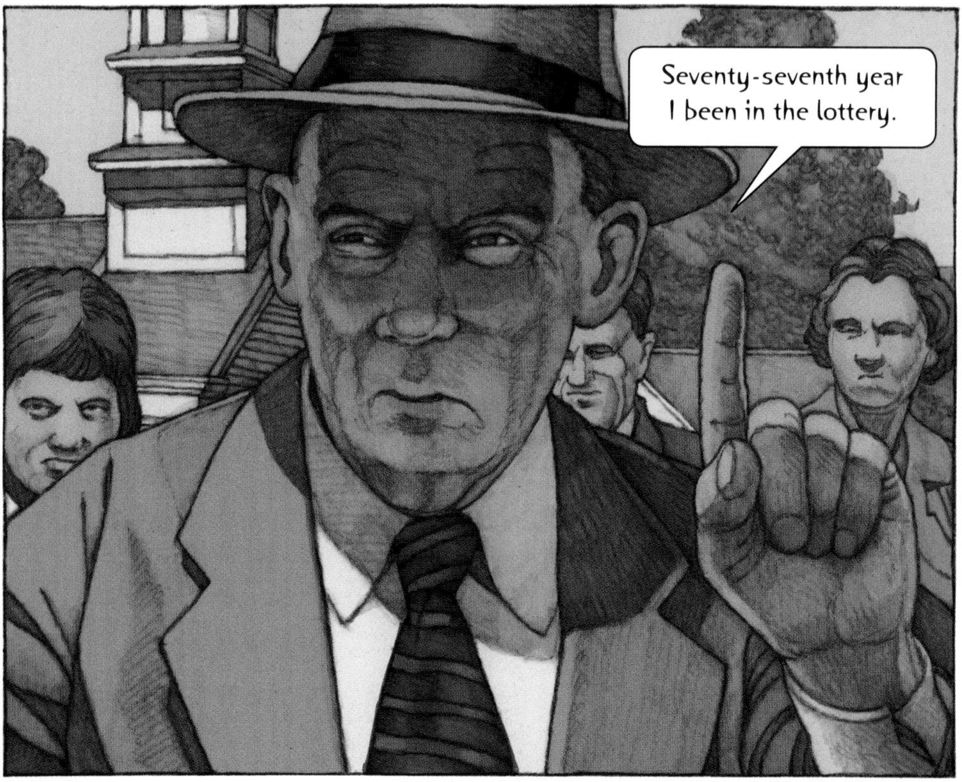
Seventy-seventh year
I been in the lottery.

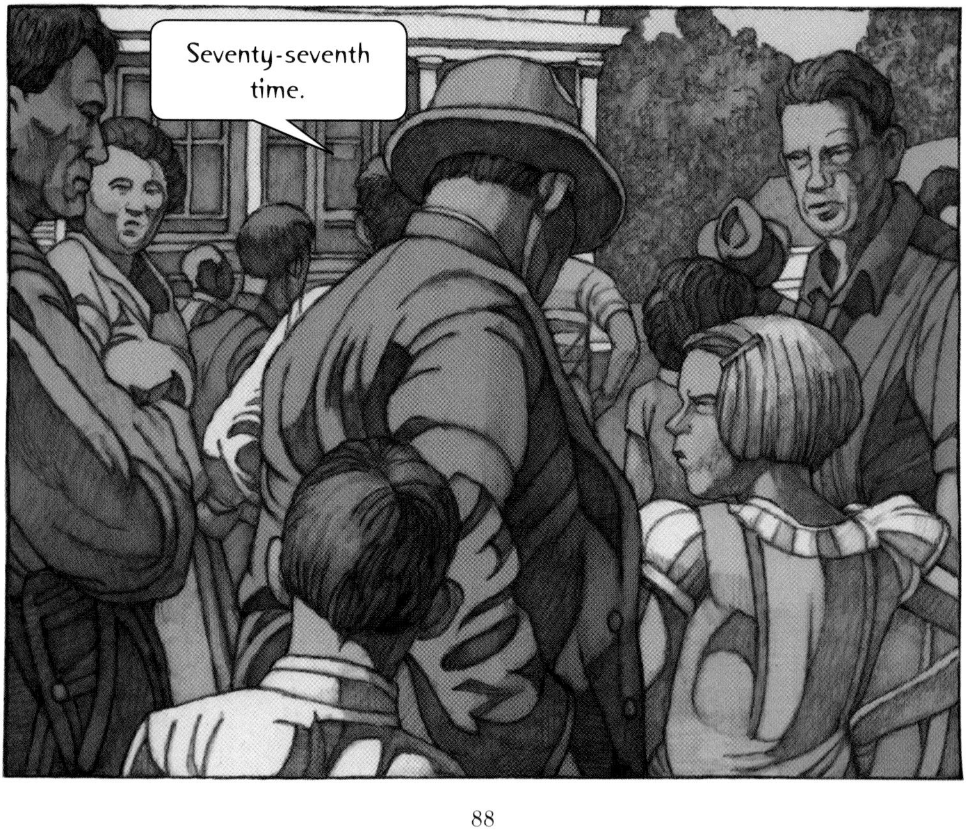
Seventy-seventh
time.

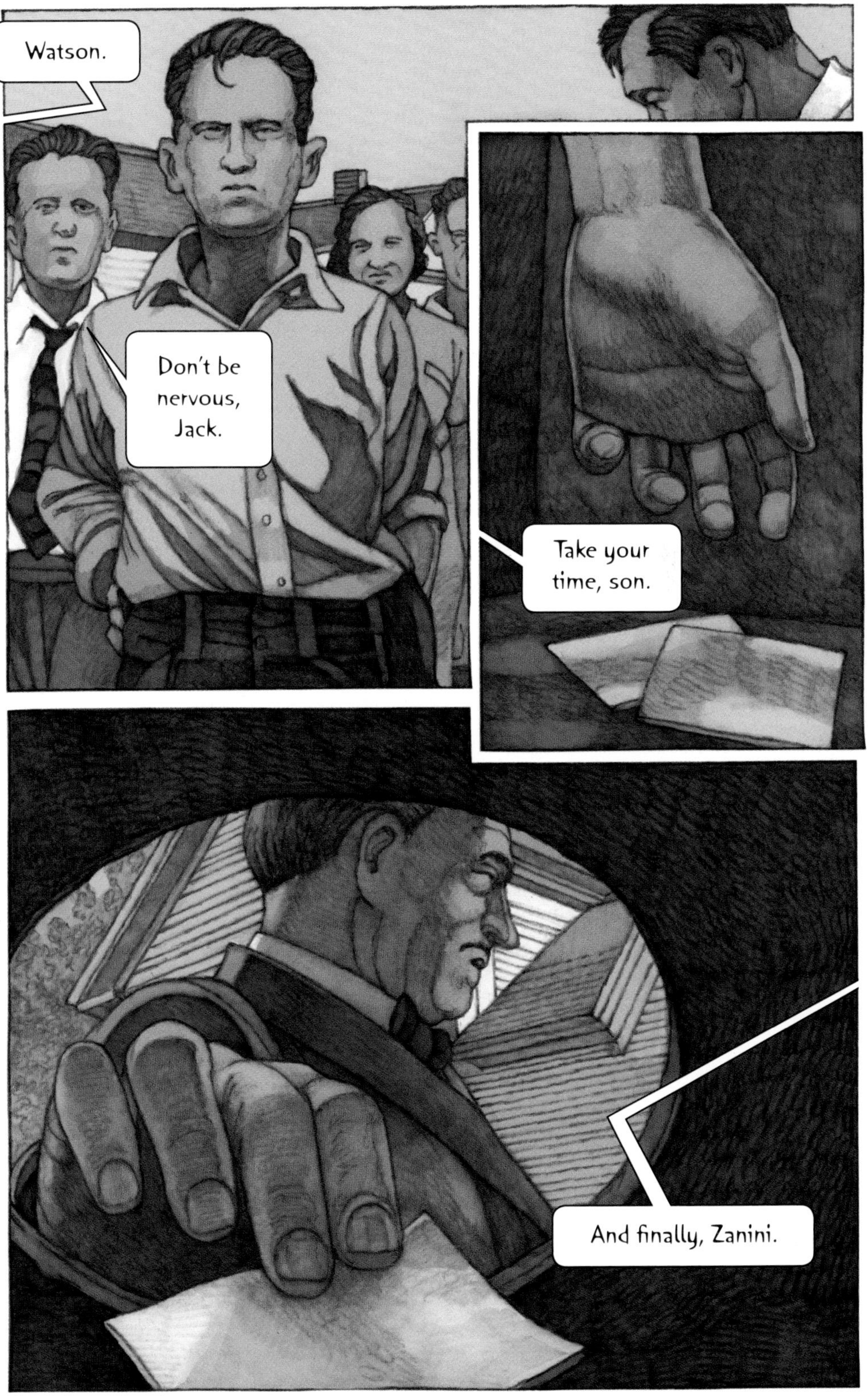
Watson.
Don't be nervous, Jack.
Take your time, son.
And finally, Zanini.

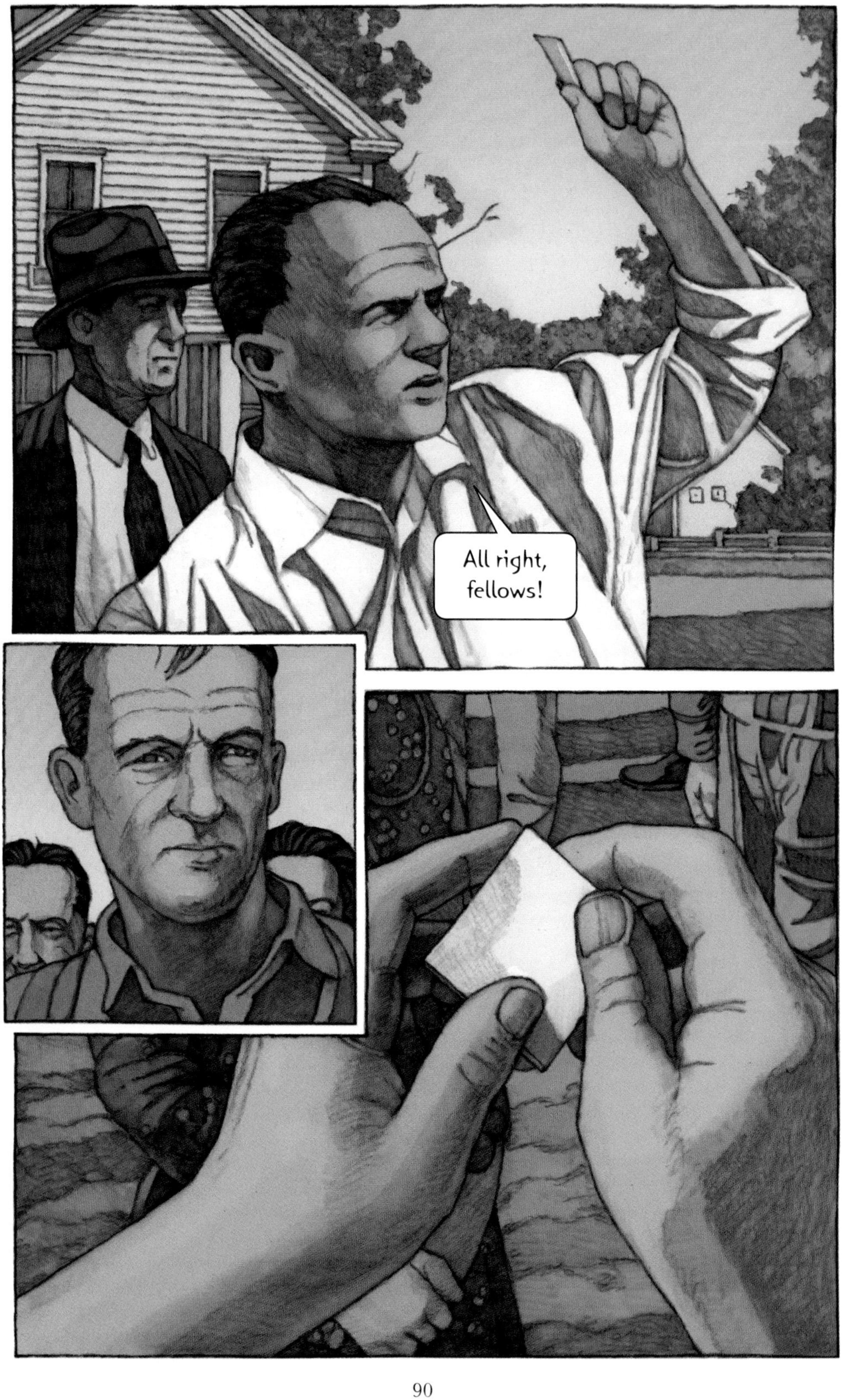
All right, fellows!

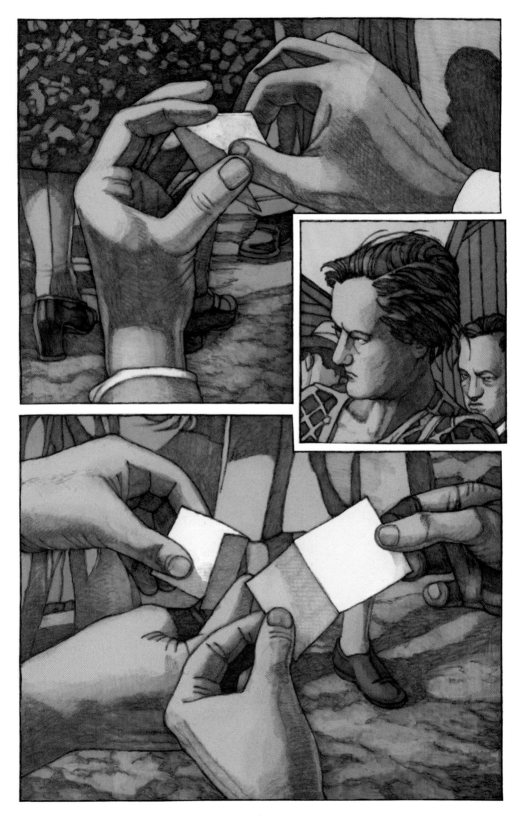

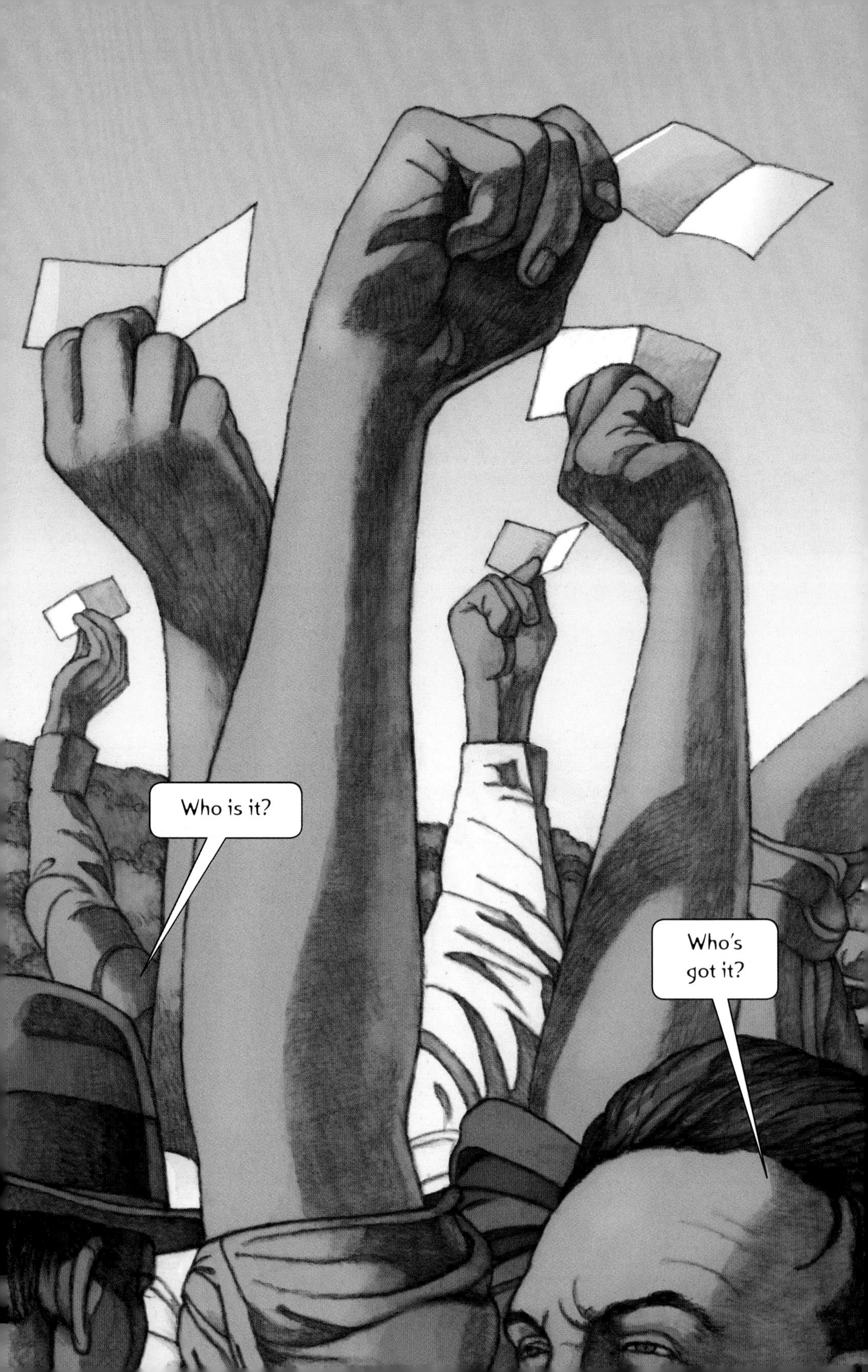
Who is it?
Who's got it?

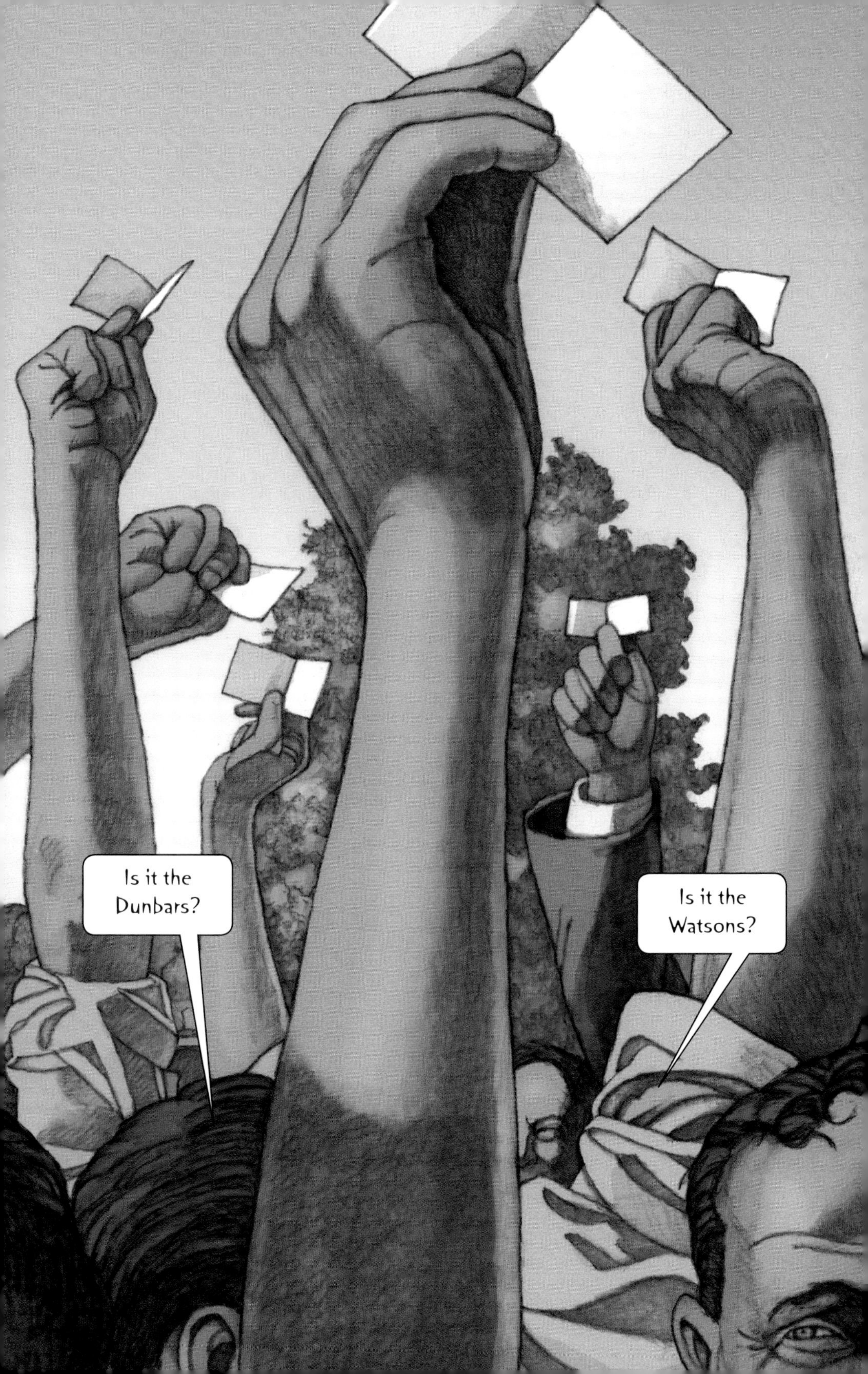
Is it the Dunbars?
Is it the Watsons?

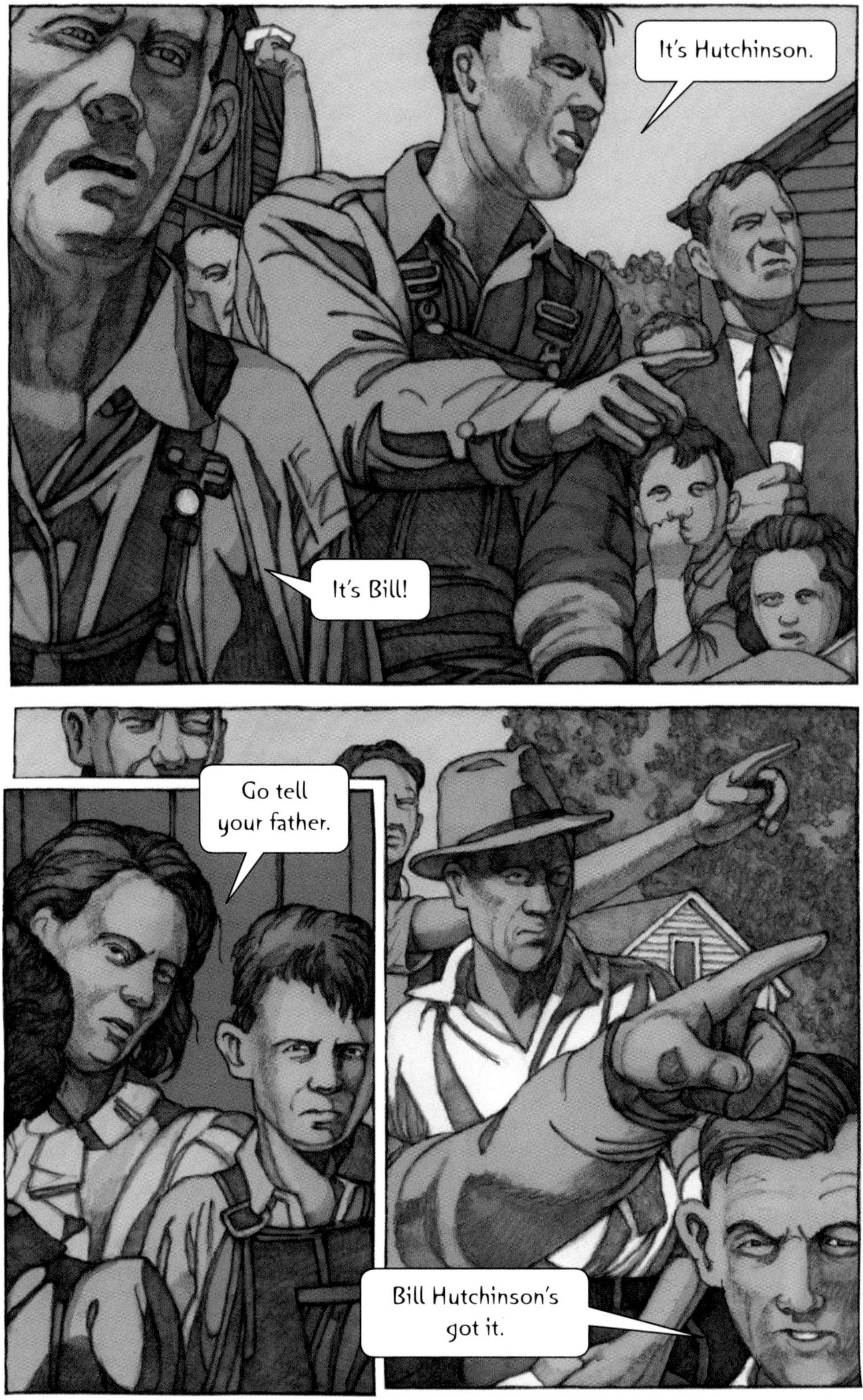
It's Hutchinson.
It's Bill!
Go tell your father.
Bill Hutchinson's got it.

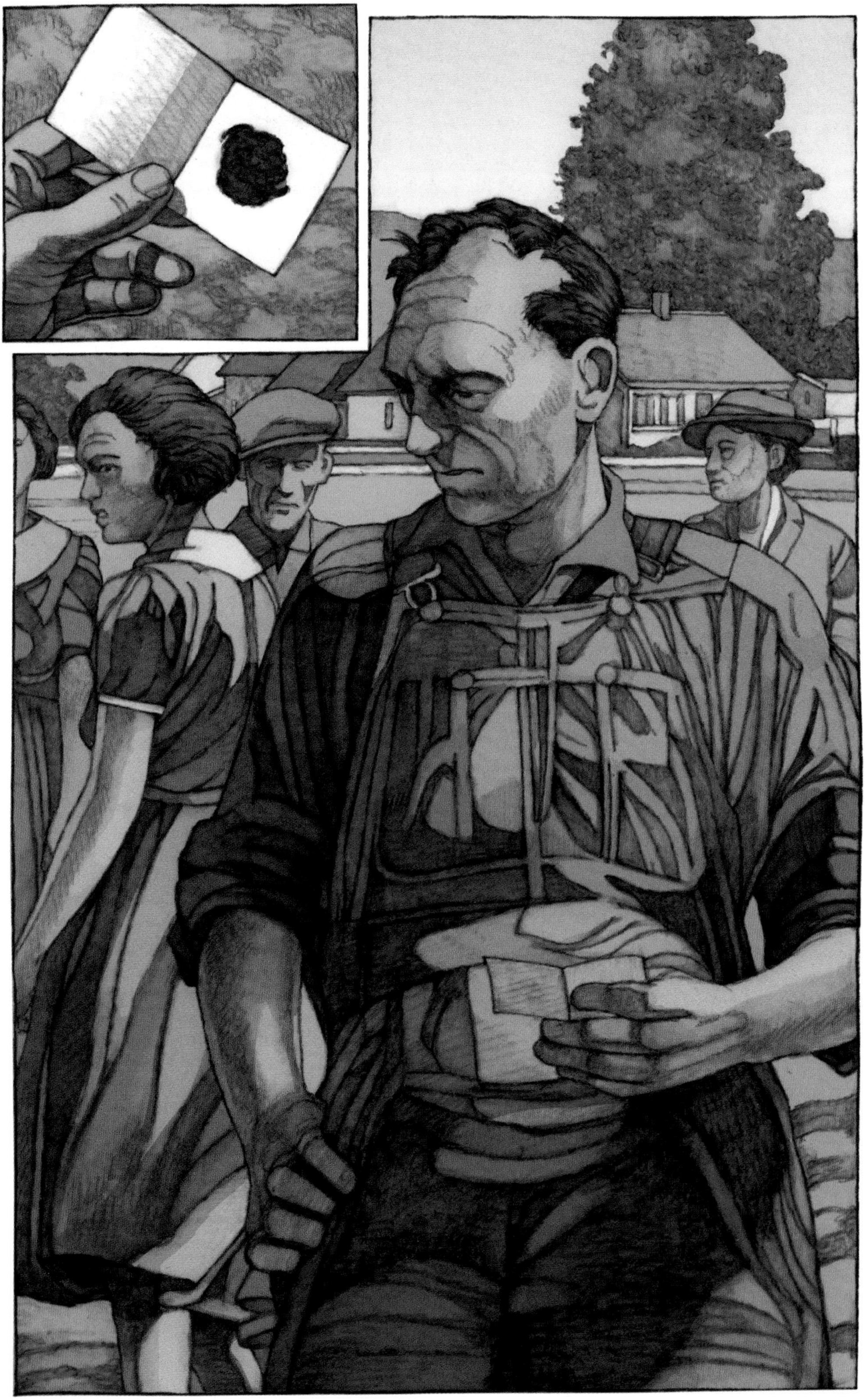

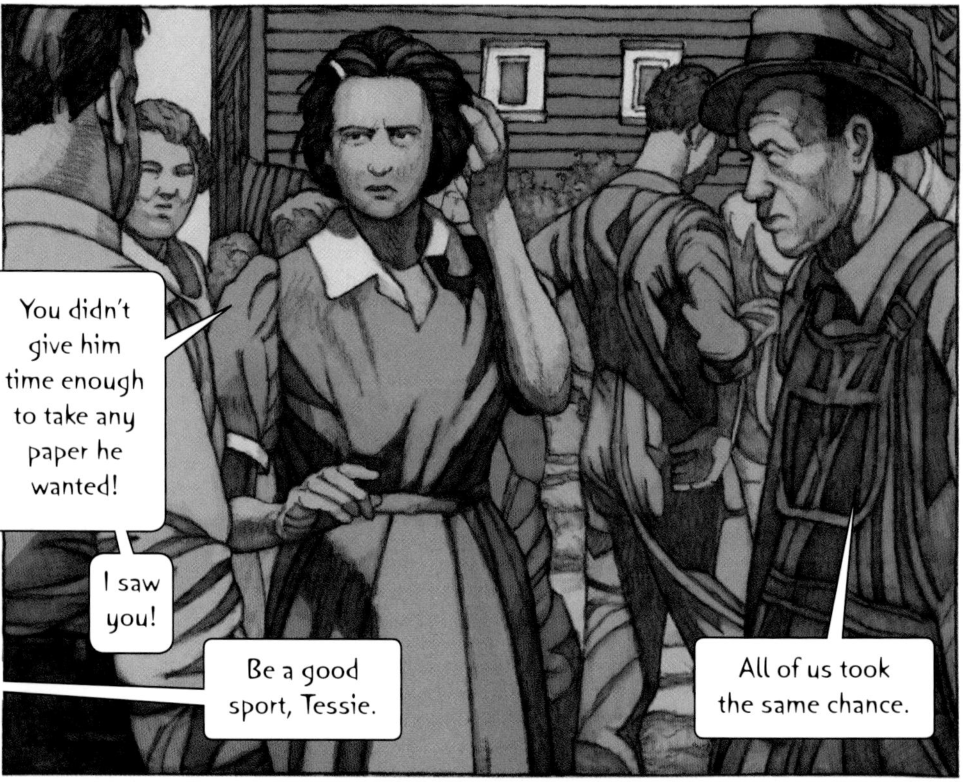
You didn't give him time enough to take any paper he wanted!
I saw you!
Be a good sport, Tessie.
All of us took the same chance.

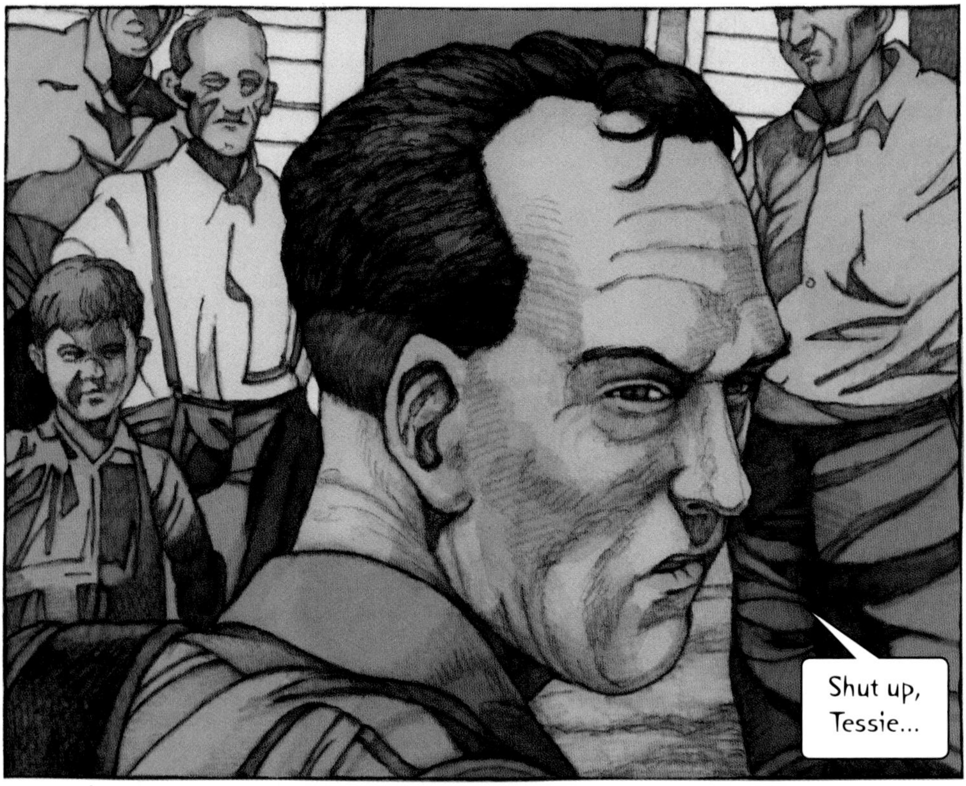
Shut up, Tessie...

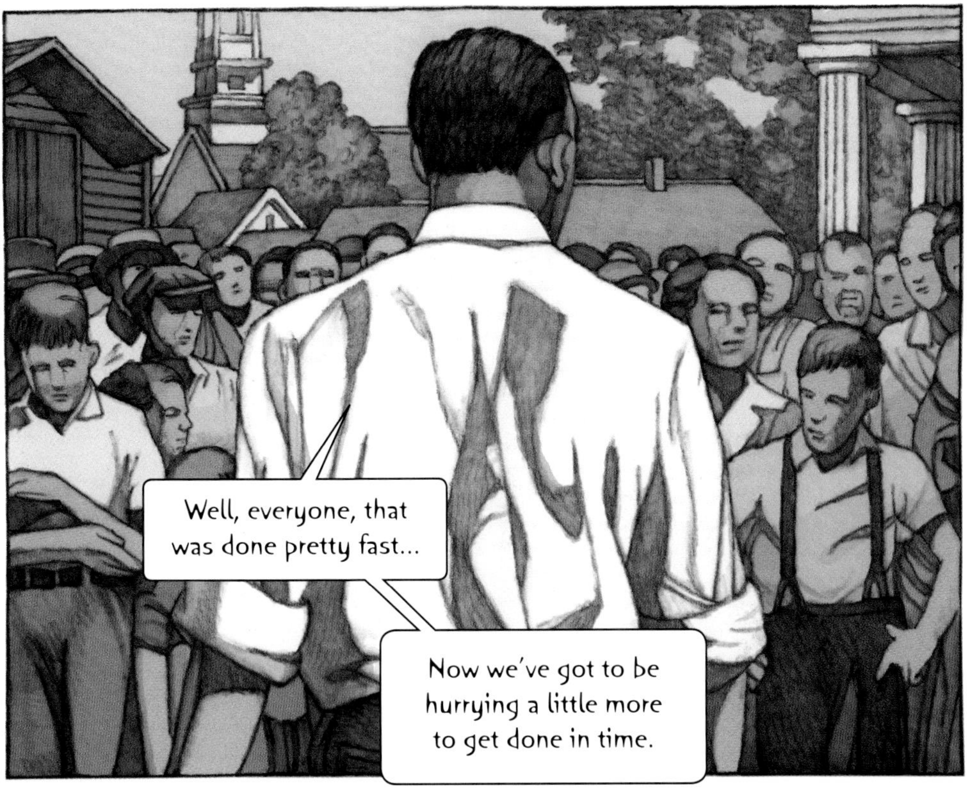
Well, everyone, that was done pretty fast...
Now we've got to be hurrying a little more to get done in time.

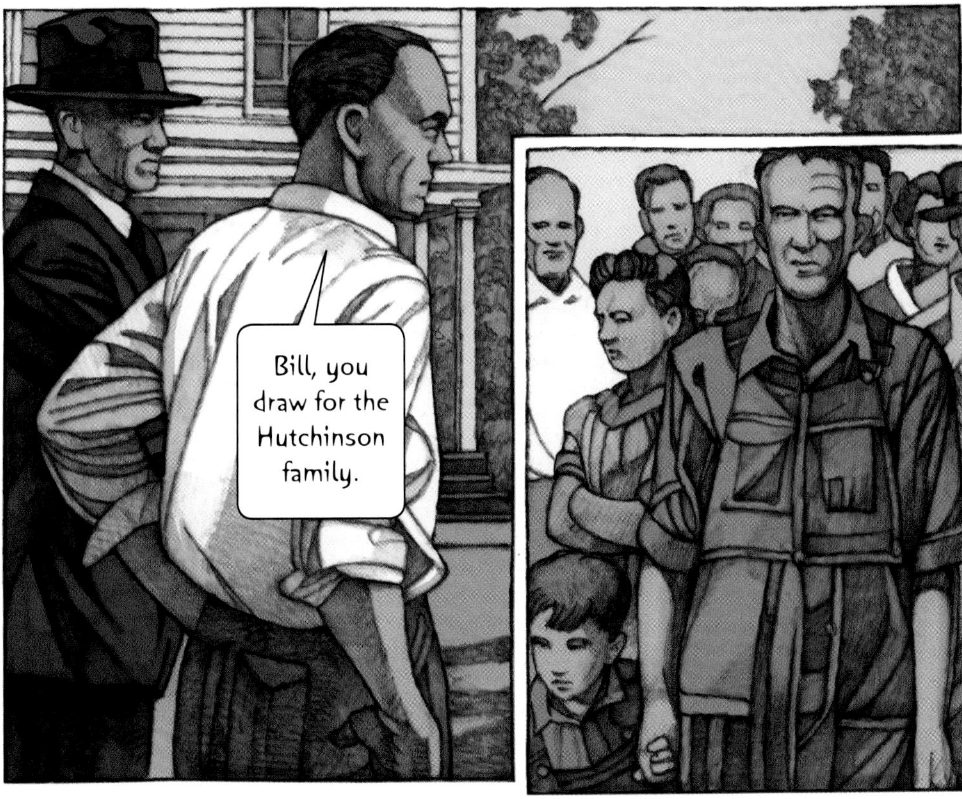
Bill, you draw for the Hutchinson family.

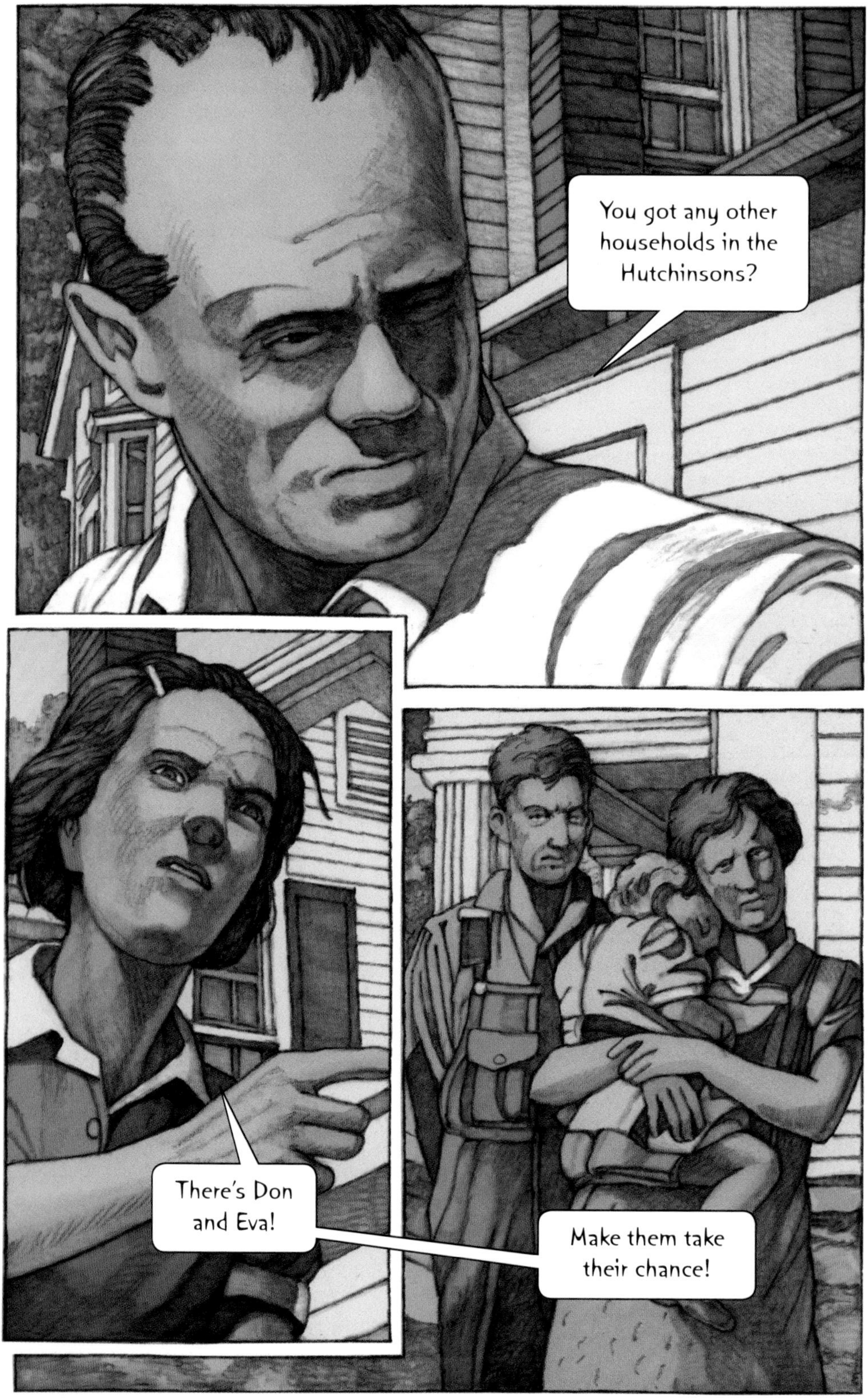
You got any other households in the Hutchinsons?
There's Don and Eva!
Make them take their chance!

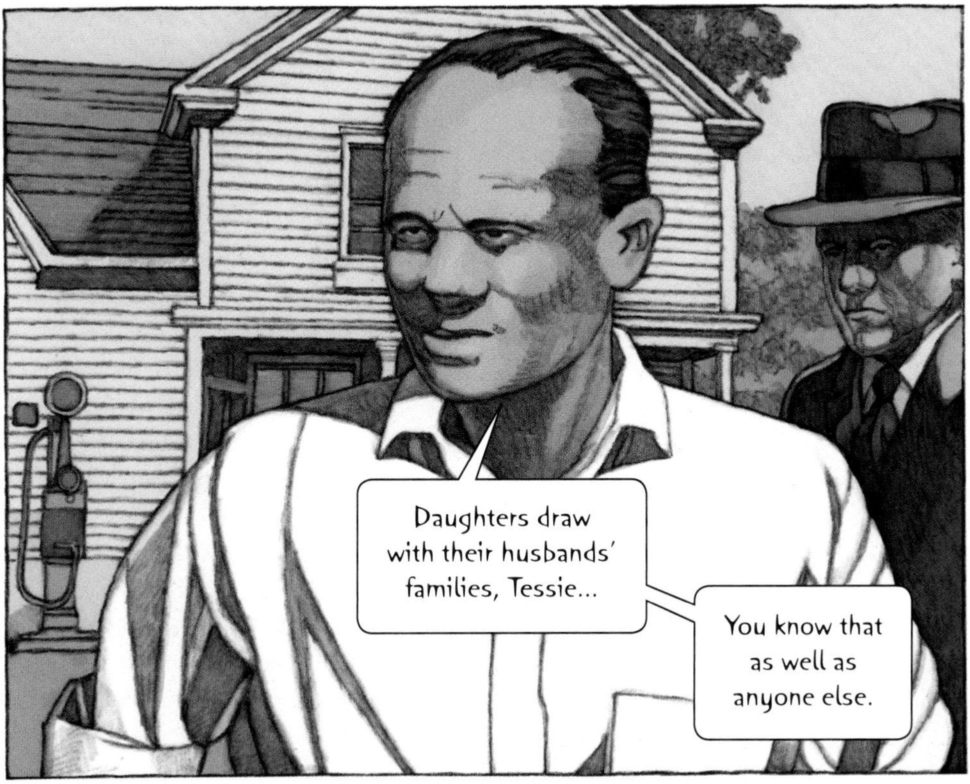
Daughters draw with their husbands' families, Tessie...
You know that as well as anyone else.

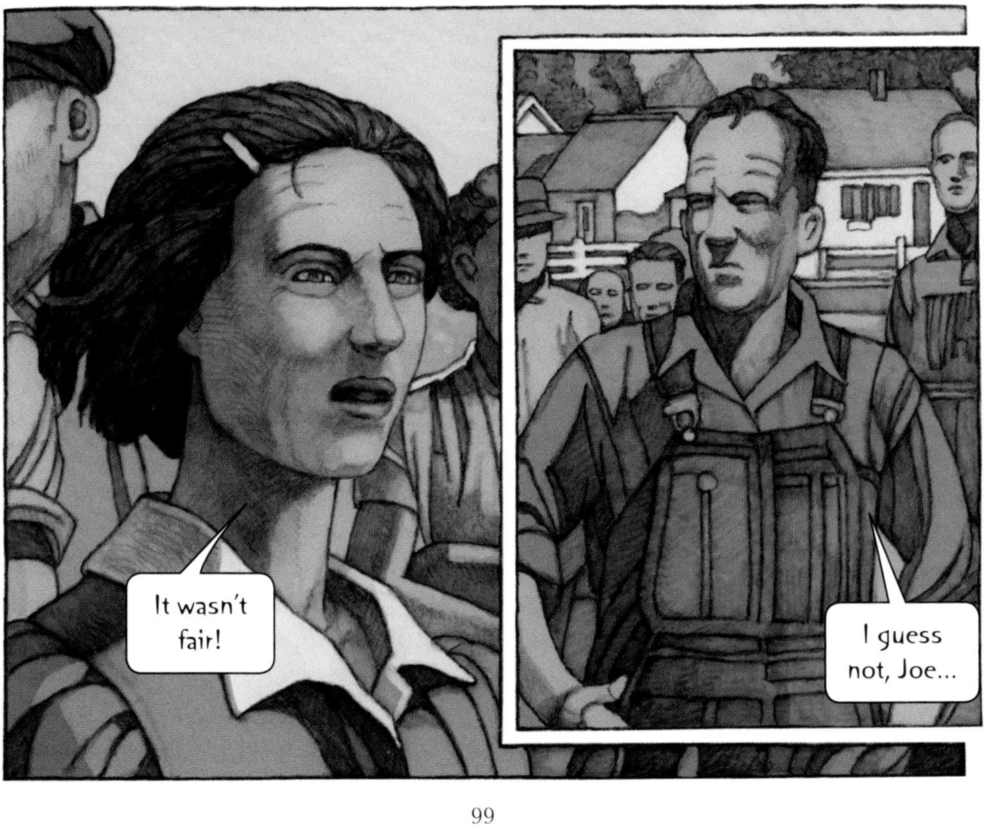
It wasn't fair!
I guess not, Joe...

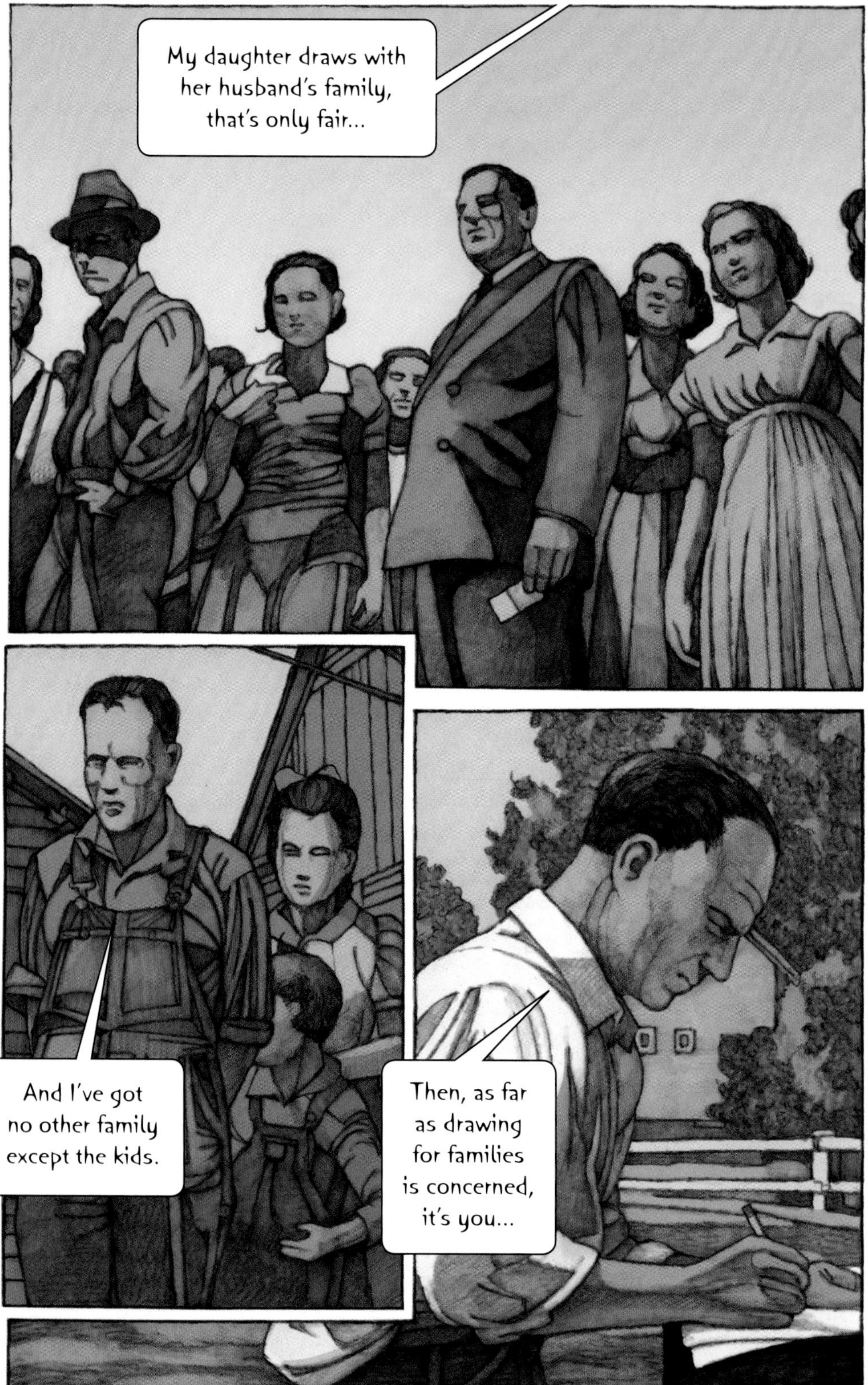
My daughter draws with her husband's family, that's only fair...
And I've got no other family except the kids.
Then, as far as drawing for families is concerned, it's you...

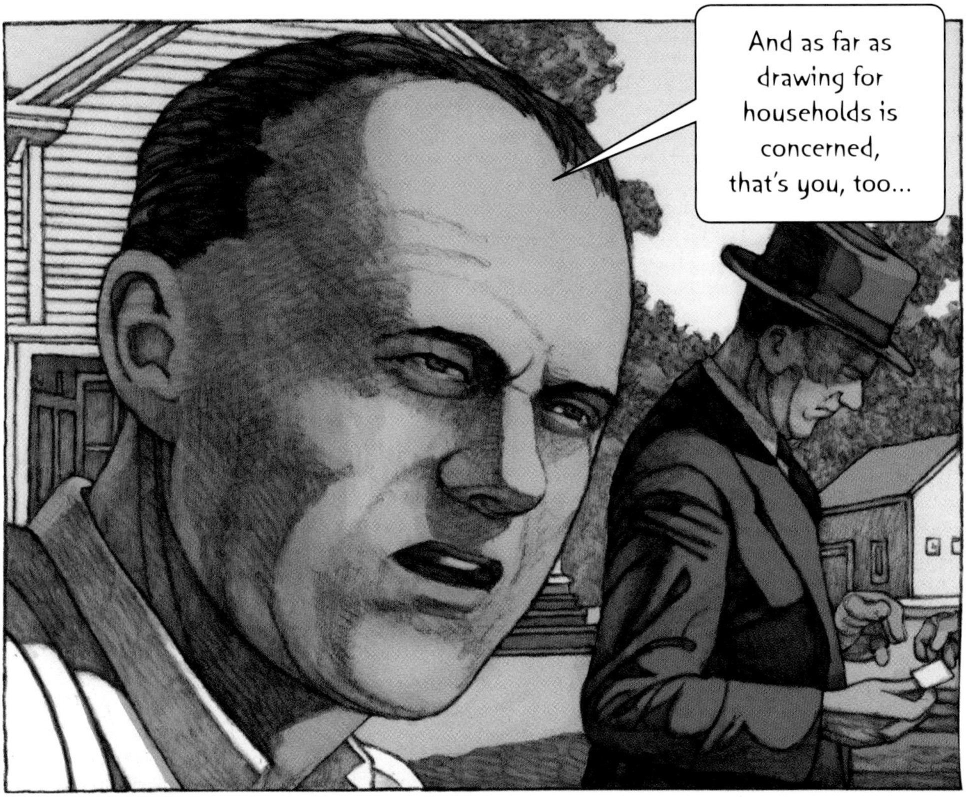
And as far as drawing for households is concerned, that's you, too...

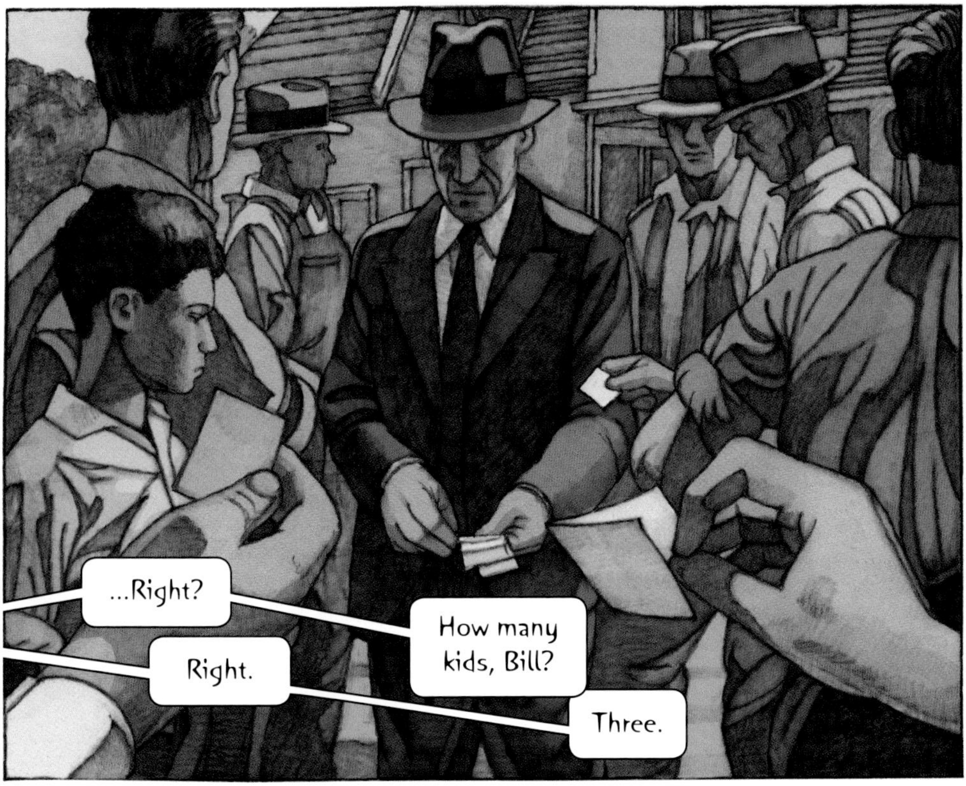
...Right?
Right.
How many kids, Bill?
Three.

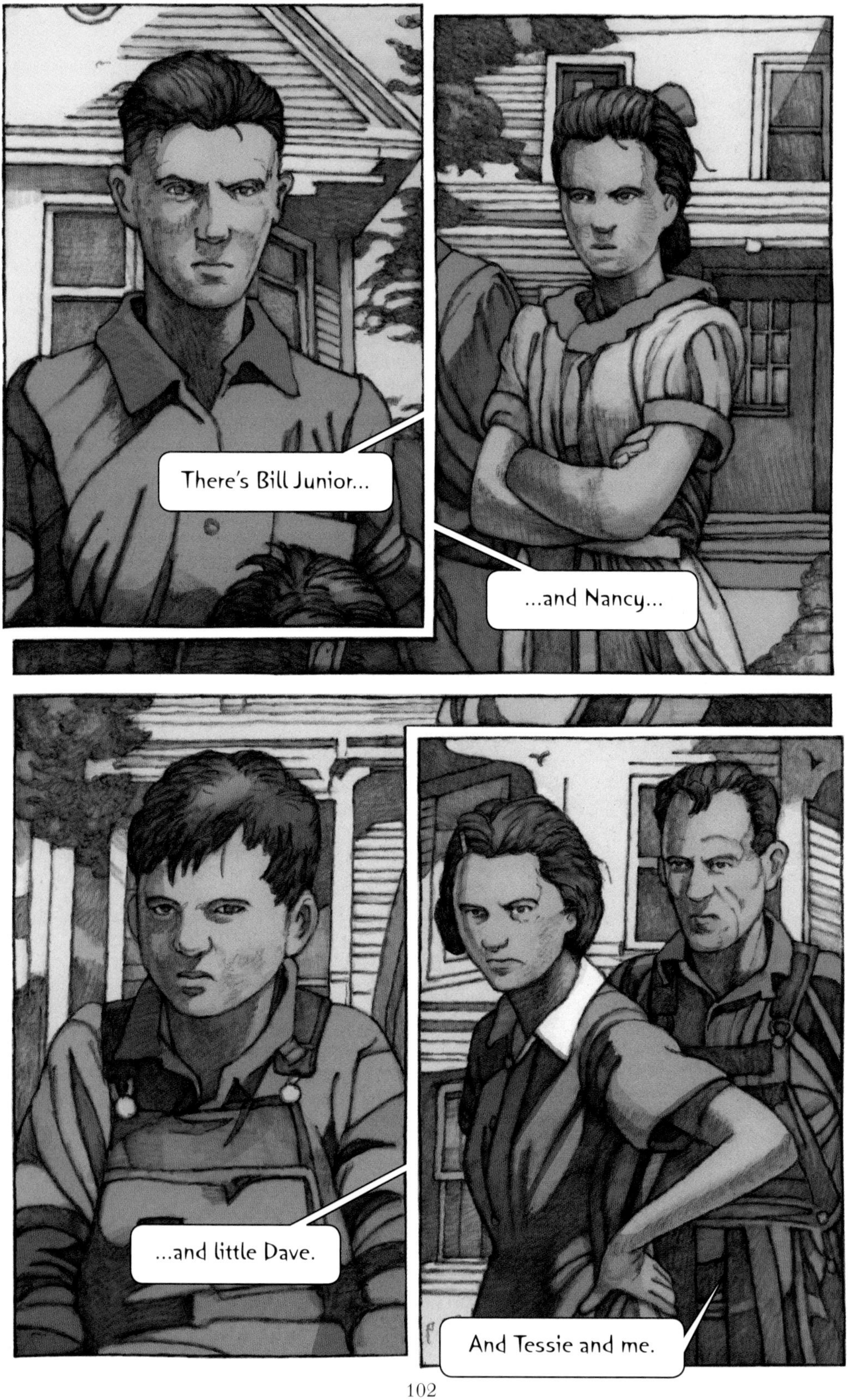
There's Bill Junior...
...and Nancy...
...and little Dave.
And Tessie and me.

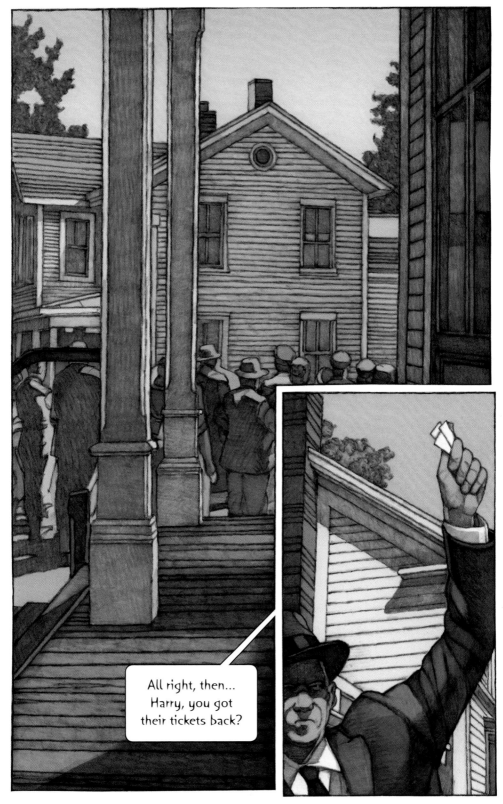

All right, then... Harry, you got their tickets back?

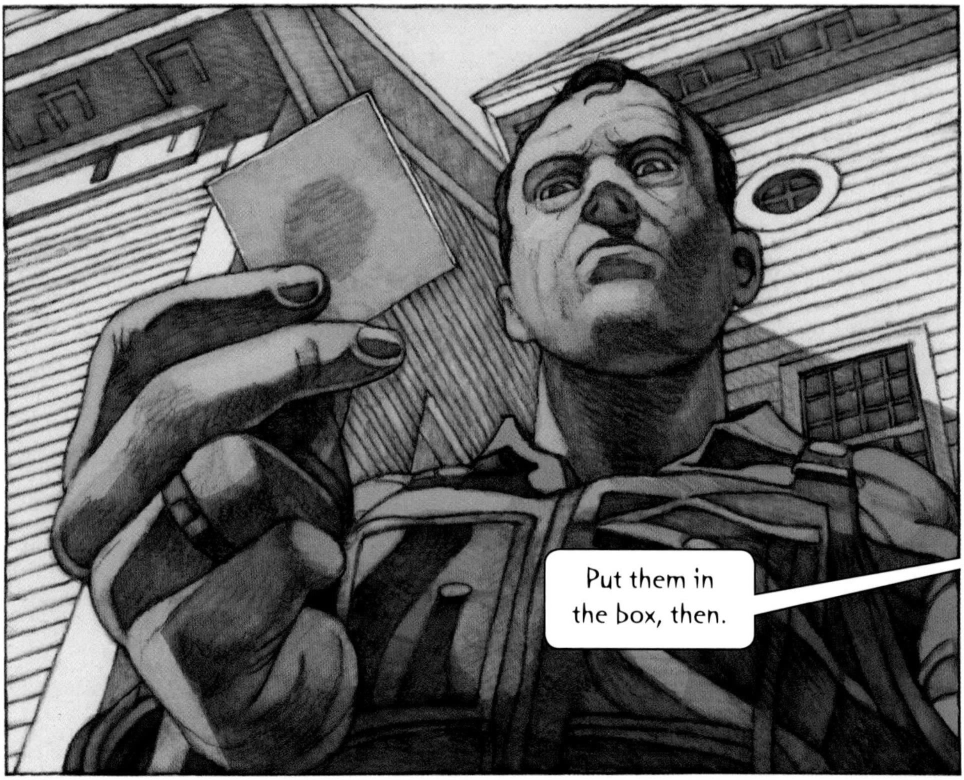
Put them in the box, then.

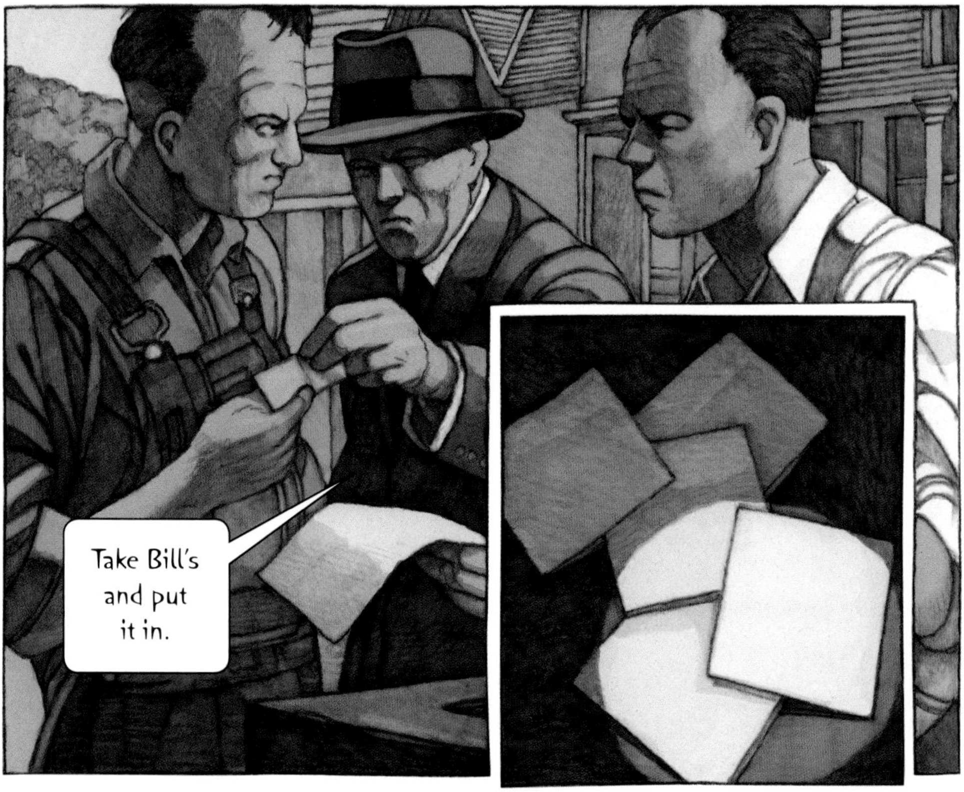
Take Bill's and put it in.

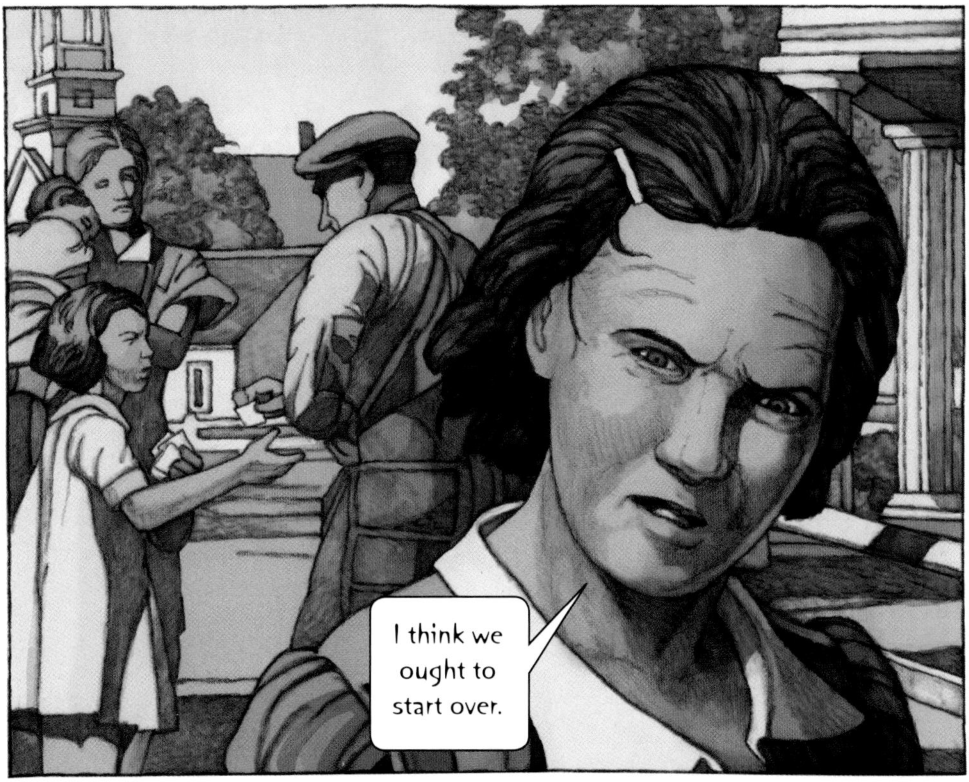
I think we ought to start over.

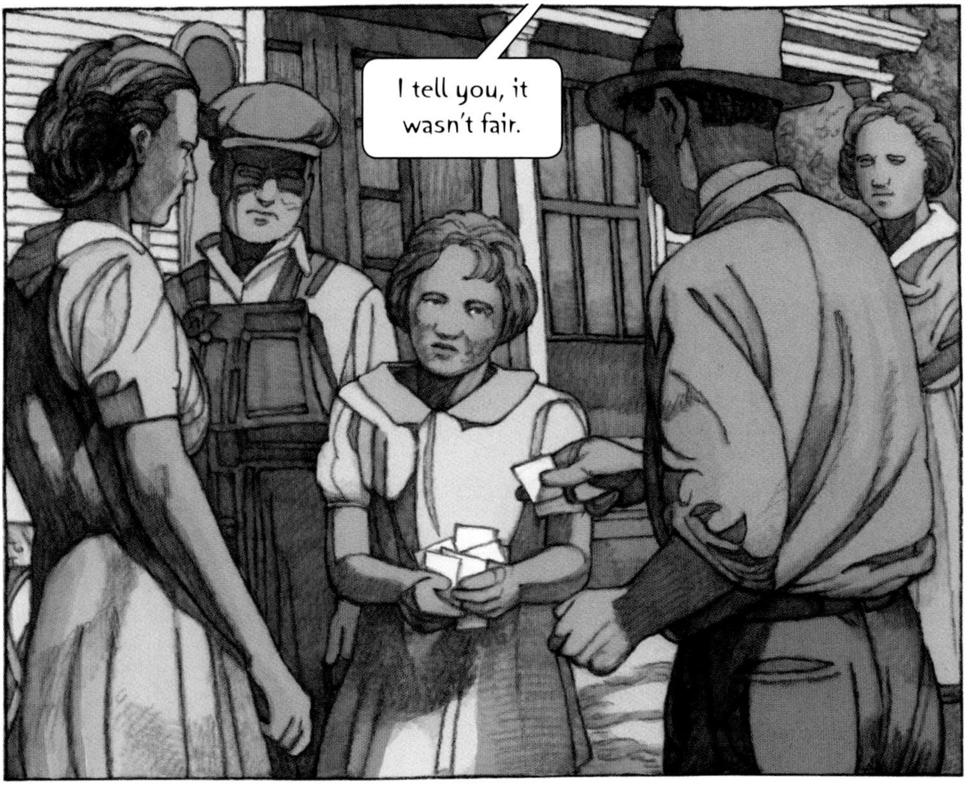
I tell you, it wasn't fair.

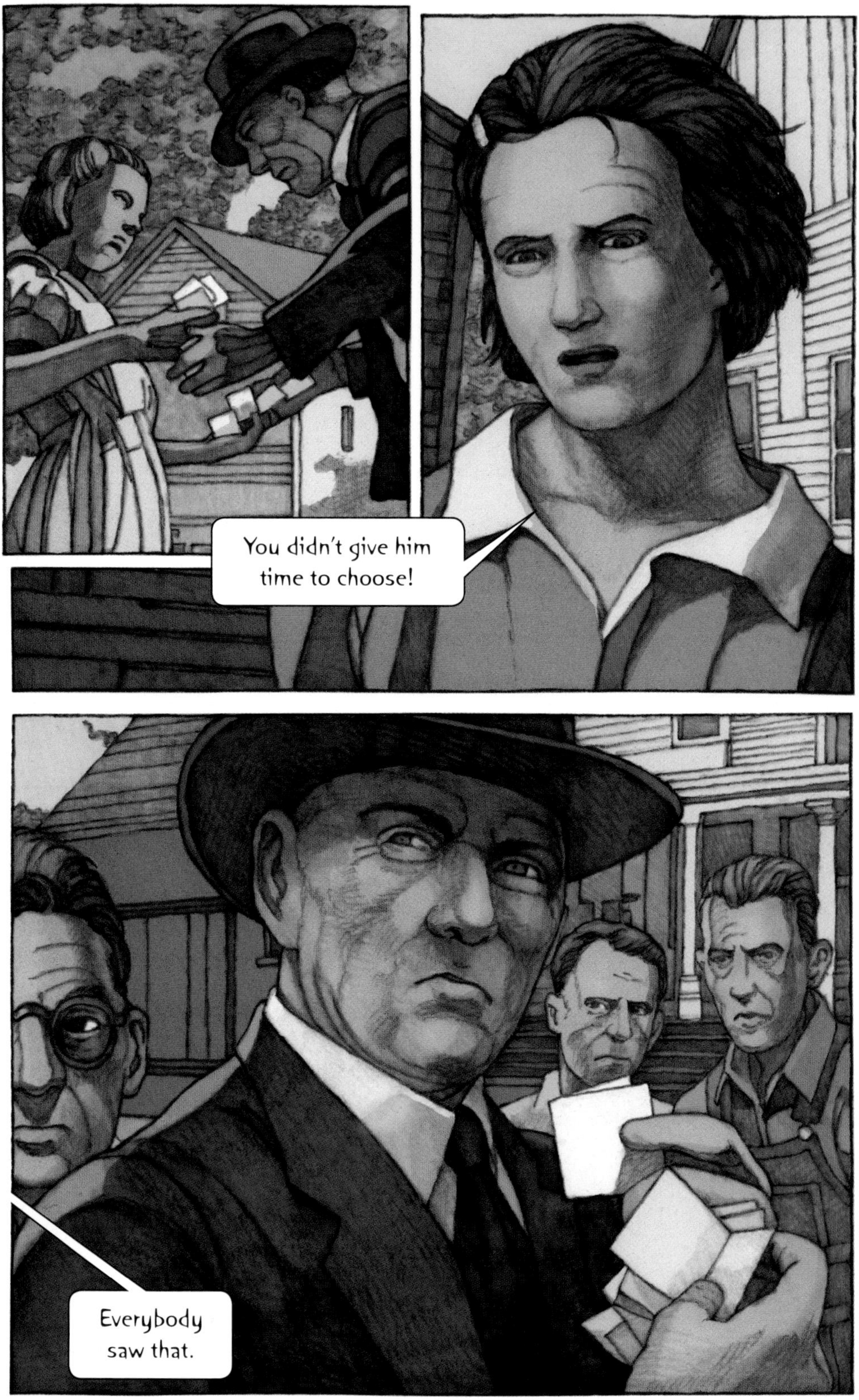
You didn't give him time to choose!
Everybody saw that.

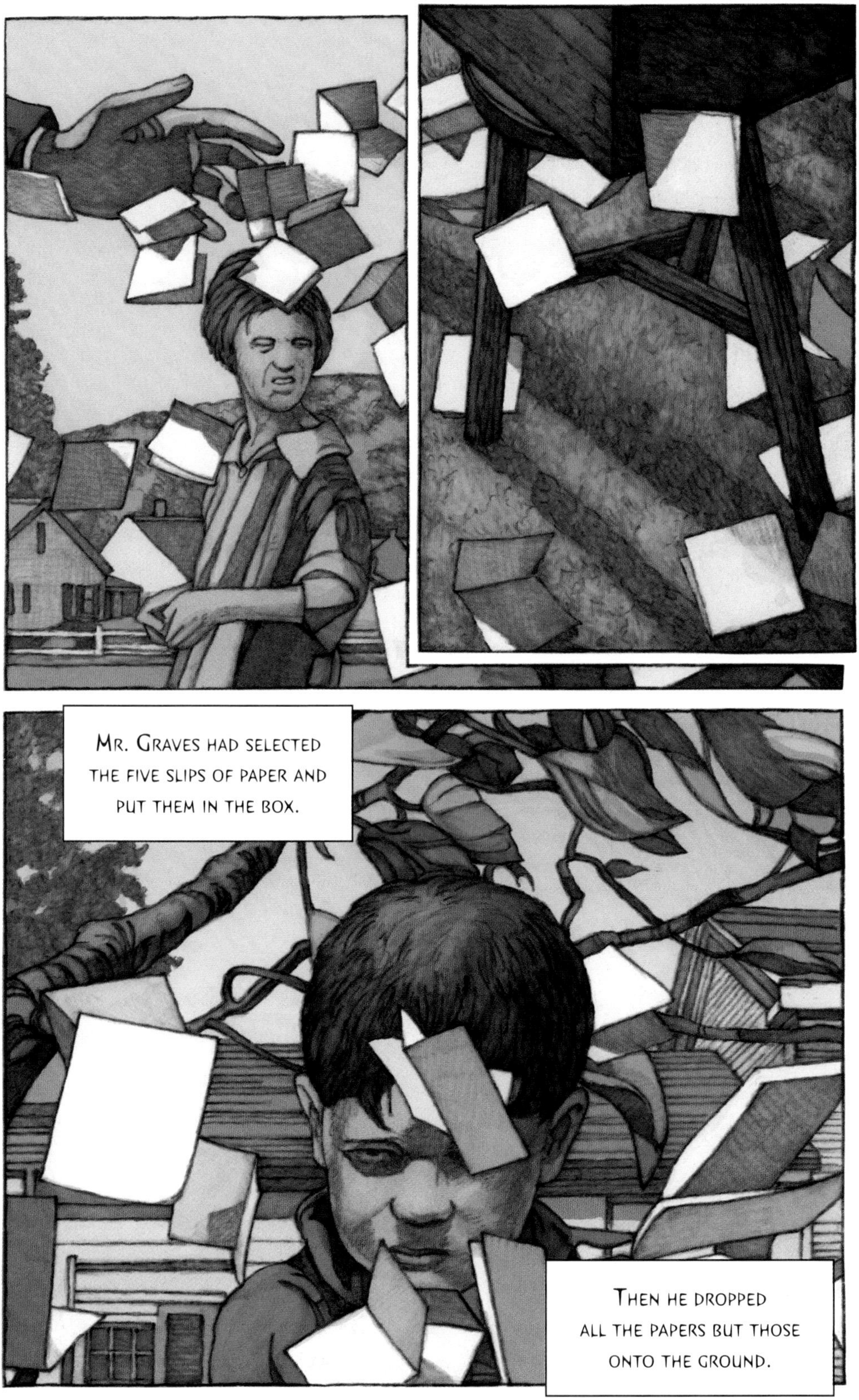
MR. GRAVES HAD SELECTED THE FIVE SLIPS OF PAPER AND PUT THEM IN THE BOX.
THEN HE DROPPED ALL THE PAPERS BUT THOSE ONTO THE GROUND.

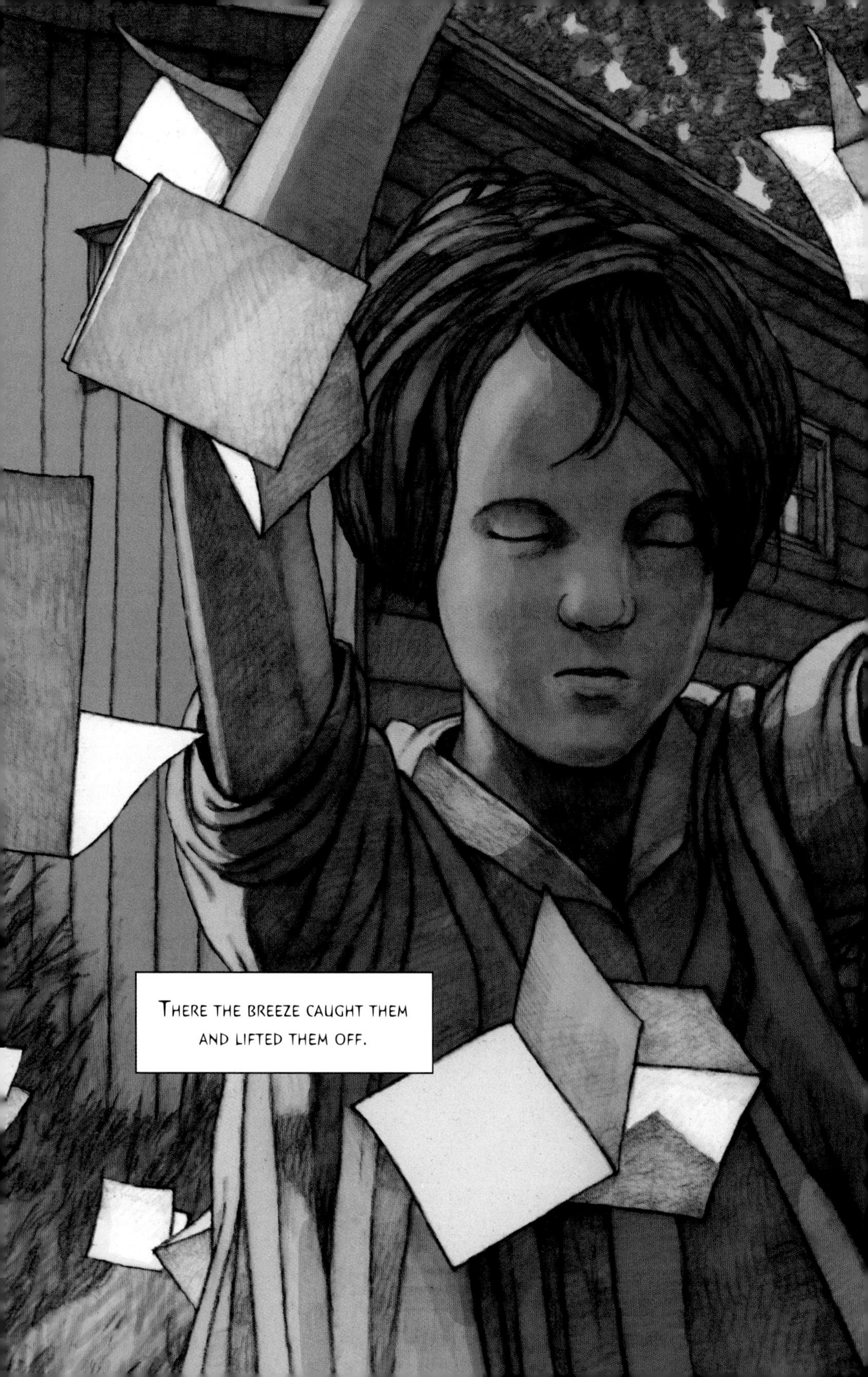
THERE THE BREEZE CAUGHT THEM AND LIFTED THEM OFF.

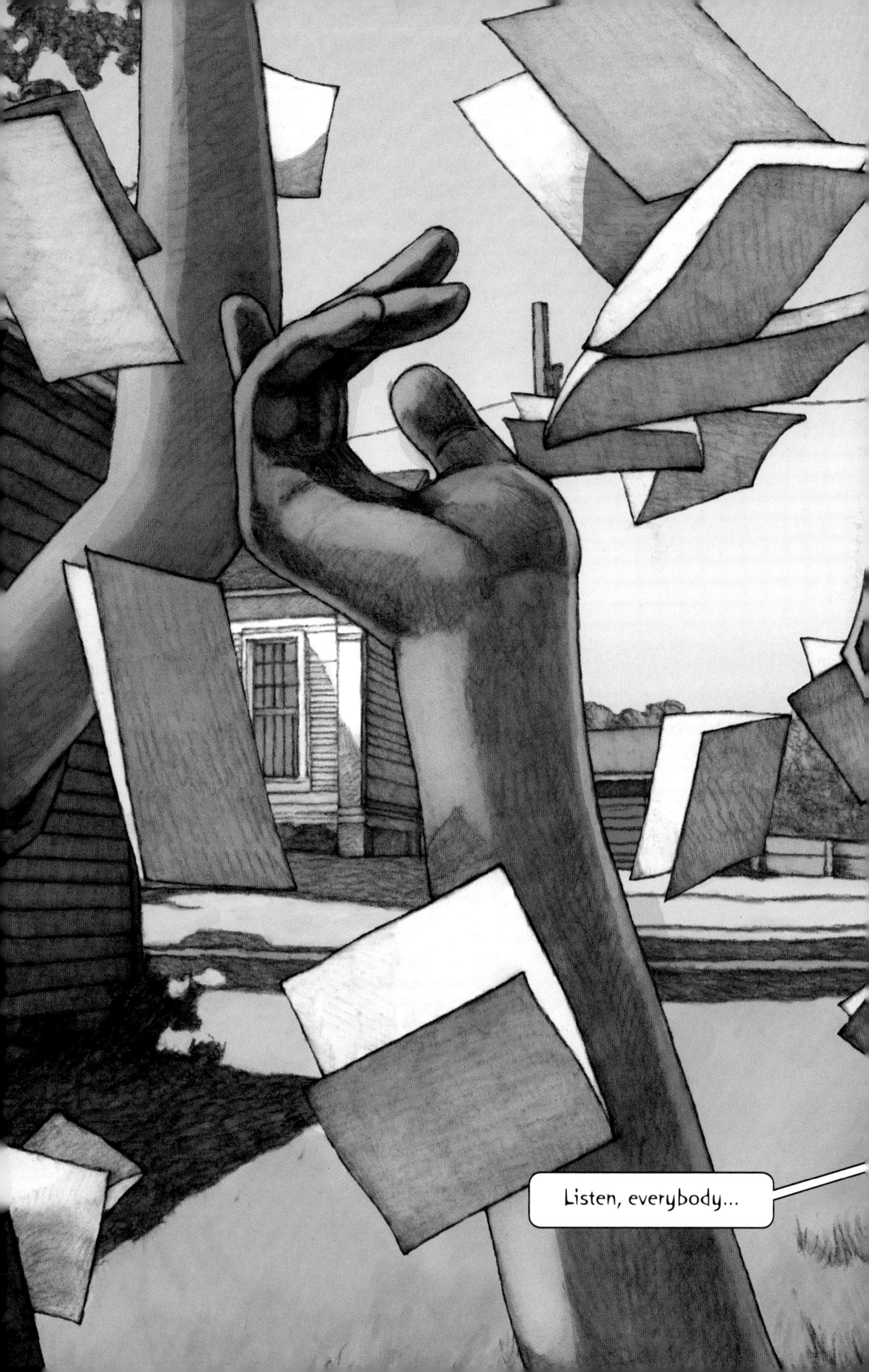
Listen, everybody...

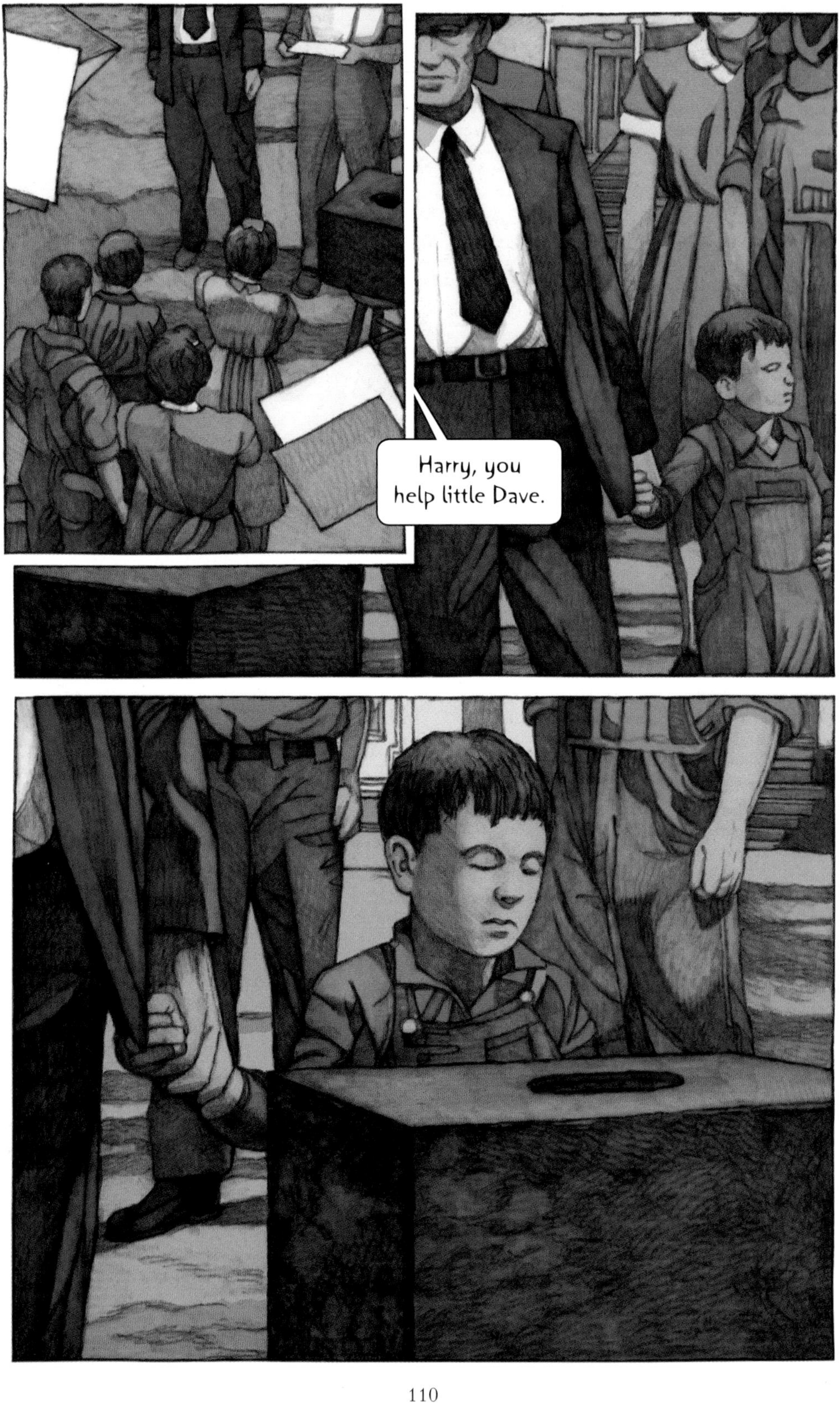
Harry, you help little Dave.

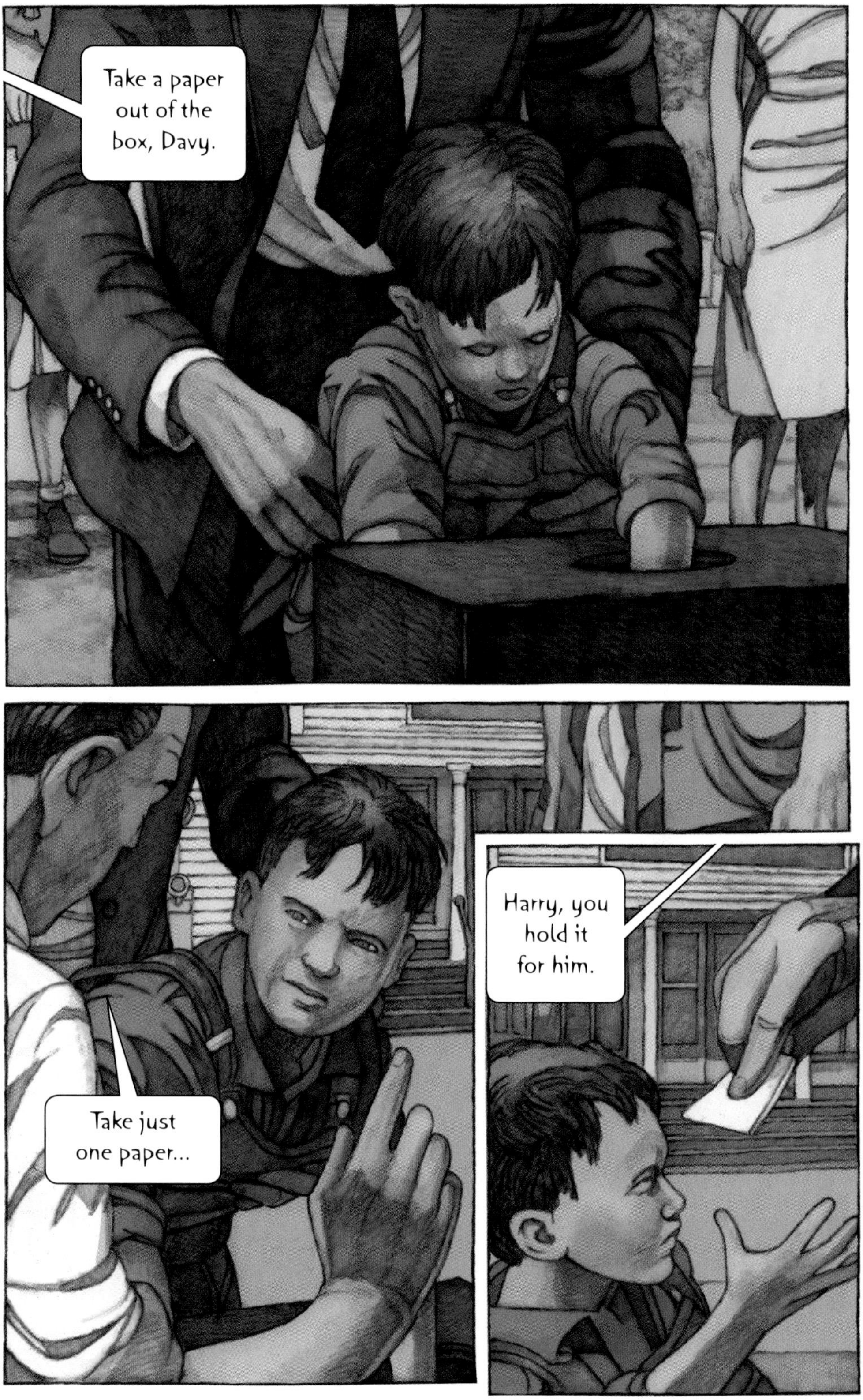
Take a paper out of the box, Davy.
Take just one paper...
Harry, you hold it for him.

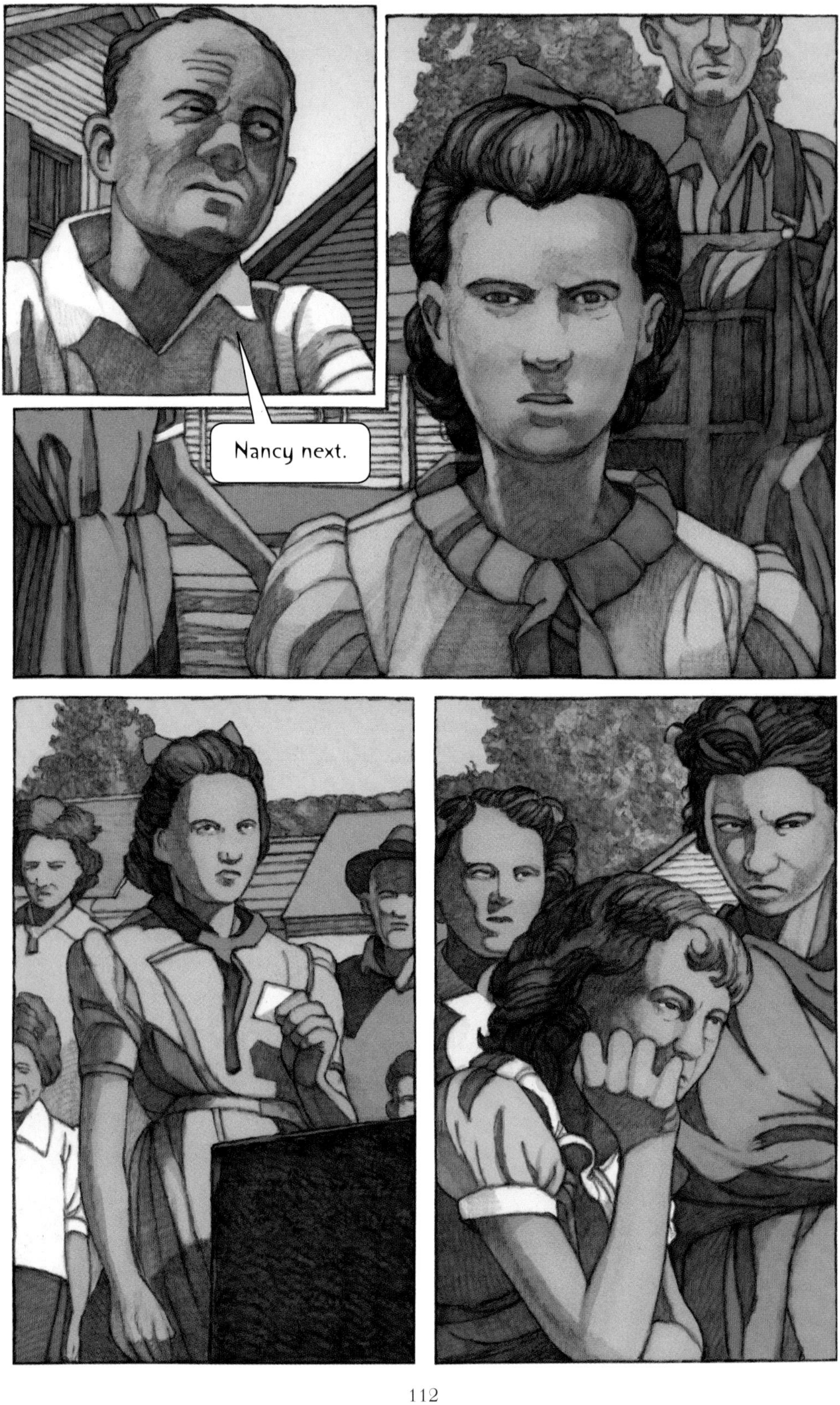
Nancy next.

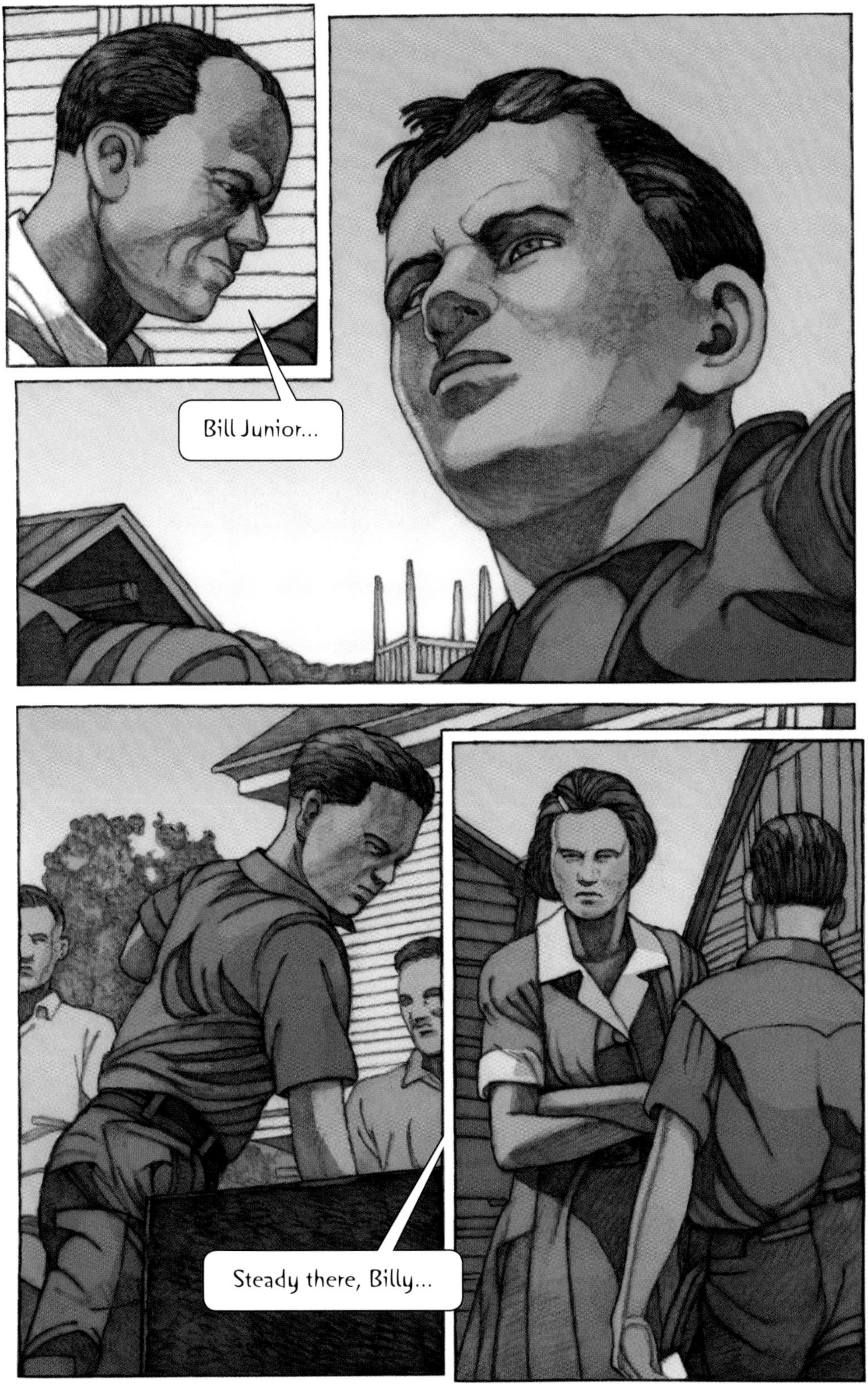
Bill Junior...
Steady there, Billy...

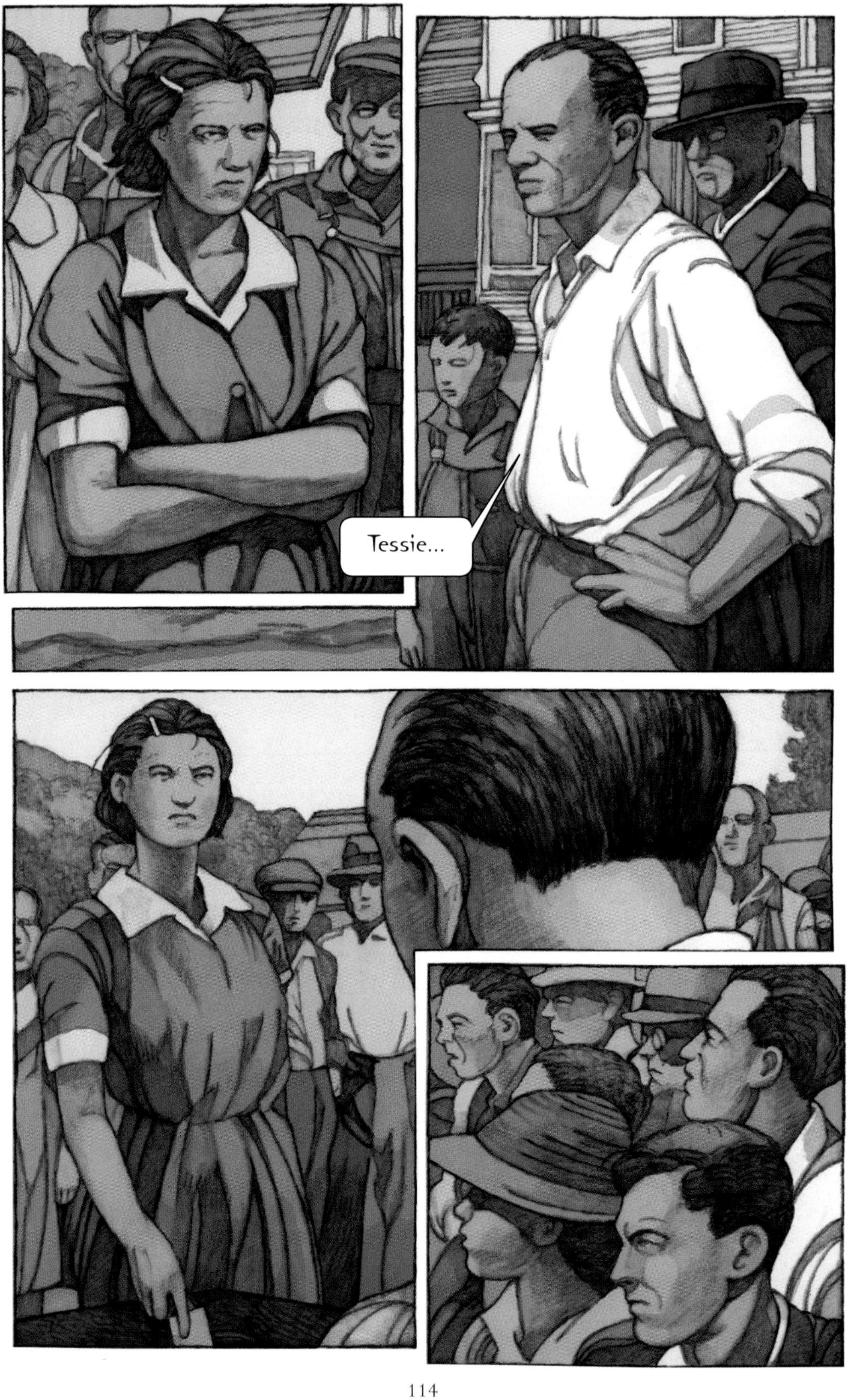
Tessie...

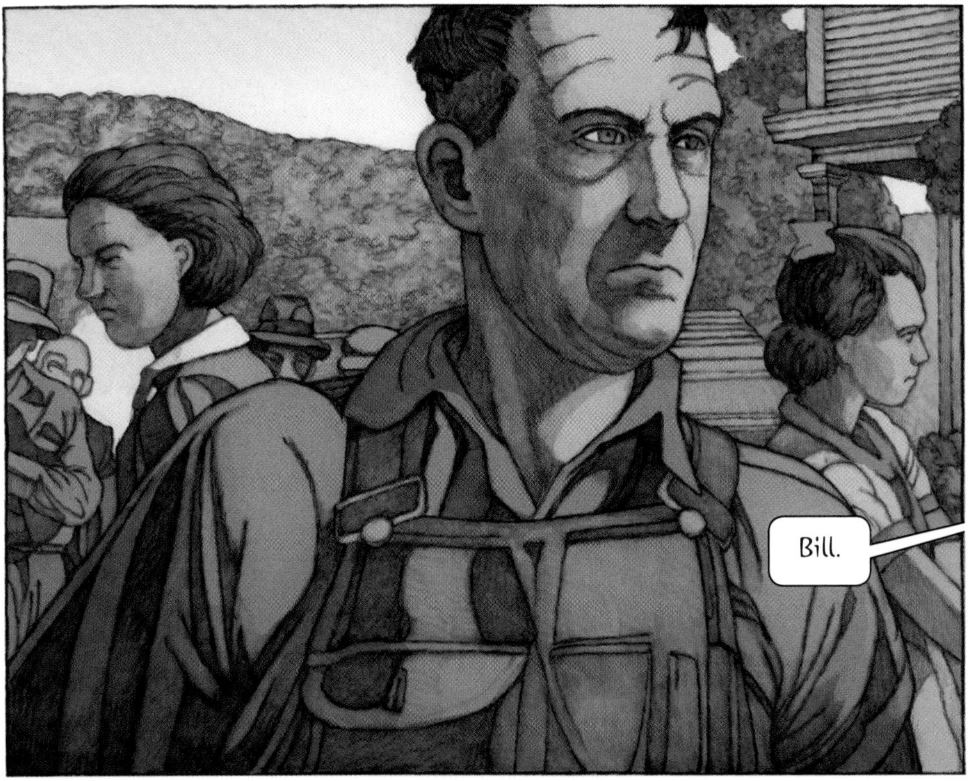
Bill.

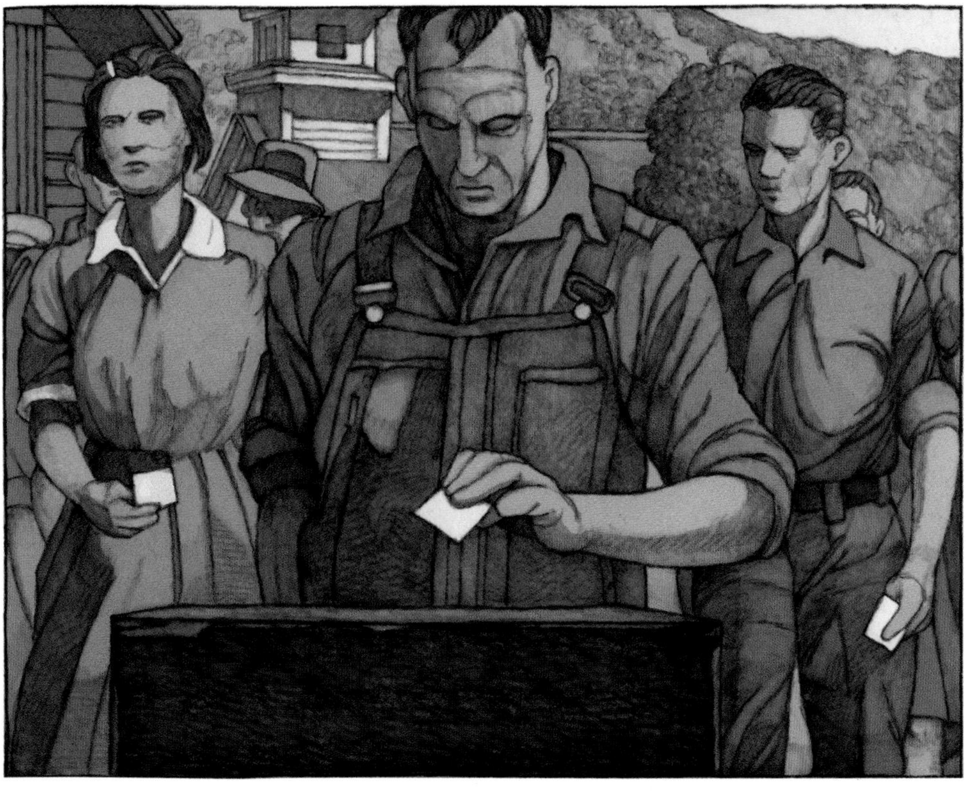

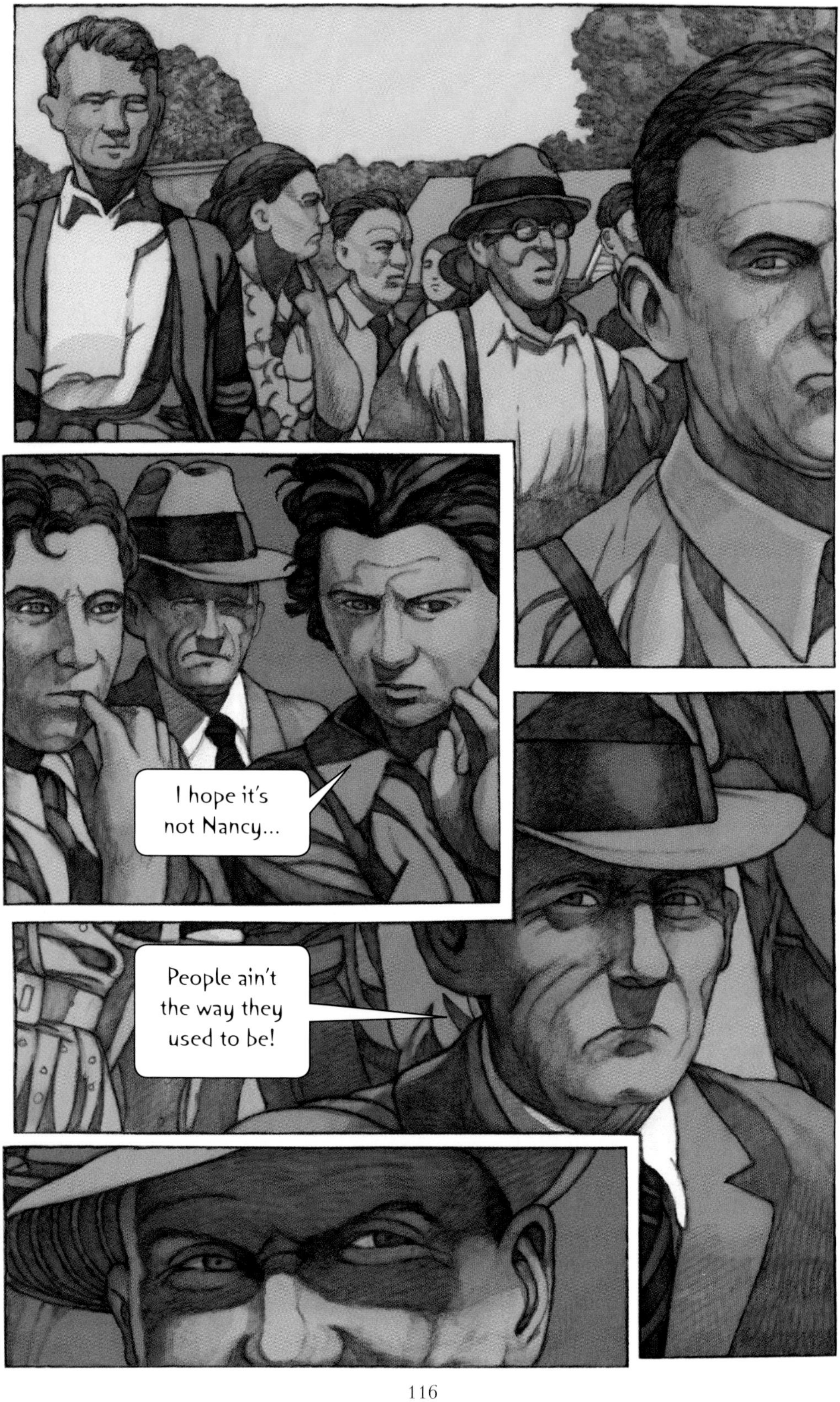
I hope it's not Nancy...
People ain't the way they used to be!

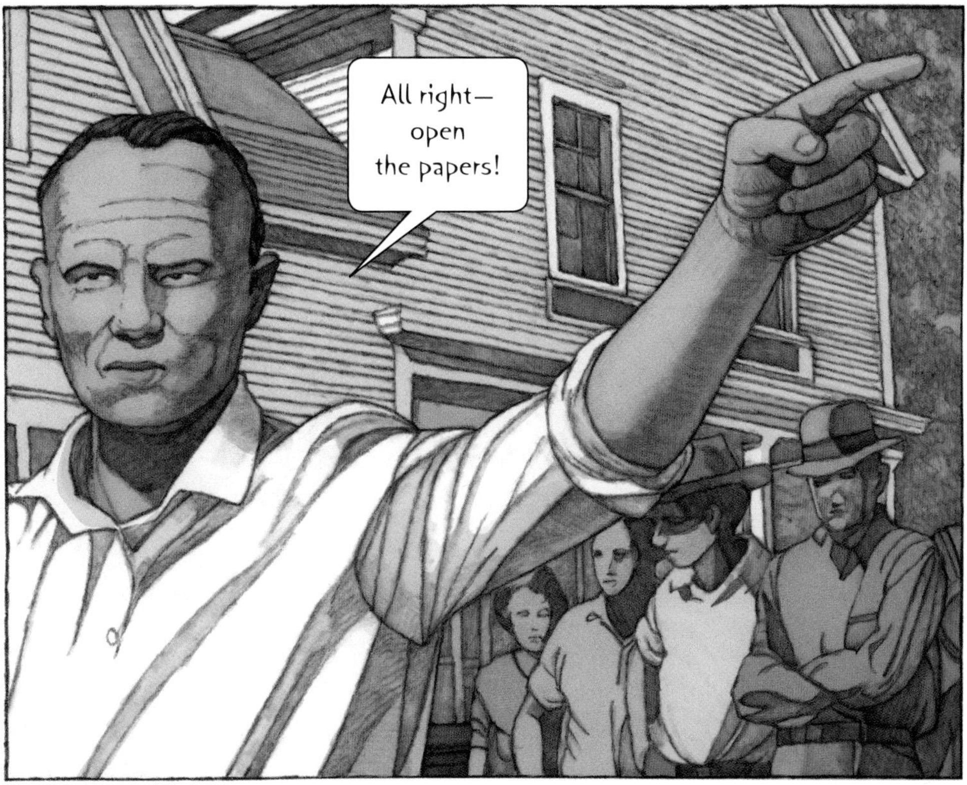
All right—
open
the papers!

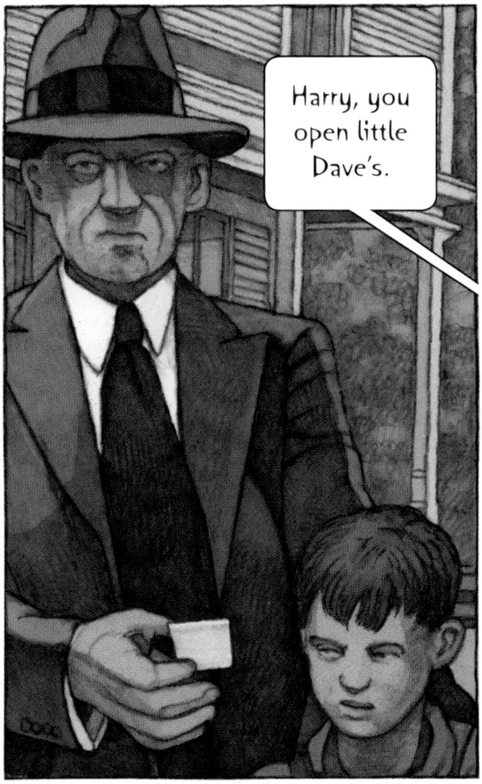
Harry, you
open little
Dave's.

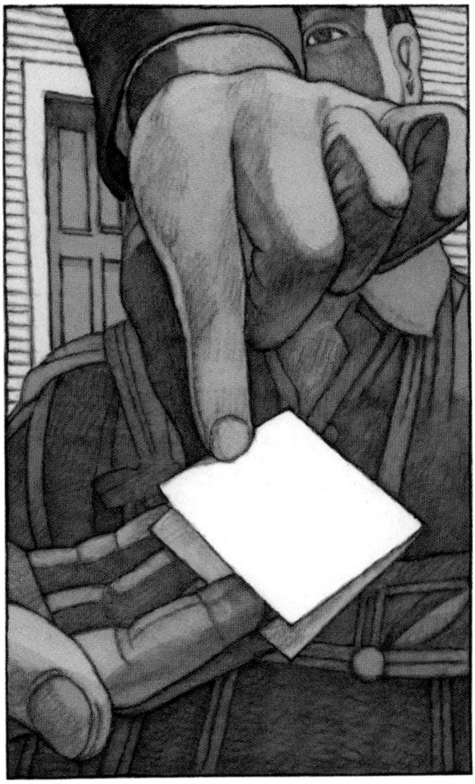

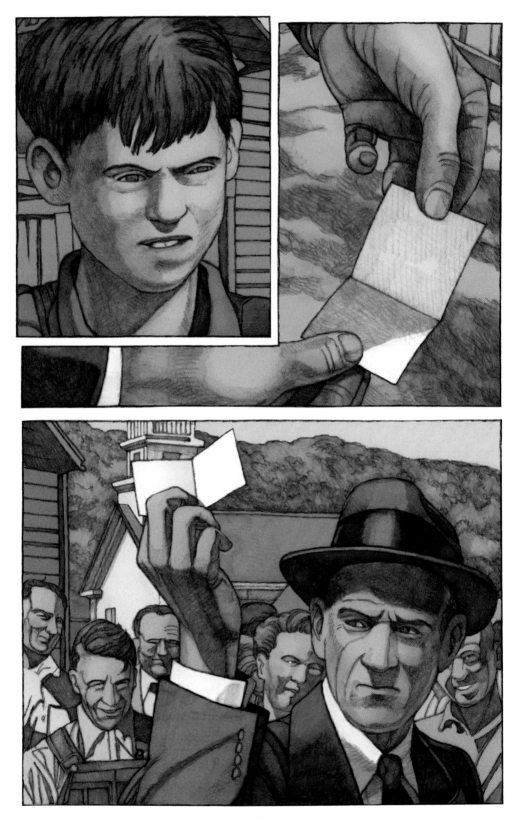

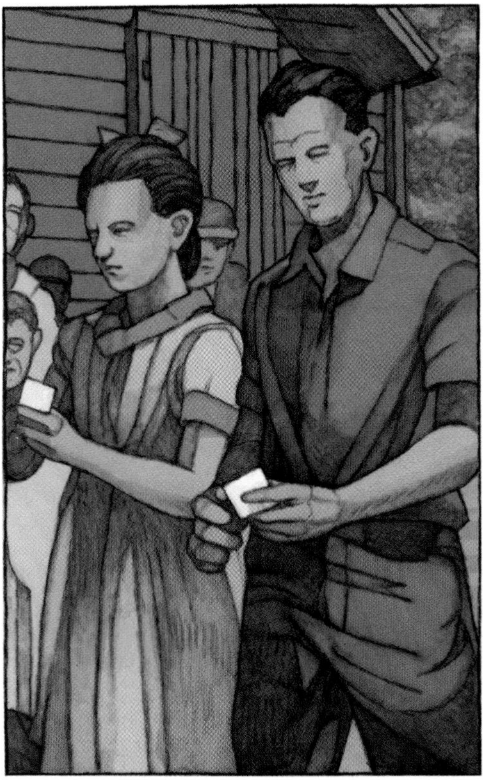

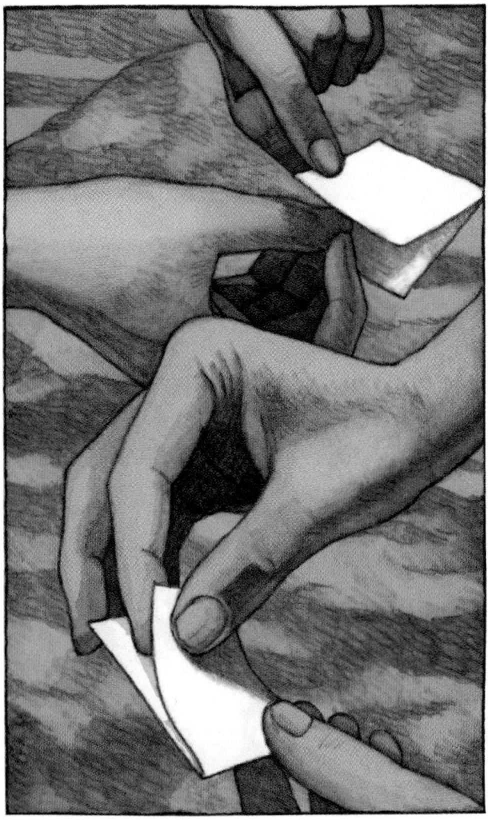

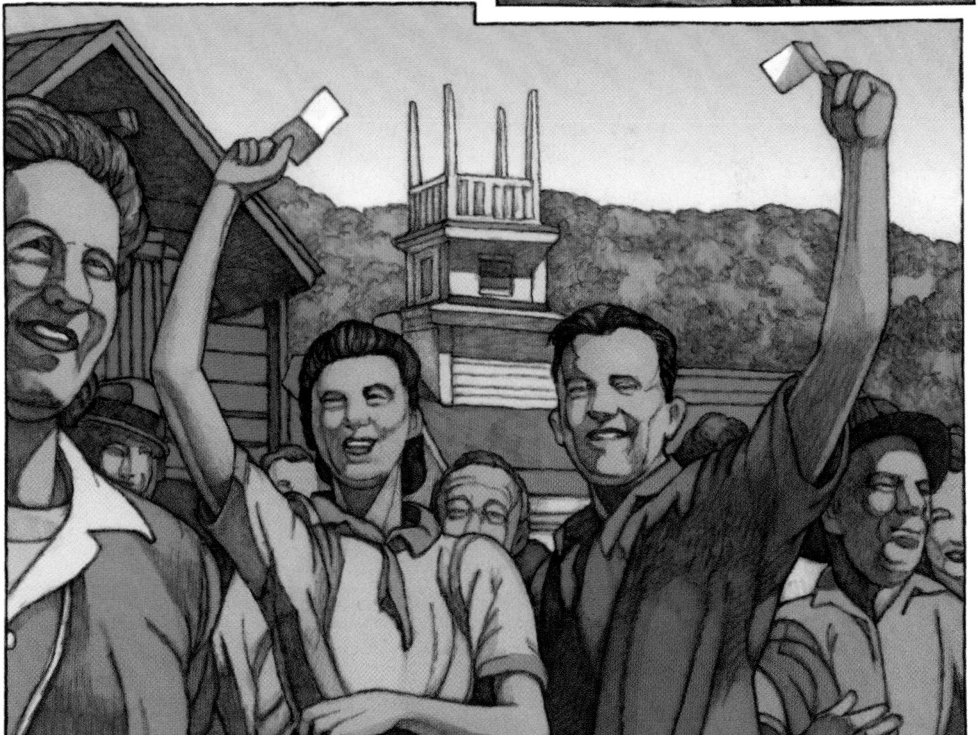

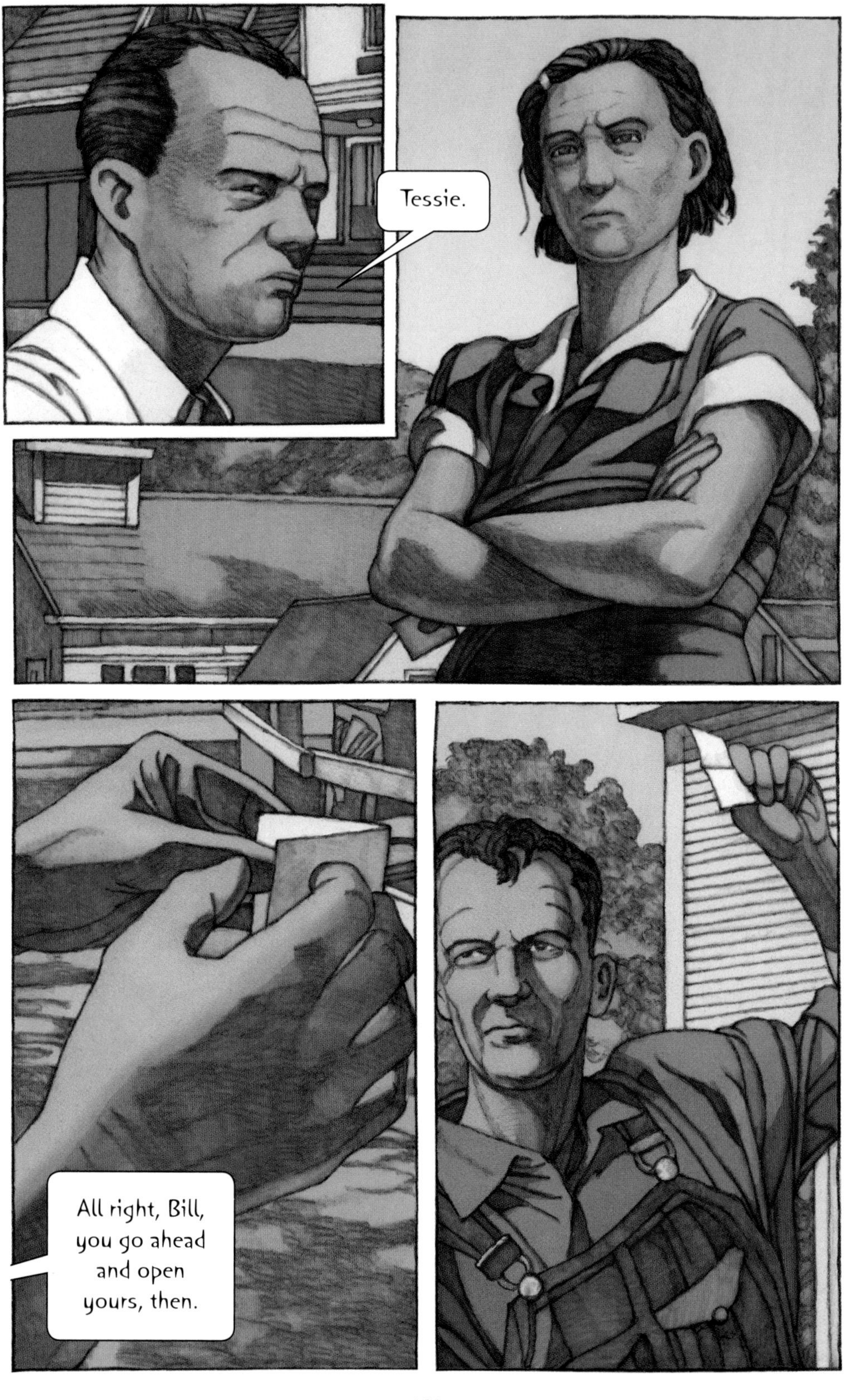
Tessie.
All right, Bill, you go ahead and open yours, then.

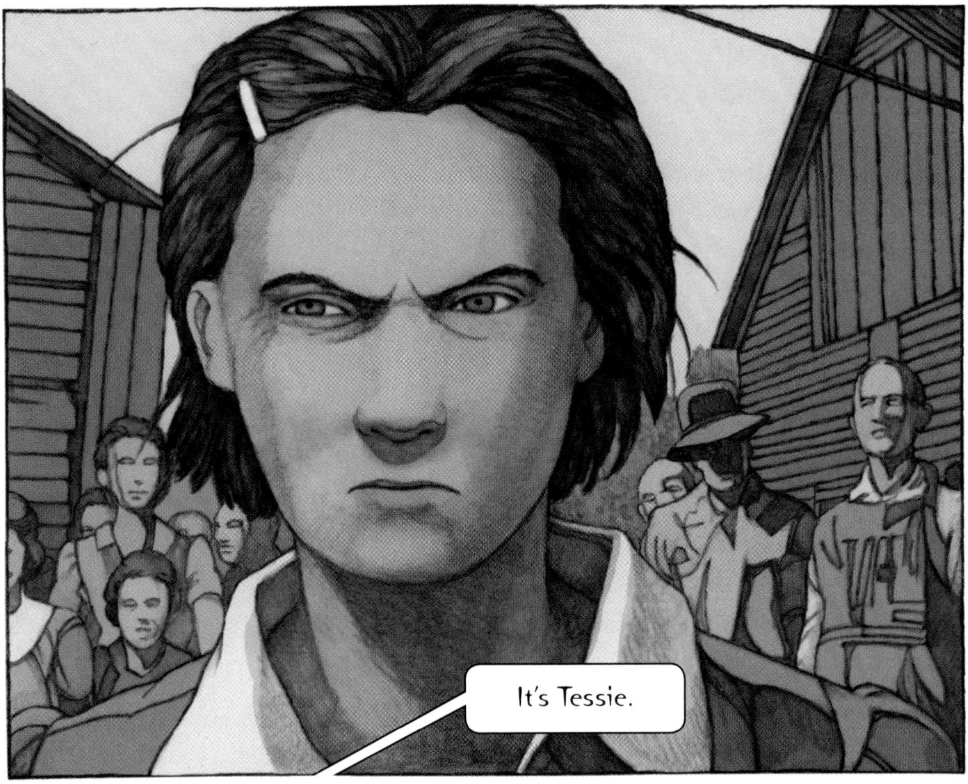
It's Tessie.

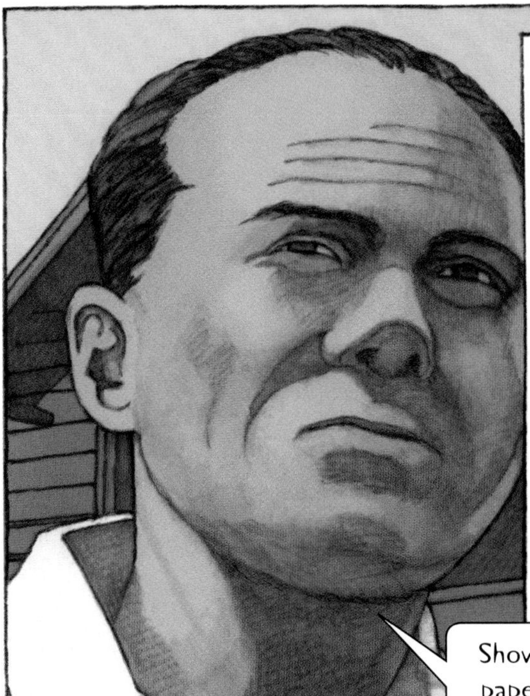
Show us her
paper, Bill...

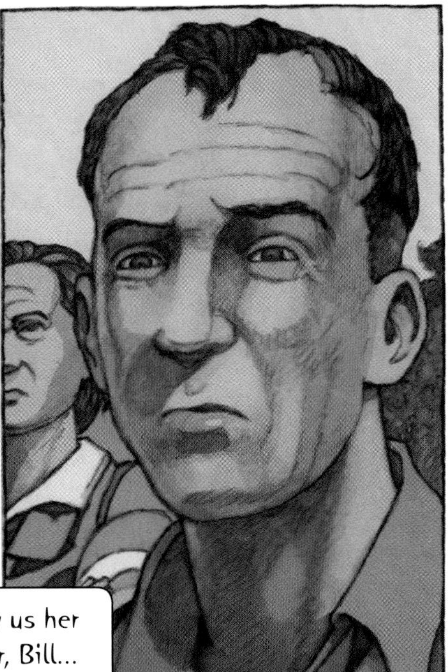

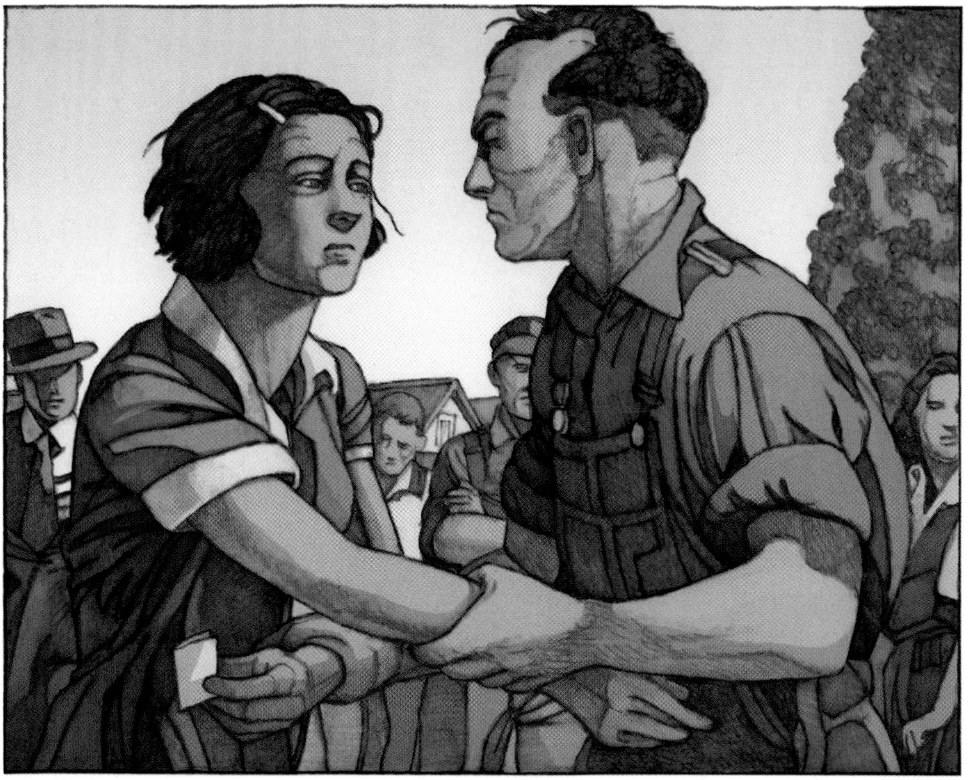

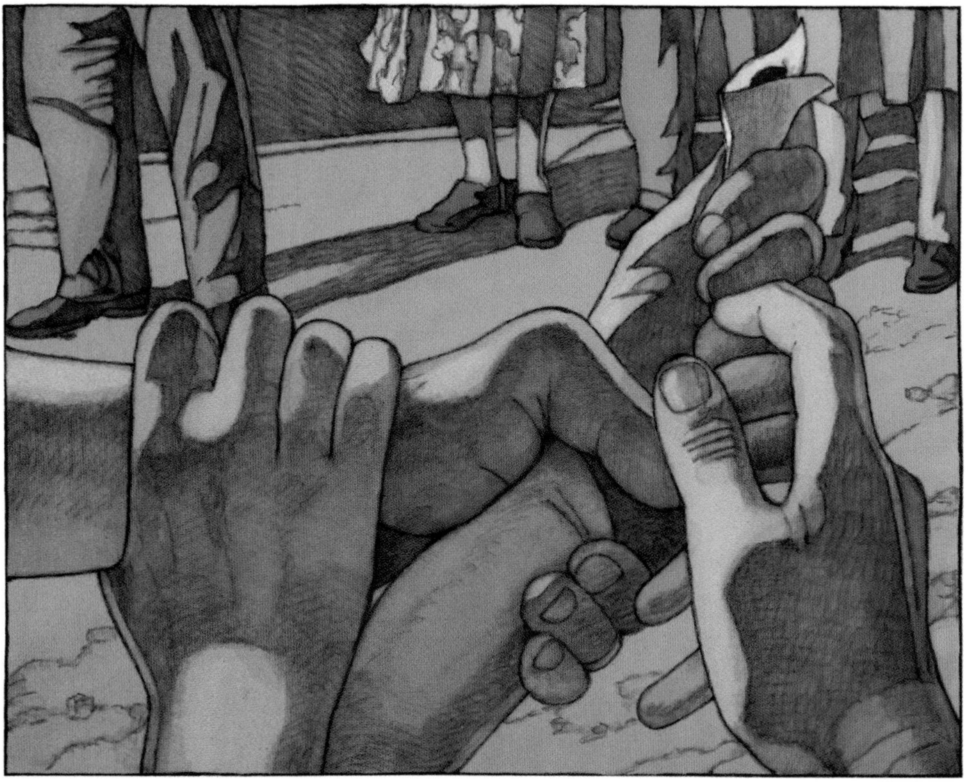

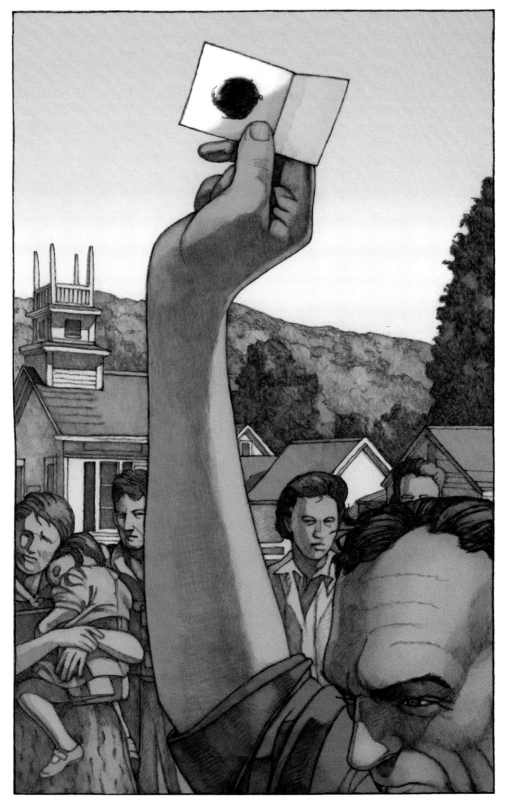

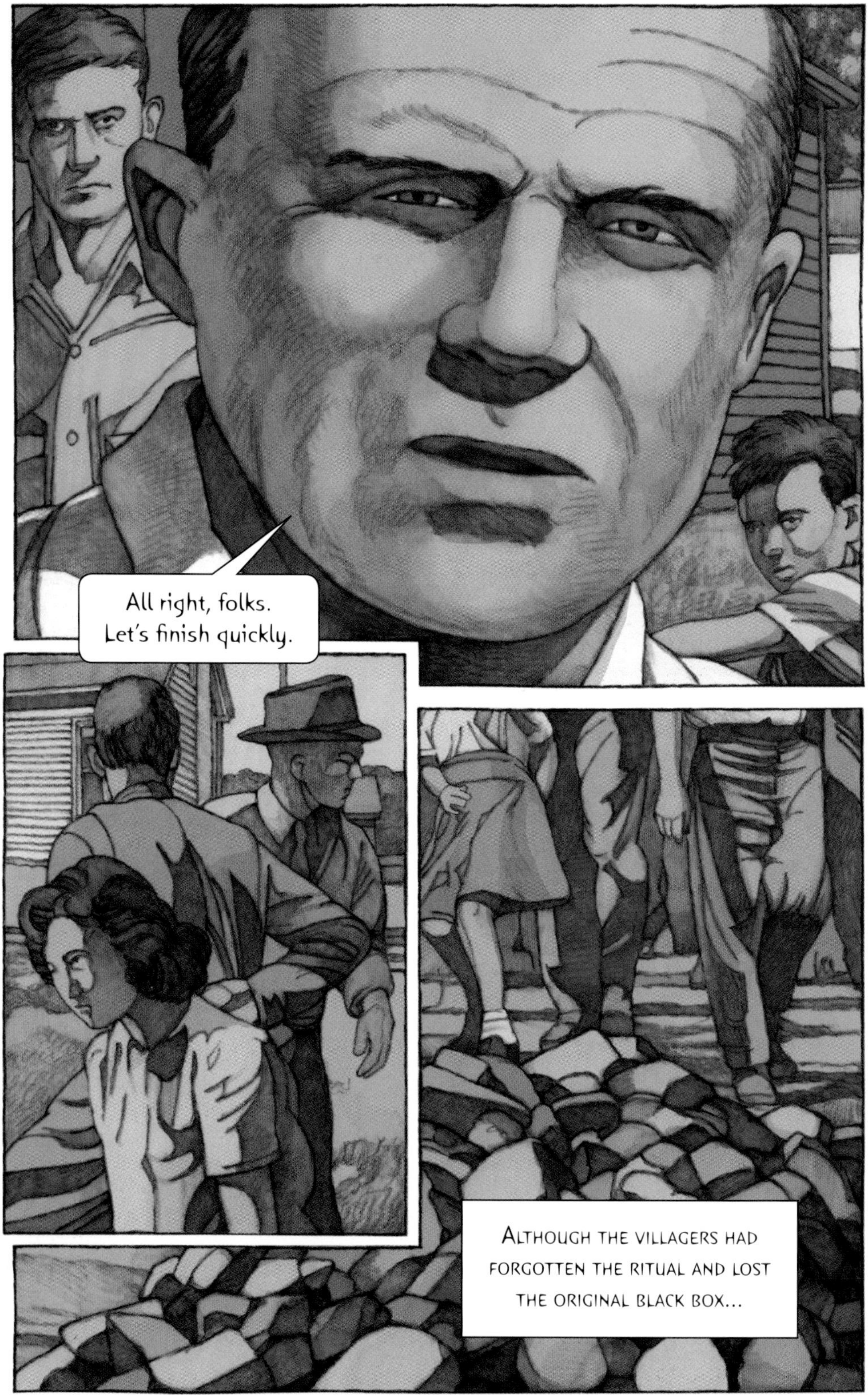
All right, folks. Let's finish quickly.
Although the villagers had forgotten the ritual and lost the original black box...

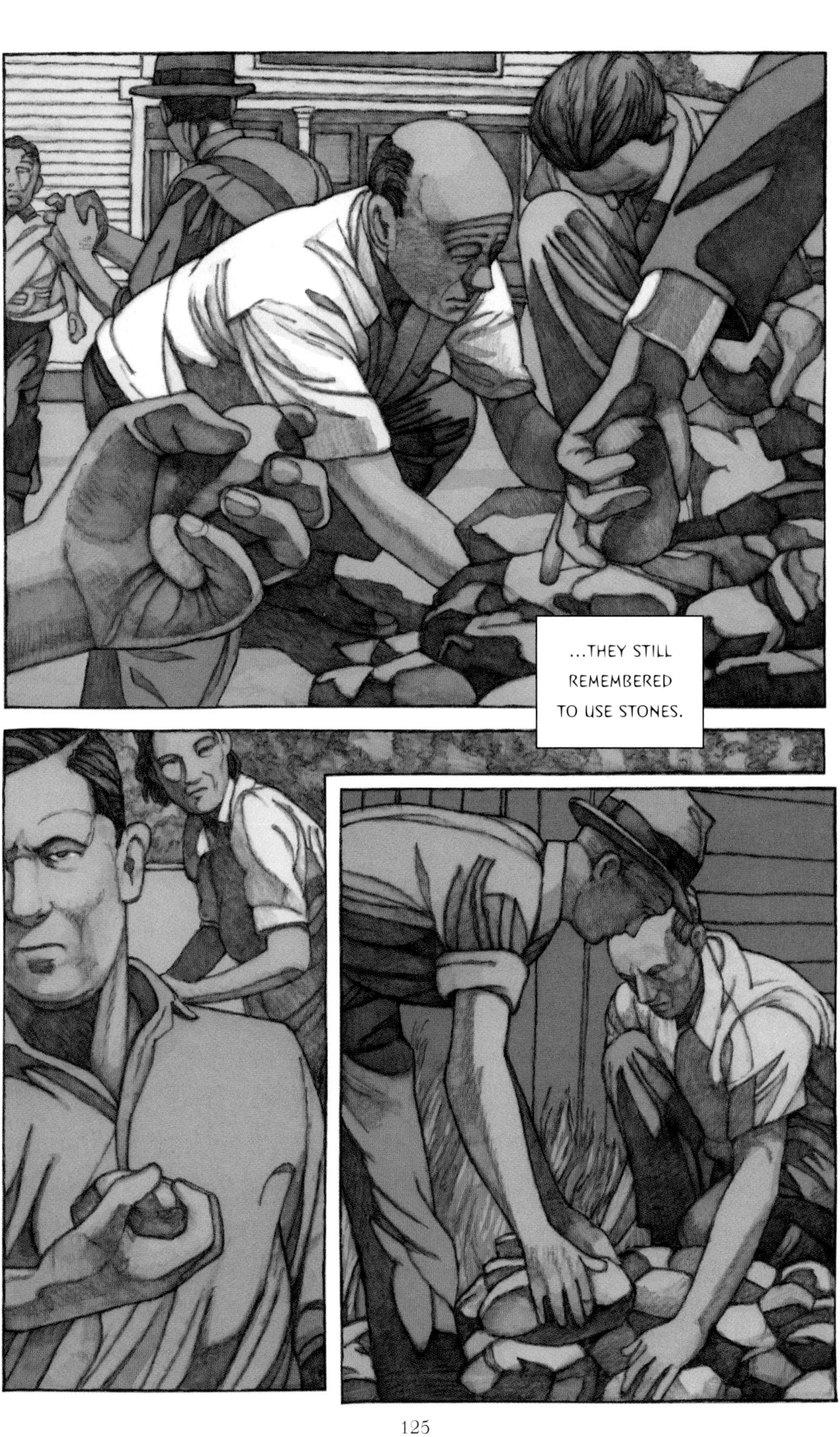
...THEY STILL REMEMBERED TO USE STONES.

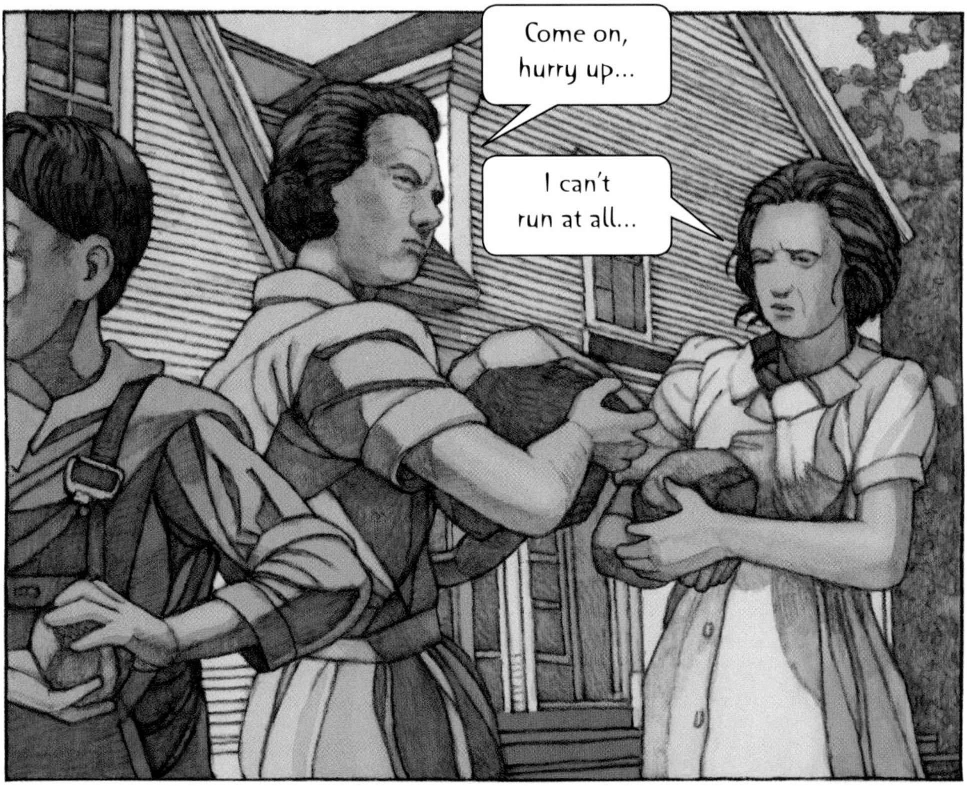
Come on,
hurry up...
I can't
run at all...

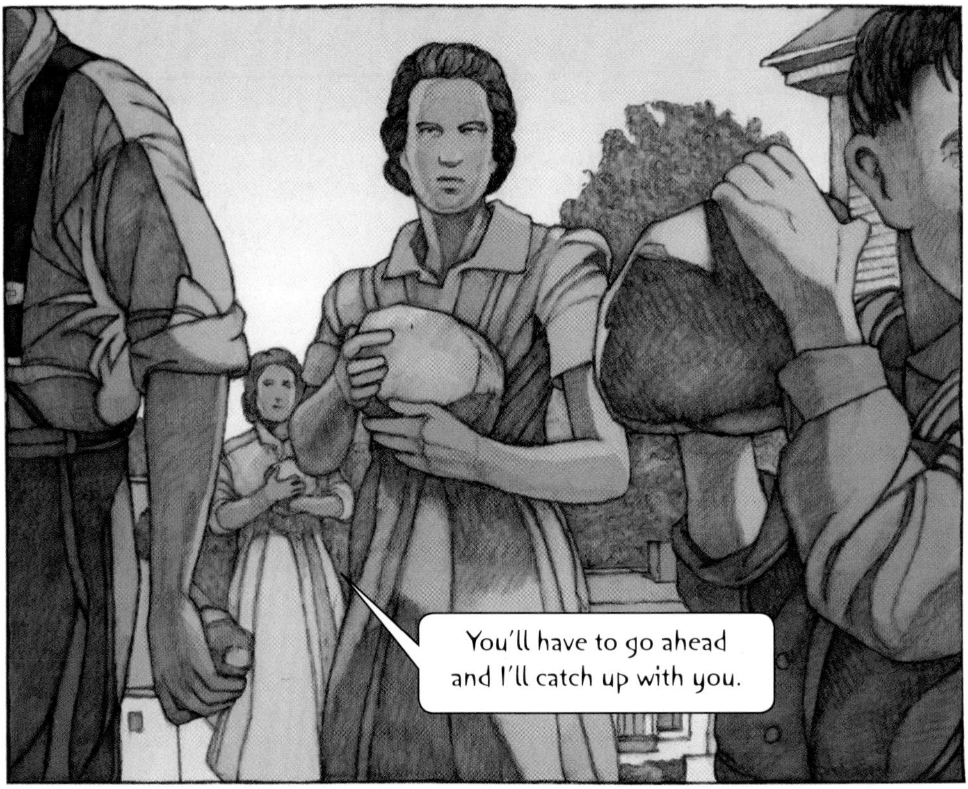
You'll have to go ahead
and I'll catch up with you.

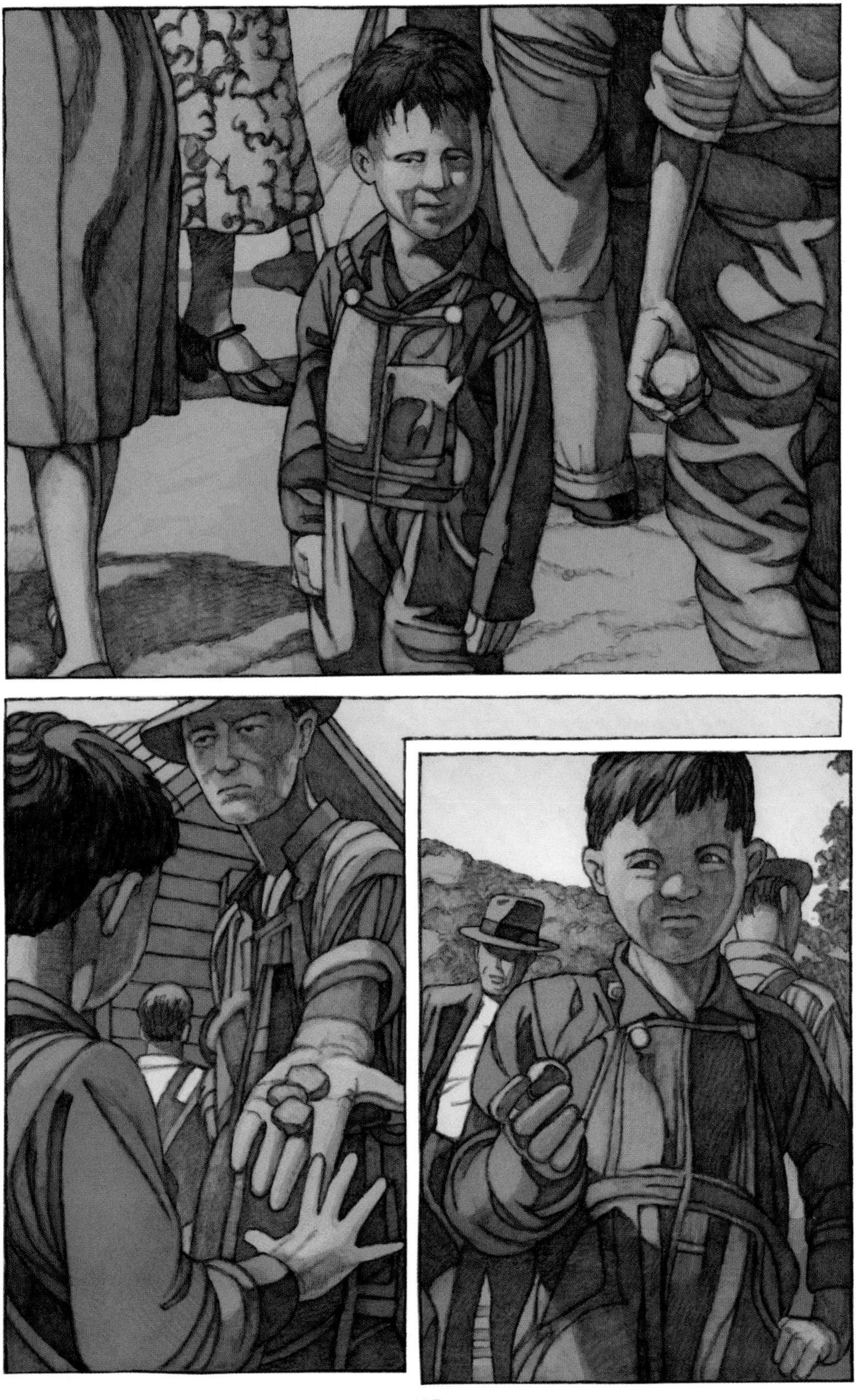

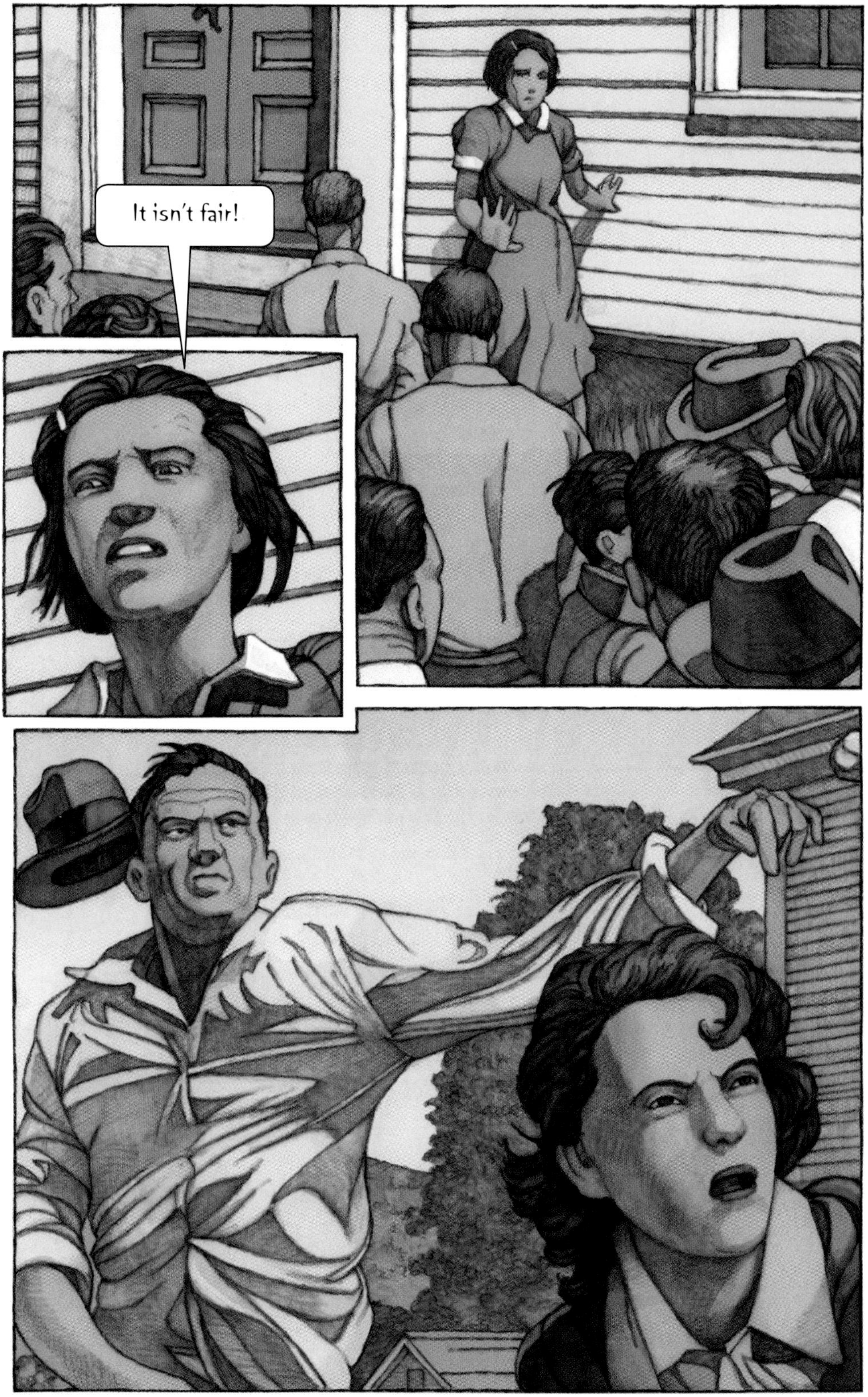
It isn't fair!

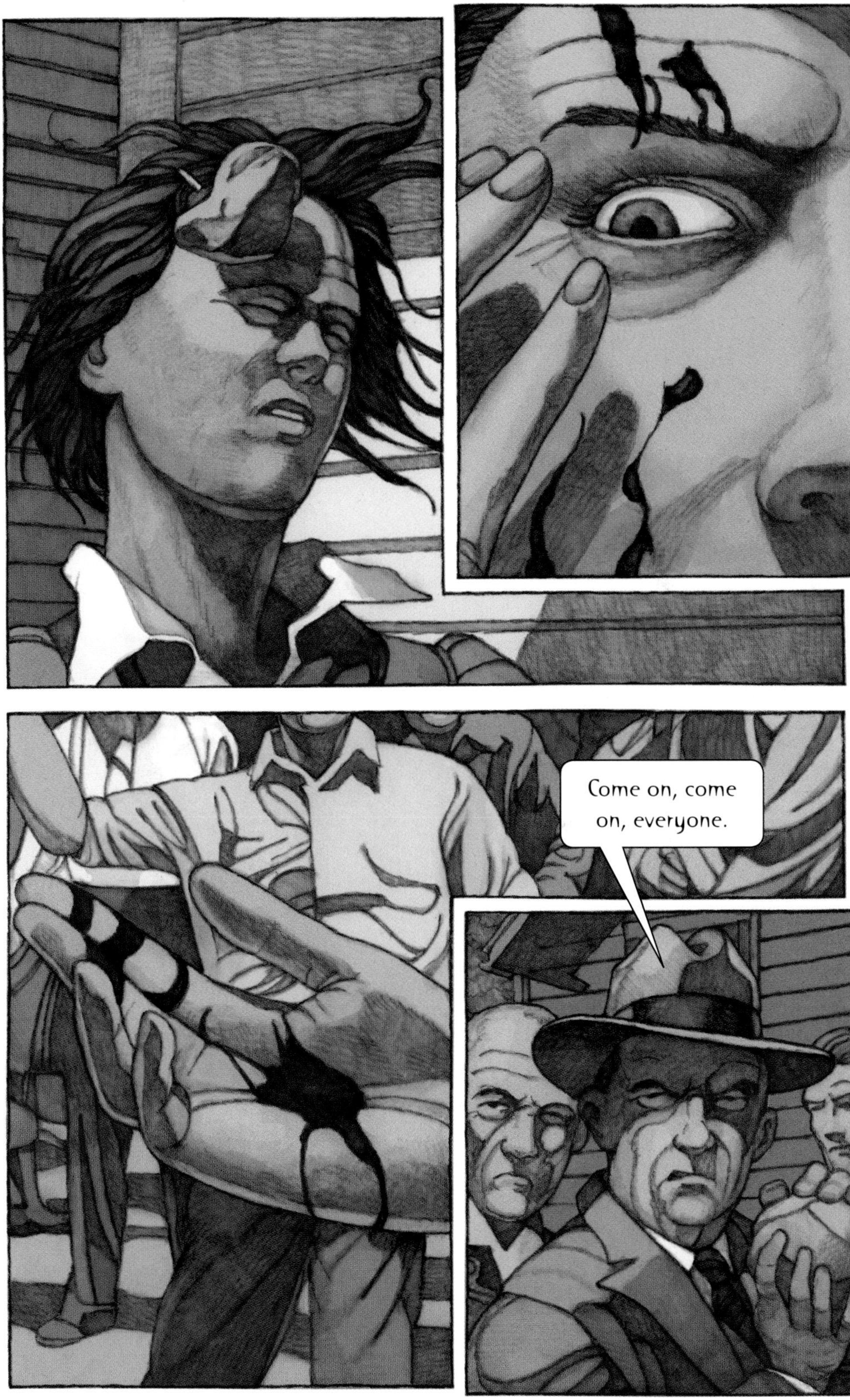
Come on, come on, everyone.

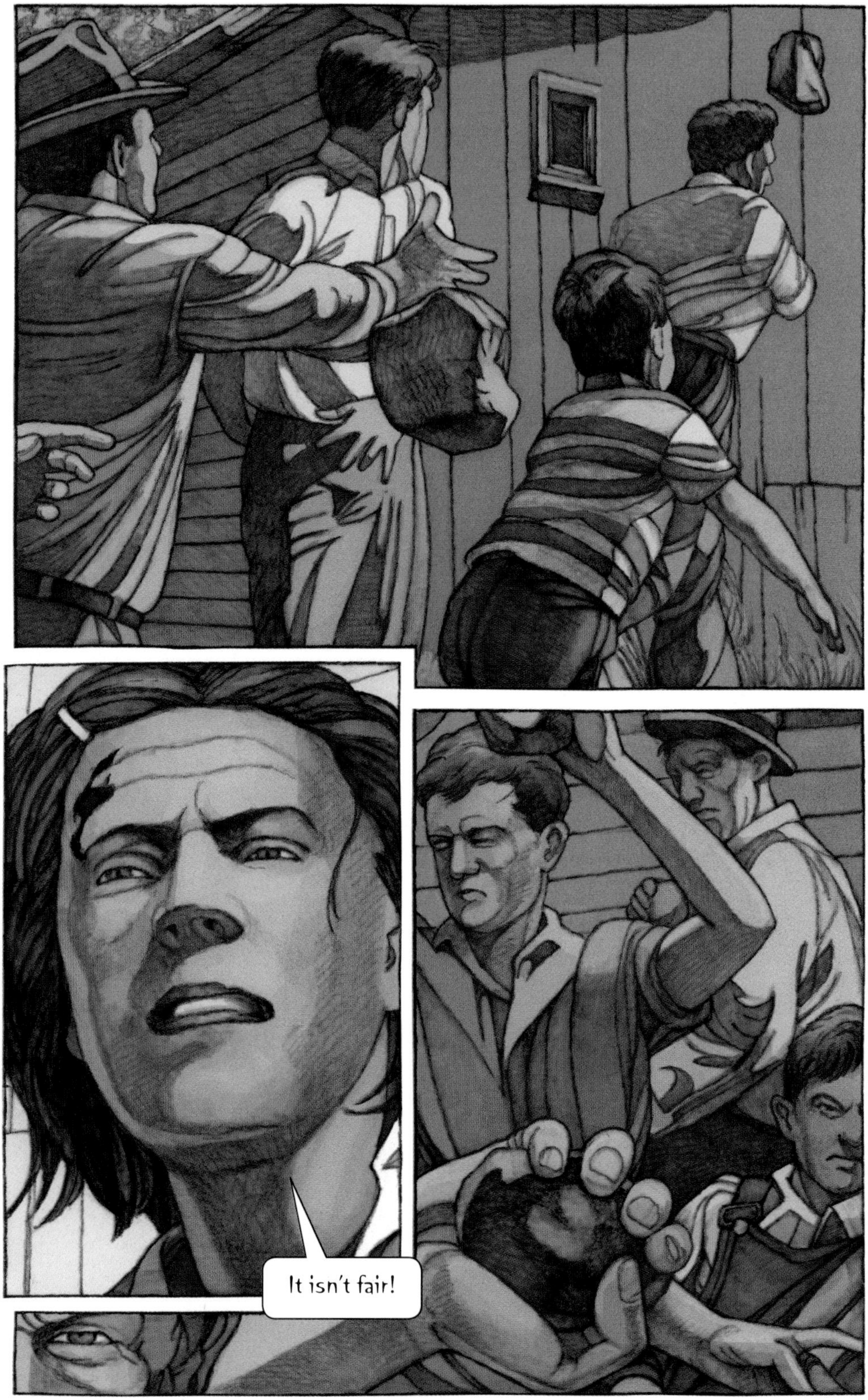
It isn't fair!

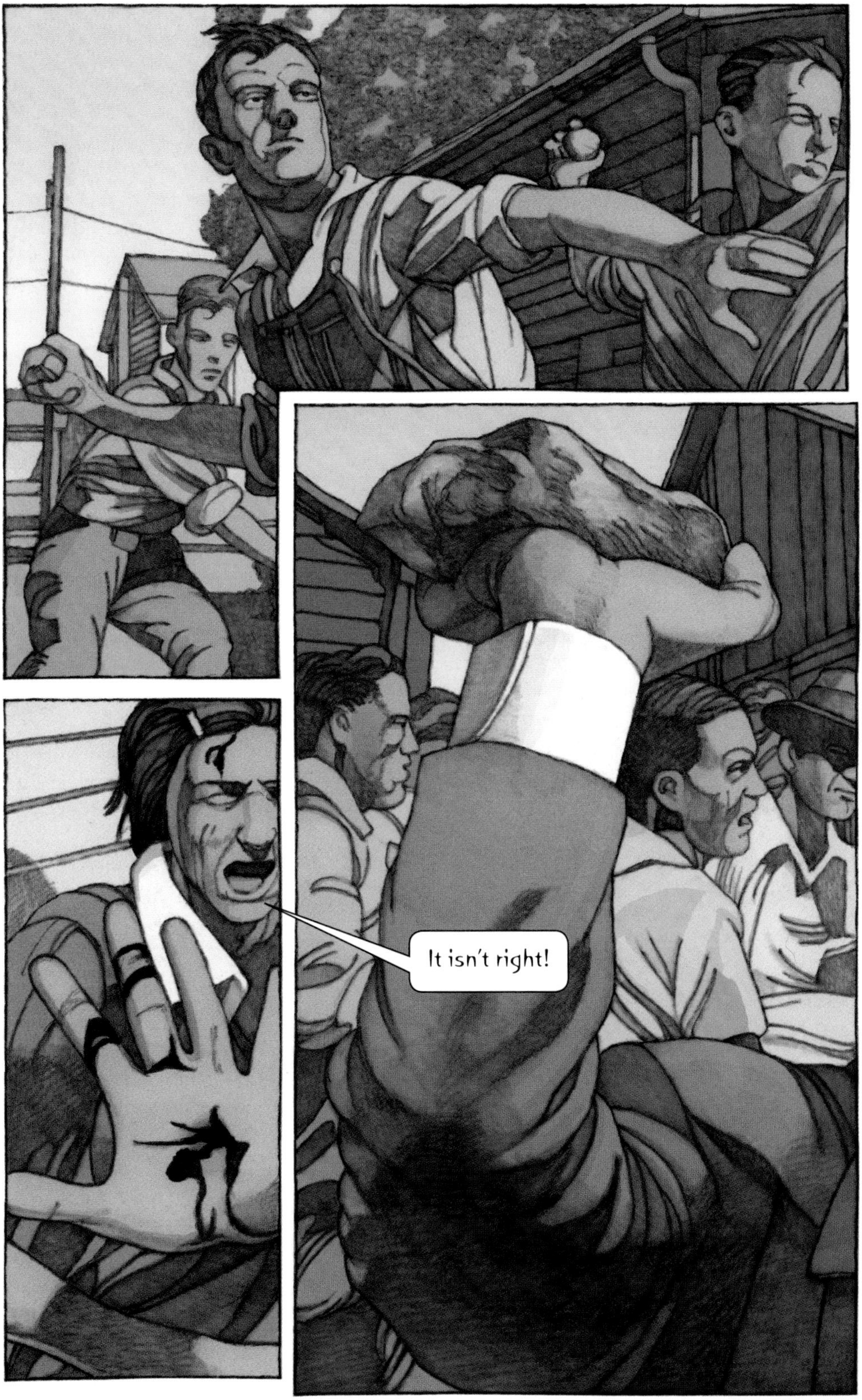
It isn't right!

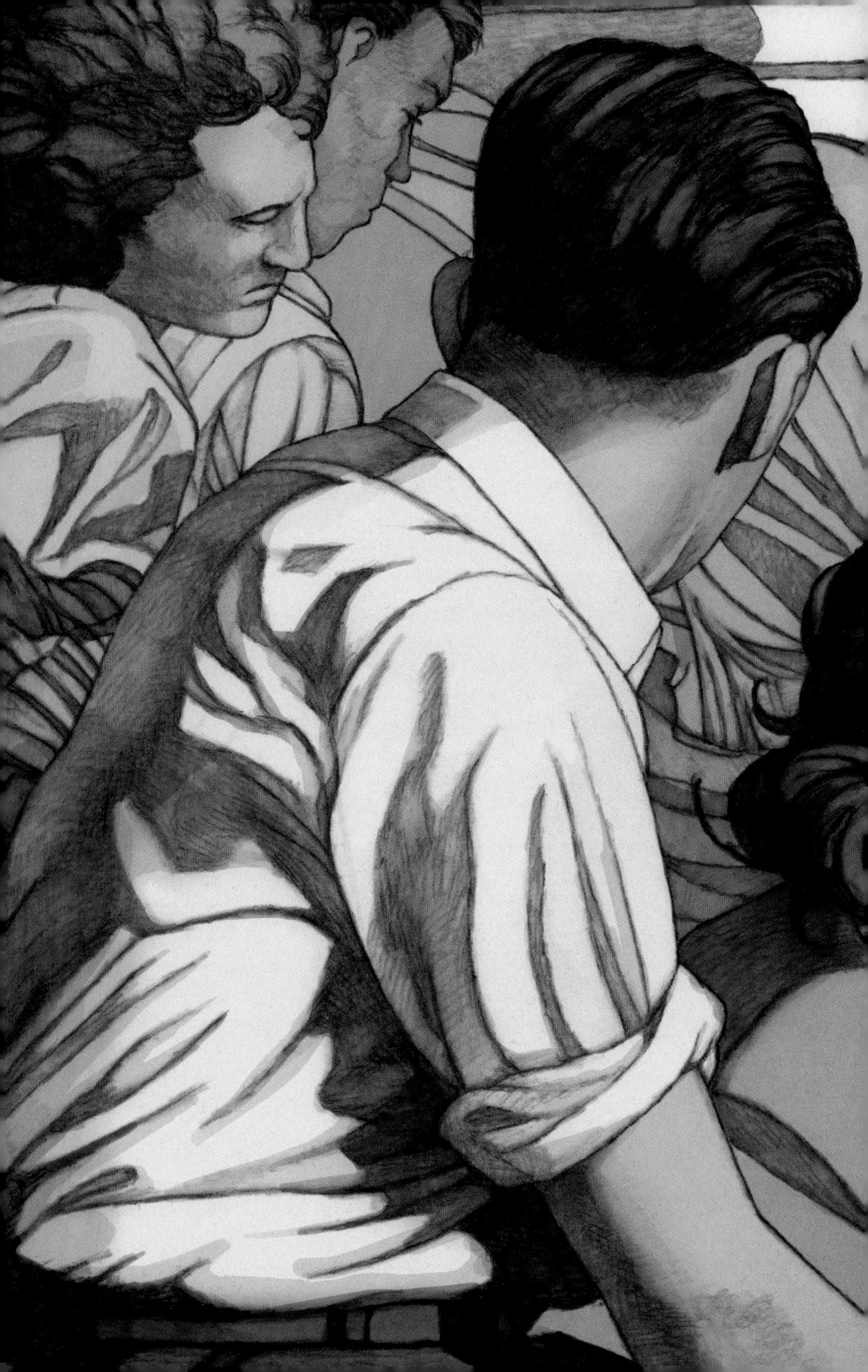

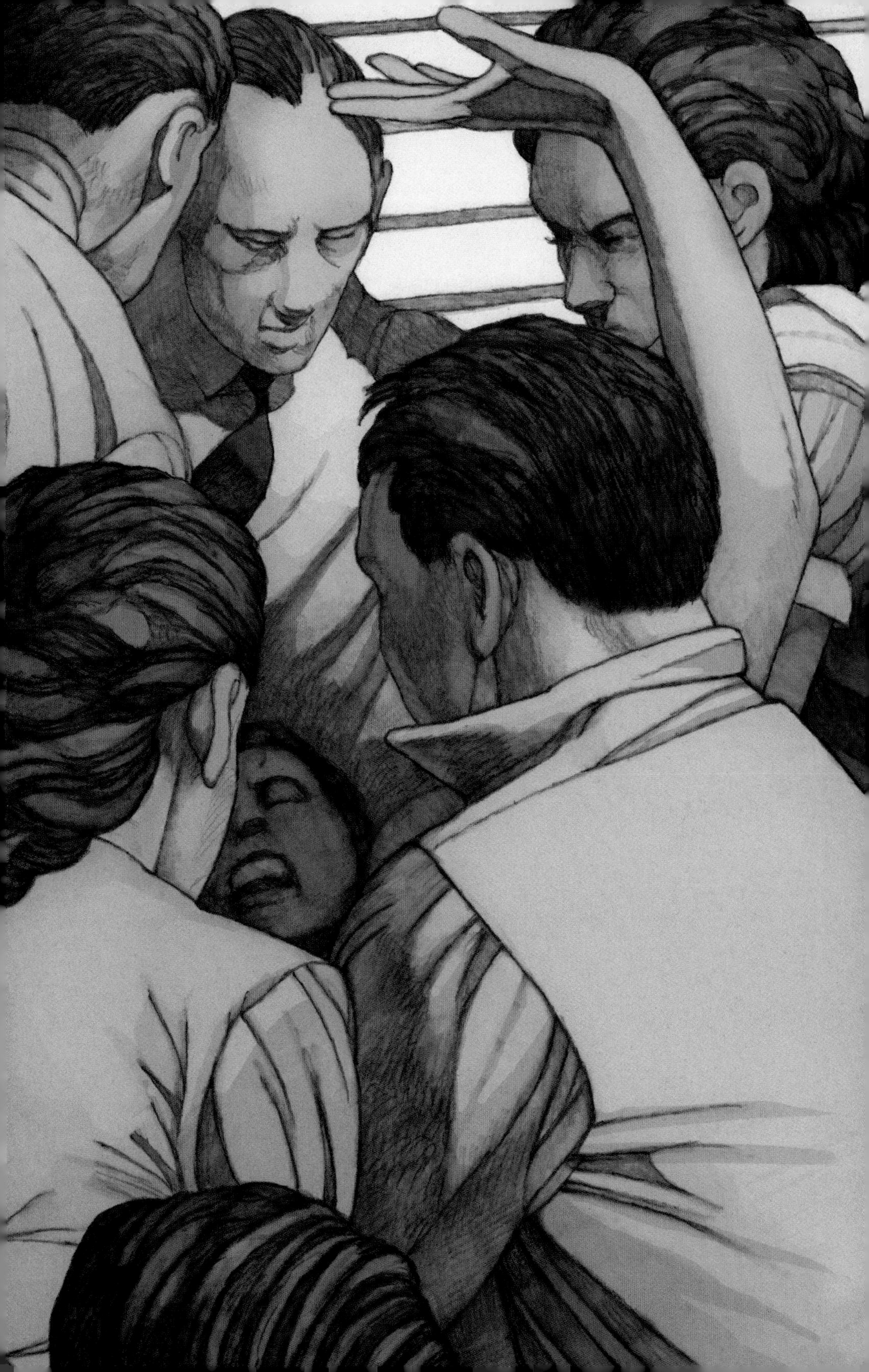

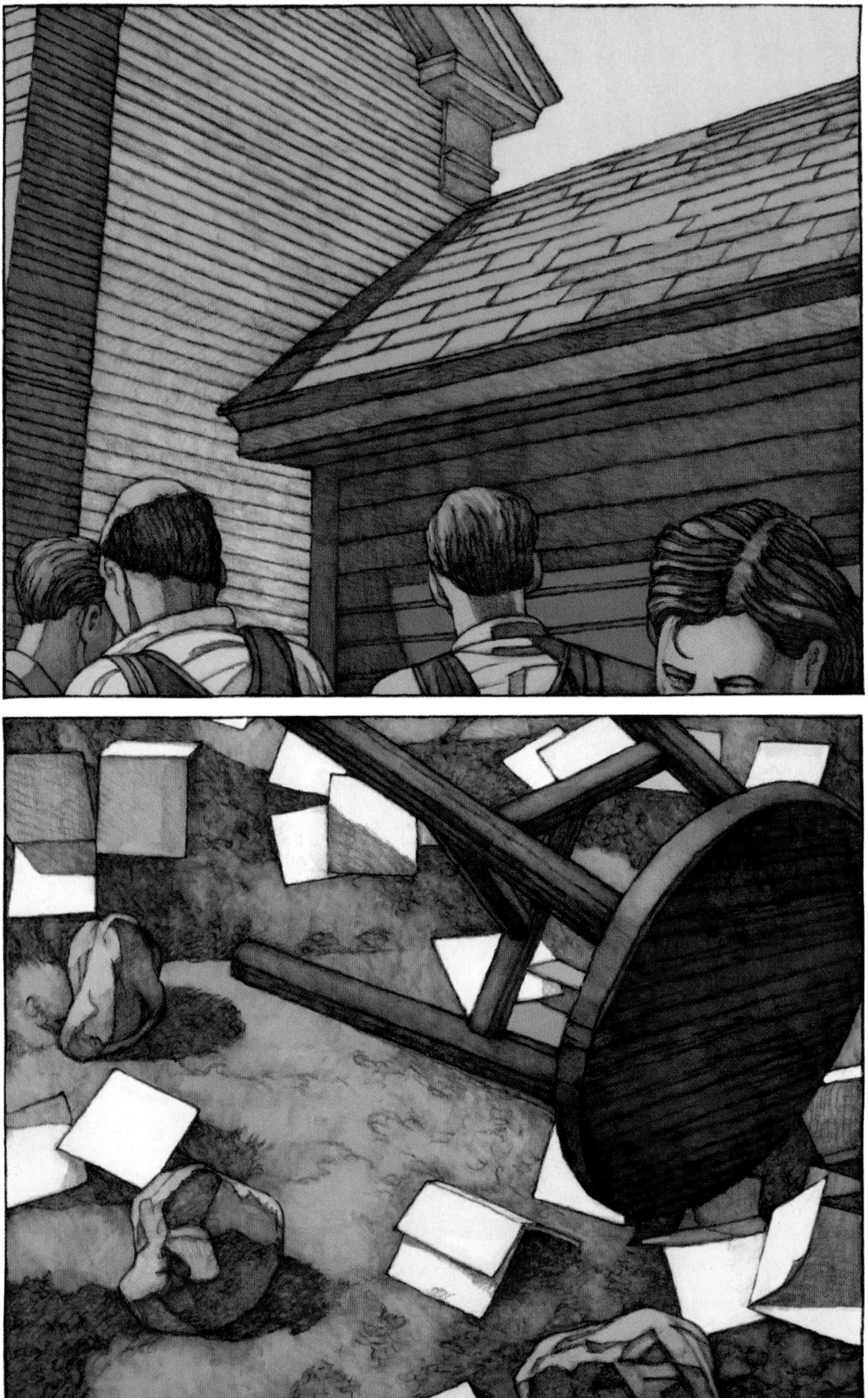

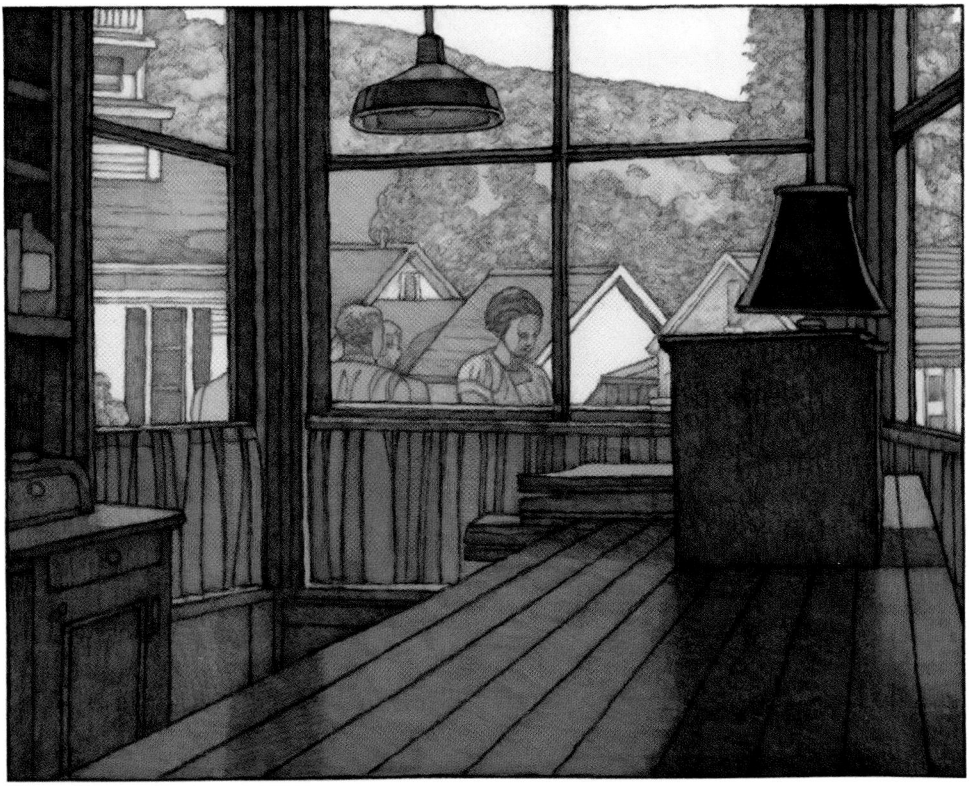

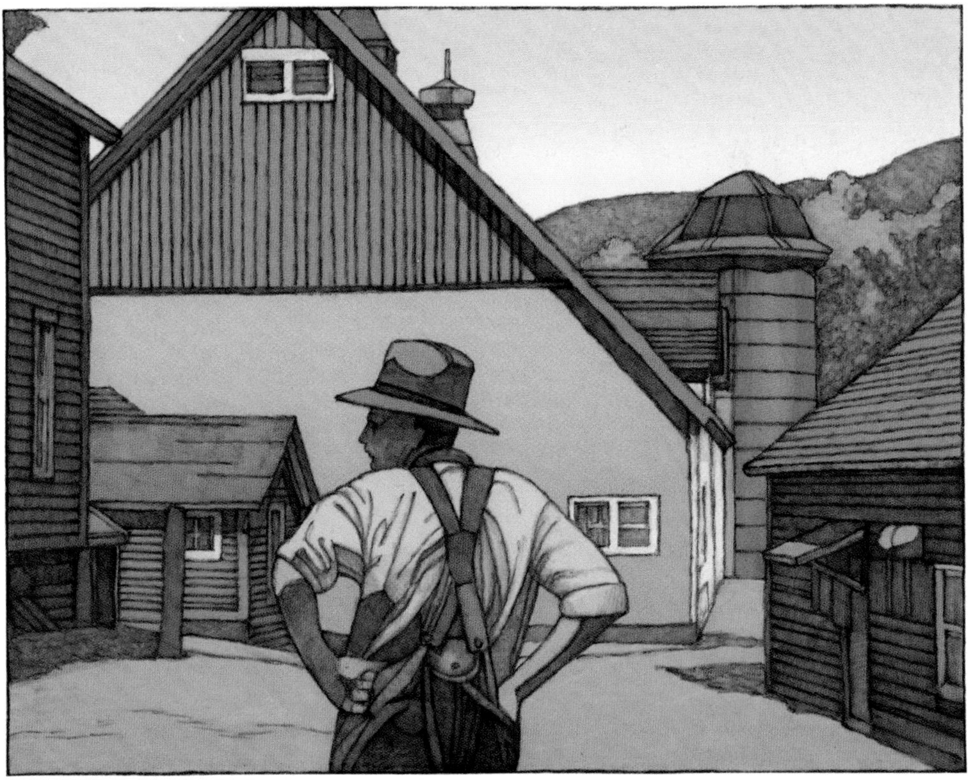

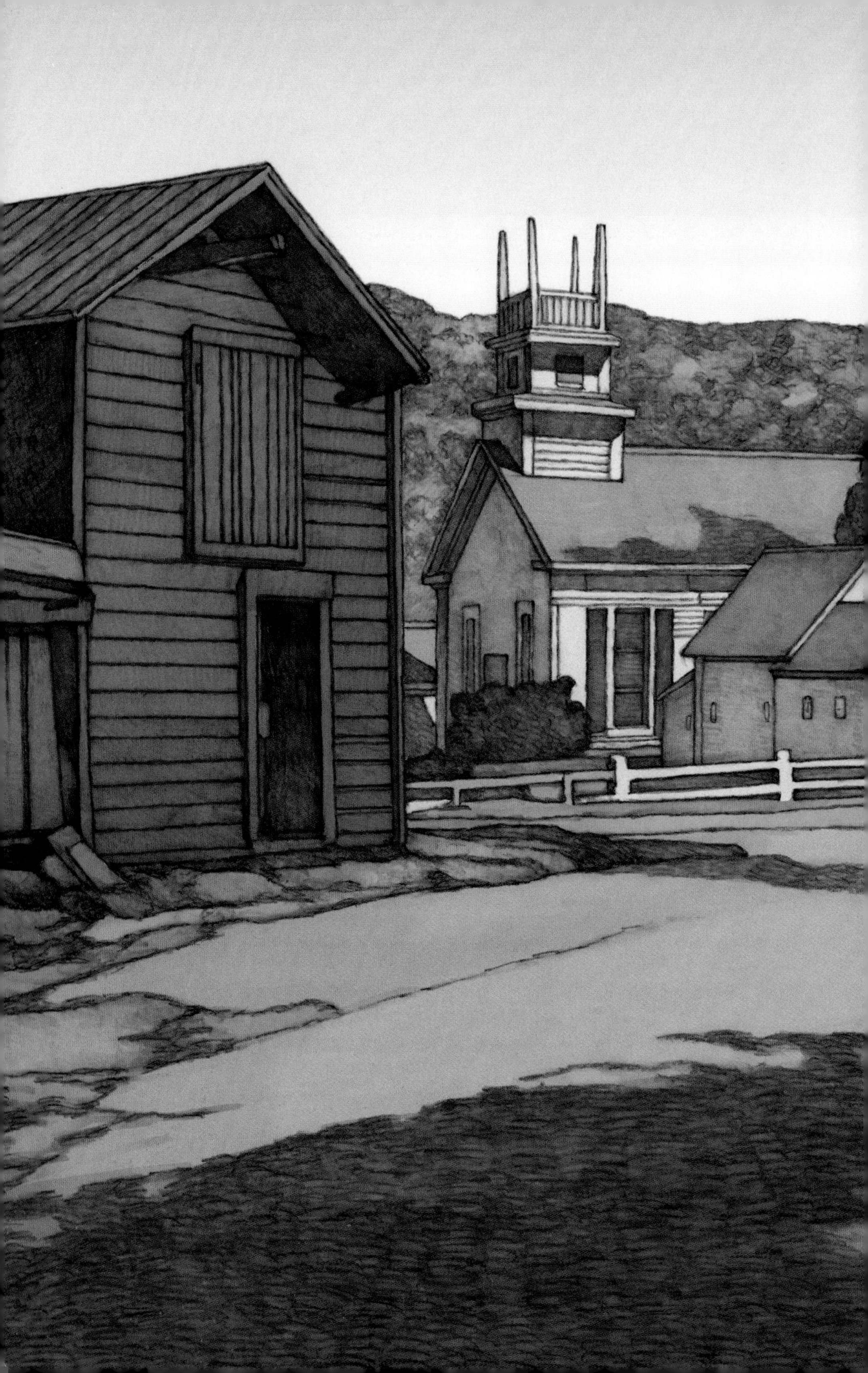

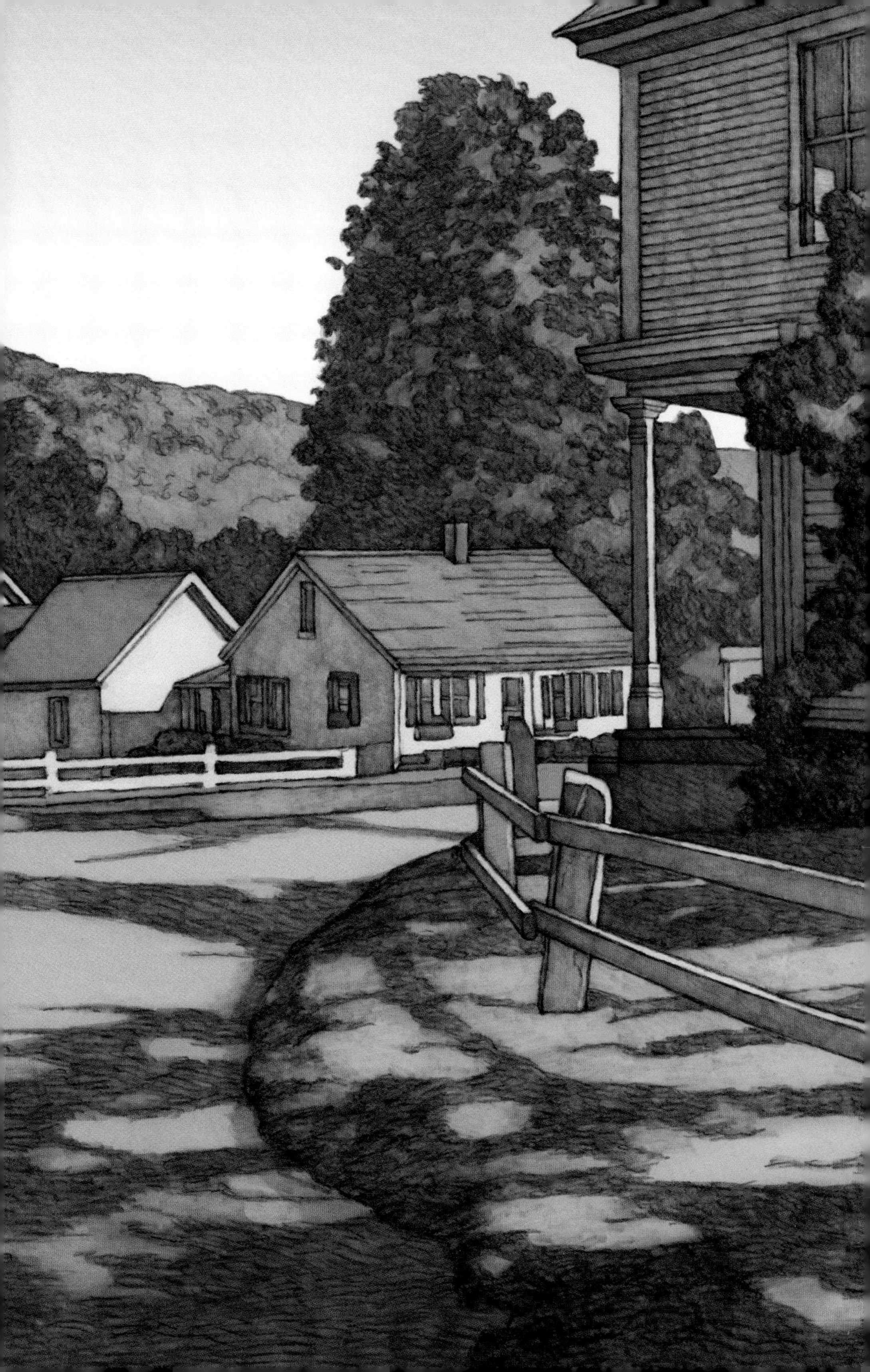

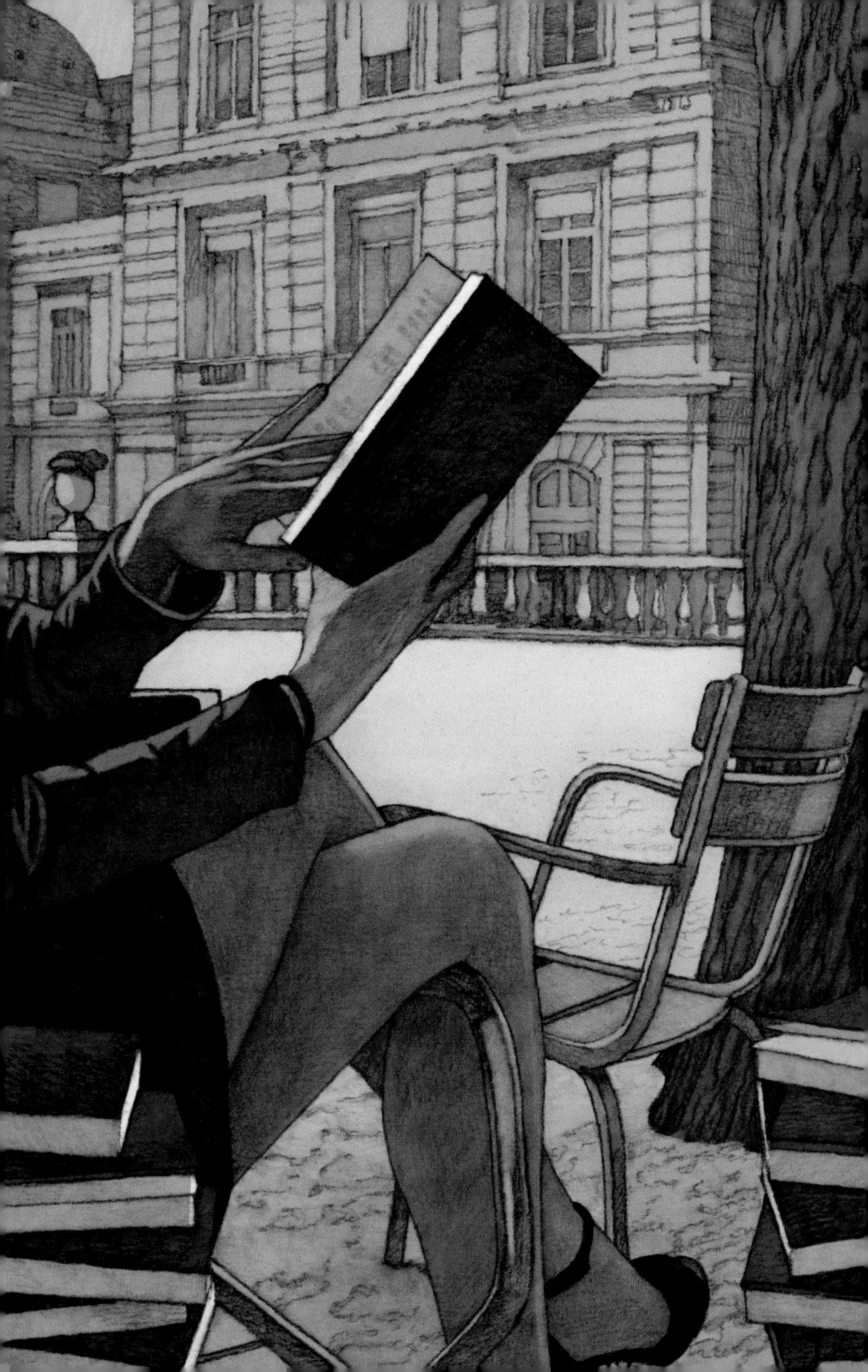

Acknowledgments

I'm deeply grateful to those friends and family who came together to help create this graphic adaptation of "The Lottery."

First of all I owe a very special thanks to my wife, Carole Schilling-Hyman, whose encouragement, guidance, and immense creative talent made this book possible.

Thanks as well to my father, Laurence Jackson Hyman, whose precious advice on the adaptation was indispensable; and to my daughter Juliette Hyman, who turned my sprawling breakdown of "The Lottery" into a coherent script.

I'd like to express my gratitude to Murray Weiss of Catalyst Literary Management, who bravely piloted this project from its earliest stages through to its completion.

And of course I owe enormous thanks to everyone at Farrar, Straus and Giroux who worked so hard to make this book a success: Amanda Moon, Scott Borchert, Stephen Weil, and Jonathan Lippincott.

Finally, I'd like to thank Benoît Mouchart for his suggestion that I adapt one of my grandmother's stories, as well as everyone at Casterman: Christine Cam, Charlotte Gallimard, Basile Béguerie, Kathy Degreef, Marie-Thérèse Vieira, Nathalie Rocher, and Néjib Belhadj-Kacem.

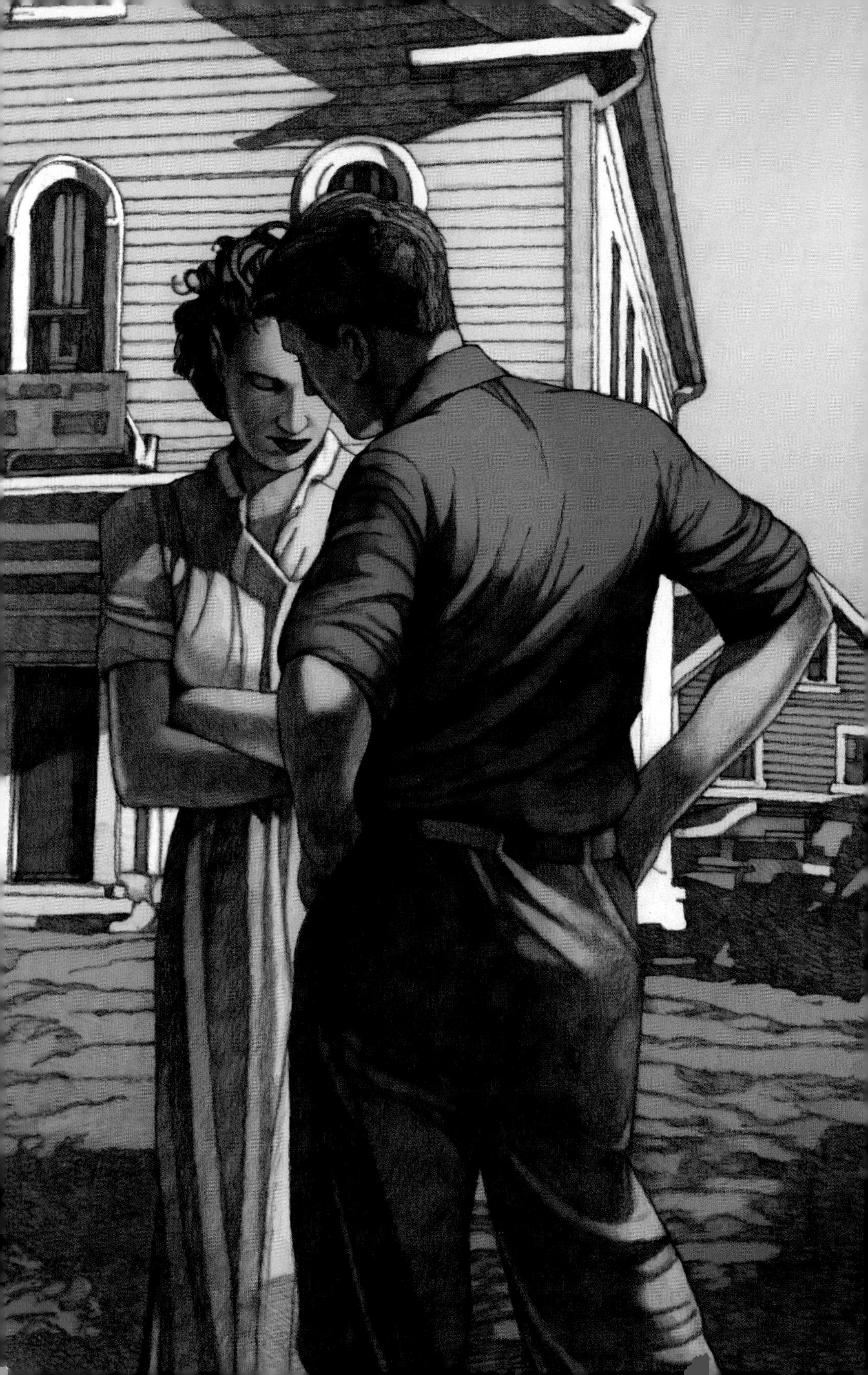

A Note About the Artist

Miles Hyman was born in Vermont. He attended Wesleyan University, where he studied literature as well as printmaking with David Schorr before moving to Paris to attend the École des Beaux-Arts. Hyman specializes in graphic novels and adaptations of classic literature. His work has been shown in galleries around the world and has appeared in publications such as *Le Monde*, *Libération*, *GQ*, *The New Yorker*, and *The New York Times*. He is the grandson of Shirley Jackson. He lives in Paris.

You can learn more about Miles Hyman's work by visiting him online at www.mileshyman.com or www.facebook.com/mileshyman.visualarts.

You can also learn more about the making of this book on our Facebook page: www.facebook.com/thelotterygraphicnovel.

Selected Titles by Miles Hyman

Graphic Novels
L'Homme à Deux Têtes*
Nuit de Fureur*
Images Interdites*
The Black Dahlia

Illustrator
Ouest*
Manhattan Transfer, by John Dos Passos*
The Secret Agent, by Joseph Conrad*
Lorsque Lou, by Philippe Djian*
A Place in the World Called Paris, edited by Steven Barclay
The Chess Garden, by Brooks Hansen
Nine Magic Wishes, by Shirley Jackson
The Sundial, by Shirley Jackson
Miles Hyman/Drawings *

*Published in French